THE DEFENSE OF THE FAITH

THE DEFENSE OF THE FAITH

BY

CORNELIUS VAN TIL

PRESBYTERIAN AND REFORMED PUBLISHING CO.
Phillipsburg, New Jersey

ISBN: 0-87552-483-4

SECOND EDITION
Revised and Abridged
1963

THIRD EDITION
Revised, 1967

Library of Congress Catalog Card Number 55-7140

PRINTED IN THE UNITED STATES OF AMERICA

TO MY WIFE

CONTENTS

CONTENTS

PREFACE

Except for minor corrections and additions, primarily in the form of footnotes, this third edition is the same as the second. Discussion of more recent movements in theology and philosophy, both orthodox and neo-orthodox, may be found in later writings by the present writer, and, more exactly, in unpublished class syllabi available through the Presbyterian and Reformed Publishing Co. or from Westminster Theological Seminary.

Acknowledgment is again made to publishers who kindly gave permission to quote from various books: To the Macmillan Company for permission to quote from *Religious Realism*, copyright, 1931, and from A. E. Taylor's *Does God Exist?* copyright-reprint 1947; to the Cambridge University Press for permission to quote from James Jeans' *The Mysterious Universe;* to William B. Eerdman's Co. for permission to quote from Edward Carnell's *An Introduction to Christian Apologetics;* to F. S. Crofts and Company for permission to quote from Martin, Clarke, Clark, Ruddick: *A History of Philosophy*; to Yale University Press for permission to quote from Cassirer's *Essay on Man*, and Gilson's *God and Philosophy*; to Charles Scribner's Sons for permission to quote from Millikan's *Science and the New Civilization*; and to the estate of Felix Cohen for permission to quote from Morris R. Cohen's *Reason and Nature*, copyrighted, revised 1953.

Special thanks are due to the Rev. Rousas John Rushdoony for carefully reading the entire manuscript; and to my former student, Robert G. DeMoss, Th.M., for painstaking help in the technical details of the manuscript.

I am indebted to Mr. Edward Robert Geehan for editorial work in connection with the revision of this volume.

Cornelius Van Til
October, 1967

INTRODUCTION

There are many who share with the writer of this book the conviction that if Christ is to be presented to men as a challenge to their thinking and living then he must be offered without compromise.

Yet the traditional method of presenting Christ to men, as developed chiefly by Roman Catholic theologians, does compromise him. In Roman Catholic apologetics the natural man is not challenged to make his every thought captive to the obedience of Christ. The natural man is merely asked to *add* the wisdom and work of Christ to that which man has in and of himself.

The result of this Roman Catholic compromise is twofold. Negatively it results in failure to show the natural man the internal inconsistency and futility of his effort to find meaning in life. For if Roman Catholic apologetics were to demonstrate to the natural man the futility of his position it would, at the same time, demonstrate the futility of its own position. If by means of his philosophy and natural theology the Roman Catholic apologist "proves" the existence of God, then he proves the existence of *a* god such as is "proved" by Aristotle, *a* god, who is nothing more than an abstract universal principle of being, *a* god who, instead of giving meaning to the universe, is itself in need of the contingency of this universe as correlative to itself.

Positively the traditional method of apologetics, as developed by Roman Catholics, has no Christ who could challenge the thought and life of the natural man in order to save him and his culture. The Christianity of Roman Catholic "supernatural theology" cannot be attached to the "theism" of its philosophy and natural theology without itself sinking in the bottomless pit of pure contingency.

Protestant Christians ought therefore to celebrate the grace of God their Savior unto them by noting carefully from what they have been saved and to what they are called. Their method of apologetics should be in line with their theology. In both Christ should be taught and preached unto men who are lost in all their thinking and living without him. The natural man must be shown that on his presupposition or assumption of man's autonomy human predication has no meaning at all. But this negative task cannot be accomplished except on the presupposition that in Christ life does have meaning. Only when Protestant theology thus sees its apologetics to be an aspect of its theology of free grace can the glad tidings of the gospel ring out clearly and fully to men. Only thus can those who are in the schismatic "mother church" be challenged to come into the church universal in which Christ is really supreme and really saves men from sin.

But if Protestants are thus to fulfill their task they should do so while they confess their failures. Their own apologetics has constantly come far behind their theology. The traditional or Roman Catholic method of apologetics was often brought into the Protestant fold. This is notably true of those who followed the lead of Arminian theologians. The methodology of Bishop Butler's *Analogy* is essentially the same as that of the *Contra Gentiles* of Thomas Aquinas.

But the greater burden lies upon those who have followed the lead of Reformed theologians. In his little book, *The Plan of Salvation,* B. B. Warfield shows clearly that Roman Catholic theology is defective because it is not constructed exclusively in terms of the revelation of God in Christ. Rome's notion of "freedom," argues Warfield, constitutes a compromise with the naturalist notion of autonomy.

On the Romanist view God with his grace cannot enter the penetralia of the consciousness of sinful man unless man first opens the door.

As Warfield continues, he points out that what is true of Romanism is true of Protestant theology so far as it is Arminian. In Arminian theology too God can only make salvation "possible"; he cannot actually save individual men unless they want to be saved.

The moral of Warfield's argument would seem to be easy to draw. Those who follow the lead of Reformed theologians cannot expect Arminian theology to furnish (a) a truly biblical apologetic with which to challenge the natural man and (b) an apologetic that will challenge Roman Catholics to forsake the paralyzing naturalism in their view.

A still further moral must be drawn from Warfield's telling argument. It is to the effect that Reformed theologians must put their hands in their own bosom to see whether it too is not white with the leprosy of naturalism.

Such a critical self-examination of the apologetic position of Reformed theologians is desperately needed in the present day. Modern theology is in a crisis. The neo-orthodox position of Karl Barth and his followers carries the flag but not the content of the Reformed Faith. Neo-orthodoxy and Roman Catholicism are drawing ever closer together.

Both oppose "modernism" but both are afflicted with its naturalist assumptions. None of them have a Christ who can help sinners in need. Nothing short of the Christ of the Scriptures, as presented in historic Reformed theology, can challenge men to forsake their sin and establish them in truth and life.

If only Reformed theologians were true to their own principles and ideas! How often does it not prove true that Arminian Christians are, in practice, more truly biblical and Reformed than are those who speak of Calvin as their leader? If only the present writer, in presuming to differ from Reformed thinkers of the past and present, were true to his principles and ideals! Truly, with Augustine, our prayer should ever be for humility and more humility. Even so, necessity is laid upon us. The gospel must be heard without compromise. The whole world lies in darkness. Modern philosophers follow one another about in circles within the hollow of a sphere that they have built about themselves. They will never question their common assumption of human autonomy. Therefore those who know that they were themselves in that state but have been taken out of it by grace must proclaim that grace to those who are in darkness still.

It is this one ideal that has controlled the writing of this book. First, the main contents of the gospel of grace is briefly set forth in terms of theology (Chapter I). Then this same gospel is set forth in terms of philosophy (Chapters II-IV). Finally, this gospel is presented to the "natural man" in order that he might be saved (Chapters V-XI). It is especially in the last chapters that controversial matters have been brought in. Even so, the main goal throughout is the discovery of the most Biblical and therefore the most effective way of bringing Christ to men.

For those who, after finishing this work, wish to pursue the various areas discussed in more depth, unpublished class syllabi are available. They may be most profitably consulted in the following order: First, *The Protestant Doctrine of Scripture;* second, *Introduction to Systematic Theology;* third, *A Christian Theory of Knowledge;* fourth, *History of Christian Epistemology;* fifth, *Apologetics;* sixth, *Christian Theistic Evidences;* seventh, *Christian Theistic Ethics;* eighth, *The Triumph of Grace;* ninth, *Sovereign Grace Defended,* and finally, *The Psychology of Religion.* None of these materials, however, is to be regarded as a published work. Various papers developing particular subjects, either mimeographed or in single copies, may be found in the Westminster Theological Seminary Library, as well as publications and syllabi of the present writer which are now out of print. Material from these syllabi quoted in this book can be identified by its smaller type.

CHAPTER I

CHRISTIAN THEOLOGY

The basic structure of Christian theology is simple. Its every teaching should be taken from the Scriptures of the Old and New Testament as being the words of prophets and apostles spoken on the authority of Jesus Christ, the Son of God and Son of Man, the Saviour of sinners.

The Confessions of the Reformed Churches have sought to reproduce the content of Christ's teachings as found in his Word in order to make it effective for purposes of teaching and defense.

We may therefore speak of the "system of truth" contained in Scripture if only we are careful to note that its various doctrines are not to be obtained by way of deduction from some master concept. There is no doubt consonance between the "doctrine of God," the "doctrine of man" and the "doctrine of Christ" as found in Scripture. But even when conjoined and seen in their fullest harmony, these and other doctrines together do not begin to exhaust the riches of God's revelation to man through Christ and his Spirit.

In this work we are concerned with the defense of the "system of truth" presented in Scripture. We must begin by asking what it is we believe.

It is impossible and useless to seek to defend Christianity as an historical religion by a discussion of facts only. We say that Christ arose from the grave. We say further that this resurrection proves his divinity. This is the nerve of the historical argument for Christianity. Yet a pragmatist philosopher will refuse to follow this line of reasoning. Granted he allows that Christ actually arose from the grave, he will say that this proves nothing more than that something very unusual took place in the case of that man Jesus. The pragmatist's philosophy is that everything in this universe is unrelated and that such a fact as the resurrection of Jesus, granted it were a fact, would have no significance for us who live two thousand years after him. It is apparent from this that if we would really defend Christianity as an historical religion we must at the same time defend the theism upon which Christianity is based and this involves us in philosophical discussion.

But to engage in philosophical discussion does not mean that we begin without Scripture. We do not first defend theism philosophically by an appeal to reason and experience in order, after that, to turn to Scripture for our knowledge and defense of Christianity. We get our theism as well as our Christianity from the Bible.

The Bible is thought of as authoritative on everything of which it speaks. And *it speaks of everything*. We do not mean that it speaks of football games, of atoms, etc., directly, but we do mean that it speaks of everything either directly or indirectly. It tells us not only of the Christ and his work but it also tells us who God is and whence the universe has come. It gives us a philosophy of history as well as history. Moreover, the information on these subjects is woven into an inextricable whole. It is only if you reject the Bible as the Word of God that you can separate its so-called religious and moral instruction from what it says, e.g., about the physical universe.

It is therefore the system of truth as contained in Scripture which we must present to the world. The various theological disciplines contribute to the setting forth of this system. It is the business of dogmatic or systematic theology to set forth this system under several main headings. So we take the headings of systematic theology as we find them worked out, for instance, in such manuals as Professor Louis Berkhof has written. In them we find discussions on (a) the doctrine of God, (b) the doctrine of man, (c) the doctrine of Christ, (d) the doctrine of the church, (e) the doctrine of salvation, and (f) the doctrine of the last things.

In each case the Reformed position is shown to be that which Scripture teaches. The Romanist, the Arminian and other views are shown not to be fully Biblical. So before turning to the question of the defense of the Reformed Faith, we must know, in general, what it is.

I

The Doctrine of God

Naturally in the system of theology and in apologetics the doctrine of God is of fundamental importance. We must first ask what kind of a God Christianity believes in before we can really ask with intelligence whether such a God exists. The *what* precedes the *that*; the connotation precedes the denotation; at least the latter cannot be discussed intelligently without at once considering the former.

What do we mean when we use the word God? Systematics answers this question in its discussion of the attributes or properties of God. These attributes are divided into incommunicable and communicable. Under the incommunicable attributes we have:

First, independence or aseity of God. By this is meant that God is in no sense correlative to or dependent upon anything beside his own being. God is the source of his own being, or rather the term source cannot be applied to God. God is *absolute*. He is sufficient unto himself.

Secondly, we speak of the *immutability* of God. Naturally God does not and cannot change since there is nothing besides his own eternal Being on which he depends (Mal. 3:6; James 1:7).

Thirdly, we speak of the infinity of God. In relation to the question of time we speak of the *eternity* of God while with respect to space we speak of the *omnipresence* of God. By the term eternity we mean that there is no beginning or end or succession of moments in God's being or consciousness (Ps. 90:2; 2 Pet. 3:8). This conception of eternity is of particular importance in Apologetics because it involves the whole question of the meaning of the temporal universe: it involves a definite philosophy of history. By the term omnipresence we mean that God is neither included in space nor absent from it. God is above all space and yet present in every part of it (1 Kings 8:27; Acts 17:27).

Fourthly, we speak of the *unity* of God. We distinguish between the unity of singularity (*singularitatis*) and the unity of simplicity (*simplicitatis*). The unity of singularity has reference to numerical oneness. There is and can be only one God. The unity of simplicity signifies that God is in no sense composed of parts or aspects that existed prior to himself (Jer. 10:10; I John 1:5).

The attributes of God are not to be thought of otherwise than as aspects of the one simple original being; the whole is identical with the parts. On the other hand the attributes of God are not characteristics that God has developed gradually; they are fundamental to his being; the parts together form the whole. Of the whole matter we may say that the unity and the diversity in God are equally basic and mutually dependent upon one another. The importance of this doctrine for Apologetics may be seen from the fact that the whole problem of philosophy may be summed up in the question of the relation of unity to diversity; the so-called problem of the one and the many receives a definite answer from the doctrine of the simplicity of God.

Man cannot partake of these incommunicable attributes of God. Man cannot in any sense be the source of his own being; man cannot in any sense be immutable or eternal or omnipresent or simple. These attributes therefore emphasize the *transcendence* of God.

Under God's communicable attributes we may speak of God as light, God as the Holy One and God as Sovereign.[1] The first of these pertains to God's knowledge of himself and the world.

[1] Louis Berkhof, Reformed Dogmatics, Vol. I, p. 43.

The second pertains to his moral nature and its significance for man and the world. The third pertains to God's power and its relation to the world.

God's knowledge of himself is self-contained. It is not dependent upon eternal ideas of truth above him. There are no hidden depths in God's being unknown to him. God's knowledge of himself may therefore be called absolute or self-referential.

God's knowledge of the world is, in the nature of the case, not obtained as the result of an investigation of the facts and laws of the world. The facts and laws of the world are what they are because of God's plan with respect to them. Therefore his knowledge of the world is involved in his plan for the world. Thus his knowledge of the facts and laws of the world precede the existence of the world.

God's holiness refers to his attribute whereby he is internally and eternally perfect. God's holy character is back of his expressed requirement of man that he must be perfect as a creature. What God says is right is right because he says it and he says it because it rests on his holy nature.

God's sovereignty refers to the fact that there is no other ultimate power beside himself and that his holy plan for the world will prevail over all opposition against it.

The incommunicable attributes of God stress his transcendence and the communicable attributes stress his immanence. The two imply one another. A Christian notion of transcendence and a Christian notion of immanence go together.

It is not a sufficient description of Christian theism when we say that as Christians we believe in both the transcendence and the immanence of God while pantheistic systems believe only in the immanence of God and deistic systems believe only in the transcendence of God. The transcendence we believe in is not the transcendence of deism and the immanence we believe in is not the immanence of pantheism. In the case of deism transcendence virtually means separation while in the case of pantheism immanence virtually means identification. And if we add separation to identification we do not have theism as a result. As we mean a certain kind of God when as theists we speak of God, so also we mean a certain kind of transcendence and a certain kind of immanence when we use these terms. The Christian doctrine of God implies a definite conception of the relation of God to the created universe. So also the Christian doctrine of God implies a definite conception of everything in the created universe.

a. *The Personality of God*

What we have discussed under the attributes of God may also be summed up by saying that God is *absolute personality*. The attributes themselves speak of self-conscious and moral activity on the part of God. Recognizing that for this intellectual and moral activity God is dependent upon nothing beyond his own being, we see that we have the Reformed doctrine of the *personality* of God. There were no principles of truth, goodness or beauty that were next to or above God according to which he patterned the world. The principles of truth, goodness, and beauty are to be thought of as identical with God's being; they are the attributes of God. Non-Christian systems of philosophy do not deny personality to God, at least some of them do not, but, in effect, they all agree in denying absolute personality to God. As Christians we say that we can be like God and must be like God in that we are persons but that we must always be unlike God in that he is an absolute person while we are finite persons. Non-theists, on the other hand, maintain that though God may be a greater person than we can ever hope to be yet we must not maintain this distinction between absolute and finite personality to be a qualitative one.

b. *The Trinity*

Another point in the Christian doctrine of God that needs to be mentioned here is the trinity. We hold that God exists as a tri-personality. "The trinity is the heart of Christianity."[2] The three persons of the trinity are co-substantial; not one is derived in his substance from either or both of the others. Yet there are three distinct persons in this unity; the diversity and the identity are equally underived.

We have now before us in bare outline the main points of the Christian doctrine of God. Christianity offers the triune God,

[2] H. Bavinck: *Gereformeerde Dogmatiek*, II, 289.

the absolute personality, containing all the attributes enumerated, as the God in whom we believe. This conception of God is the foundation of everything else that we hold dear. Unless we can believe in this sort of God, it does us no good to be told that we may believe in some other sort of God, or in anything else. For us everything depends for its meaning upon this sort of God.

II

The Doctrine of Man

The whole question with which we deal in Apologetics is one of the relation between God and man. Hence, next to the doctrine of God the doctrine of man is of fundamental importance.

a. *The Image of God in Man*

Man is created *in God's image.* He is therefore like God in everything in which a creature can be like God. He is like God in that he too is a personality. This is what we mean when we speak of the image of God in the wider or more general sense. Then when we wish to emphasize the fact that man resembles God especially in the splendour of his moral attributes we say that when man was created he had true knowledge, true righteousness and true holiness. This doctrine is based upon the fact that in the New Testament we are told that Christ came to restore us to true knowledge, righteousness and holiness (Col. 3:10; Eph. 4:24). We call this the image of God in the narrower sense. These two cannot be completely separated from one another. It would really be impossible to think of man having been created only with the image of God in the wider sense; every act of man would from the very first have to be a moral act, an act of choice for or against God. Hence man would even in every act of knowledge manifest true righteousness and true holiness.

Then after emphasizing that man was like God and in the nature of the case had to be like God we must stress the point that man must always be different from God. Man was *created* in God's image. We have seen that some of God's attributes are incommunicable. Man can never in any sense outgrow his creaturehood. This puts a definite connotation into the expression that man is *like* God. He is like God, to be sure, but always on a creaturely scale. He can never be like God in God's aseity, immutability, infinity and unity. For that reason the church has embedded into the heart of its confessions the doctrine of the incomprehensibility of God. God's being and knowledge are absolutely comprehensive; such knowledge is too wonderful for man; he cannot attain unto it. Man was not created with comprehensive knowledge. Man was finite and his finitude was originally no burden to him. Neither could man ever expect to attain to comprehensive knowledge in the future. We cannot expect to have comprehensive knowledge even in heaven. It is true that much will be revealed to us that is now a mystery to us but in the nature of the case God cannot reveal to us that which as creatures we cannot comprehend; we should have to be God ourselves in order to understand God in the depth of his being. God must always remain mysterious to man.

The significance of this point will appear more fully when we contrast this conception of mystery with the non-Christian conception of mystery that is current today even in Christian circles. The difference between the Christian and the non-Christian conception of mystery may be expressed in a word by saying that we hold that there is mystery for man but not for God while the non-Christian holds that there is either no mystery for God or man or there is mystery for both God and man.

b. *Man's Relation to the Universe*

Next to noting that man was created in God's image we must now observe that man was organically related to the universe about him. That is, man was to be prophet, priest and king under God in this created world. The vicissitudes of the world would depend upon the deeds of man. As a prophet man was to interpret this world, as a priest he was to dedicate this world to God and as a king he was to rule over it for God. In opposition to this all non-Christian theories hold that the vicissitudes of man and the universe about him are only accidentally and incidentally related to one another.

c. *The Fall of Man*

The fall of man needs emphasis as much as his creation. As we believe that man was once upon a time created by God in the image of God, so we also believe that soon thereafter man through disobedience fell into sin. After we have discussed what we mean by God and what we mean by the creation of man in the image of God, we can readily see what the nature of sin must be. As a creature of God man had to live in accordance with the law of God, that is, in accordance with the ordinances that God had placed in his creation. This law was for the most part not verbally transmitted to man but was created in his being. Man would act in accord with his own true nature only if he would obey the law of God and, vice versa, if he would live in accord with his own nature, he would obey the law of God. True, God did communicate to man over and above what was embedded in his very nature the specific commandment not to eat of the tree of knowledge of good and evil. But this was only to force an immediate and final test as to whether man would really live in accordance with the law of God as everywhere revealed within and about him.

When man fell it was therefore his attempt to do without God in every respect. Man sought his ideals of truth, goodness and beauty somewhere beyond God, either directly within himself or in the universe about him. God had interpreted the universe for him, or we may say man had interpreted the universe under the direction of God, but now he sought to interpret the universe without reference to God; we mean of course without reference to the kind of God defined above.

The result for man was that he made for himself *a false ideal of knowledge.* Man made for himself the ideal of absolute comprehension in knowledge. This he could never have done if he had continued to recognize that he was a creature. It is totally inconsistent with the idea of creatureliness that man should strive for comprehensive knowledge; if it could be attained, it would wipe God out of existence; man would then be God. And, as we shall see later, because man sought for this unattainable ideal, he brought upon himself no end of woe.

In conjunction with man's false ideal of knowledge, we may mention here the fact that when man saw he could not attain his own false ideal of knowledge, he blamed this on his finite character. *Man confused finitude with sin.* Thus he commingled the metaphysical and the ethical aspects of reality. Not willing to take the blame for sin, man laid it to circumstances round about him or within him.

III

The Doctrine of Christ

When we have discussed the doctrine of God and the doctrine of man, we have the two points between which the knowledge transaction takes place. Yet since sin has come into the world, we cannot see the whole of the picture of reality from the Christian point of view until we see how God and man are brought together after their separation. Reconciliation is possible only if God brings about salvation for man and therewith reunion with himself. Christ came to bring man back to God.

To do this he was and had to be truly God. For this reason the church has emphasized the fact that Christ was "Very God of Very God." Here it appears how important it is that we first think of the ontological trinity before we think of the economical trinity. It was the second person of the ontological trinity, who was, in respect of his essence, fully equal with the Father, who therefore existed from all eternity with the Father, who in the incarnation assumed a human nature.

This does not mean that he laid aside his divine nature or that he became a human person. Nor does it mean that he became a divine-human person. Nor does it mean that the divine and human natures were intermingled. Christ was and remained even when he was in the manger in Bethlehem a divine person but this divine person took to itself in close union with its divine nature a human nature. The Creed of Chalcedon has expressed all this by saying that in Christ the divine and the human natures are so related as to be "two natures, without confusion, without change, without division, without separation." The former two adjectives safeguard against the idea that the divine and the human are in any sense intermingled; the latter two adjectives assert the full reality of the union.

It will be noted at this point that this view of the incarnation is in full accord with the doctrine of God as above set forth. If Christ is really the second person of the ontological trinity, he shares in the incommunicable attributes of the Godhead. Accordingly, this implies that even in the incarnation Christ could not commingle the eternal and the temporal. The eternal must always remain independent of and prior to the temporal.

In addition to this brief statement about the person of Christ we must say a word about his offices.

Christ is true prophet, priest and king. The Westminster Shorter Catechism asks, "How does Christ execute the office of a Prophet?" The answer is: "Christ executeth the office of a Prophet, in revealing to us by his Word and Spirit, the will of God for our salvation." Now if we recall that man set for himself a false ideal of knowledge when he became a sinner, that is, he lost true wisdom, we may say that in Christ man was re-instated to true knowledge. In Christ man realizes that he is a creature of God and that he must not seek for comprehensive knowledge. Christ is our wisdom. He is our wisdom not only in the sense that he tells us how to get to heaven; he is our wisdom too in teaching us true knowledge about everything concerning which we should have knowledge.

Again the catechism asks: "How does Christ execute the office of a Priest?" The answer is: "Christ executeth the office of a Priest, in his once offering up himself a sacrifice to satisfy divine justice, and reconcile us to God, and in making continual intercession for us." We need not discuss this point except to indicate that Christ's work as priest cannot be separated from his work as prophet. Christ could not give us true knowledge of God and of the universe unless he *died* for us as priest. The question of knowledge is an ethical question at the root. It is indeed possible to have theoretically correct knowledge about God without loving God. The devil illustrates this point. Yet what is meant by knowing God in Scripture is *knowing and loving* God: this is *true* knowledge of God: the other is *false*.

In the third place the catechism asks: "How does Christ execute the office of a King?" The answer is: "Christ executeth the office of a King, in subduing us to himself, in ruling and defending us, and in restraining and conquering all of his and our enemies." Again we observe that this work of Christ as king must be brought into organic connection with his work as prophet and priest. To give us true wisdom or knowledge Christ must *subdue* us. He died for us to subdue us and thus gave us wisdom. It is only by emphasizing this organic connection of the aspects of the work of Christ that we can avoid all mechanical separation of the intellectual and the moral aspects of the question of knowledge.

IV

The Doctrine of Salvation

We have laid stress upon the organic relation between the offices of Christ. We must now point out that the same organic relationship exists between what Christ did *for* us and what Christ did and does *within* us. In Soteriology we deal with the application *to* us of the redemption Christ has wrought *for* us. Sin being what it is, it would be useless to have salvation lie ready at hand unless it were also applied to us. Inasmuch as we are dead in trespasses and sins, it would do us no good to have a wonderful life-giving potion laid next to us in our coffin. It would do us good only if some one actually administered the potion to us.

This point is already involved in the fact that Christ must subdue us in order to give us knowledge. But this subduing of us by Christ is done through his Spirit. It is the Spirit who takes the things of Christ and gives them unto us. If Christ is to do his own work the Spirit must do his. For that reason Christ told the disciples it would profit them if he should ascend to heaven. It would only be after his ascent that the Spirit could come and finish the work that Christ had begun to do while on earth. What Christ did while he was on earth is only a beginning of his work.

For this reason we must observe at this juncture that the Spirit who applies the work of Christ is himself also a member of the ontological trinity. He would have to be. Unless he were, the work of salvation would not be the work of God alone. If God was to be maintained in his incommunicable attributes the Spirit of God, not man, had to effect the salvation of man. The only alternative to this would be that man could at some point take the initiative in the matter of his own salvation. This would imply that the salvation wrought by Christ could be frustrated by man. Suppose that none should accept the salvation offered to them. In that case the whole of Christ's work would be in vain and the eternal God would be set at nought by temporal man. Even if we say that in the case of any one individual sinner the question of salvation is in the last analysis dependent upon man rather than upon God, that is if we say that man can of himself accept or reject the gospel as he pleases, we have made the eternal God dependent upon man. We have then, in effect, denied the incommunicable attributes of God. If we refuse to mix the eternal and the temporal at the point of creation and at the point of the incarnation we must also refuse to mix them at the point of salvation.

It will be noted that the point discussed in the preceding paragraph is the difference between Arminianism and Calvinism. It may be asked whether we should not in Apologetics ignore the difference that exists between different theological schools and defend the "common faith."

From what we have said above, however, it ought to appear that we cannot take this attiude. The difference between Calvinism and Arminianism is a difference in the conception of the relation of the eternal God and temporal man. Now since we hold that only such a view of theology as holds without compromise at any point to the conception of God as absolutely independent of man can really be said to represent the consistently Christian position, and since the whole debate between the Christian and the non-Christian position revolves about the question of the relation of the eternal to the temporal or of God to man, it will be apparent that we must hold that Arminianism can offer no effective Apologetic for Christianity. It is up to the Arminian to show, if he can, that his view offers a better Apologetic for Christianity than that offered by the Calvinist. Certain it is that the difference between Calvinism and Arminianism cannot be ignored. He who tries to ignore it has in effect already taken the Arminian position. We shall not make much progress against the common enemy if we ignore such differences between ourselves. A Calvinist naturally thinks that the Arminian is letting the enemy into the fort in spite of what he thinks he is doing; on the other hand an Arminian thinks that the Calvinist is letting the enemy into the fort without knowing it.

V

The Doctrine of the Church

"The catholic or universal church, which is invisible, consists of the whole number of the elect, that have been, are, or shall be gathered into one, under Christ the head thereof; and is the spouse, the body, the fullness of him that filleth all in all." Such is the Westminster Confession's definition of the church. This definition contains the same conception of the relation of the eternal to the temporal as is manifest in the doctrine of salvation. In the last analysis, it is the eternal that precedes the temporal; it is God who determines the salvation of man; the church, that is, the invisible church, is the "whole number of the elect." This does not preclude human responsibility. The Confession has spoken of man's responsibility and "free will" in preceding articles. It only brings out clearly that God is absolute, here as elsewhere.

It is this fact of God's absoluteness as expressed in his election of men that gives us courage in preaching and in reasoning with men. Sin being what it is, we may be certain that all our preaching and all our reasoning with men will be in vain unless God brings men to bay. Men cannot be brought to bay if they have any place to which they can go. And they do have a place to which they can go if they have the inherent ability to accept or reject the gospel, in which case they need not feel uneasy about rejecting it today, because they can accept it tomorrow.

VI

The Doctrine of the Last Things

When we come to the Christian conception of the "last things," we see once more how diametrically the Christian position is set over against that of its opponents. It becomes especially plain here that in the Christian conception of things interpretation precedes facts. Every Christian who trusts his future to God believes that God controls the future. He believes that God has interpreted the future; he believes that the future will come to pass as God has planned it. Prophecy illustrates this point. Belief in the promises of God with respect to our eternal salvation is meaningless if God does not control the future. We look forward to the facts to come because we accept the interpretation of them given us by God.

Here too we see again that we cannot separate man from the universe around him. Christ spoke of the "regeneration of all things" when he spoke of the end of the world. The promises for the future include a new heaven and a new earth in which righteousness shall dwell. This righteousness includes the fact that the wolf and the lamb shall feed together and that the animal will do man no harm. We interpret nature only by the light of the interpretation of God. Then too the time when all this will happen is exclusively in God's hand. If we seek to interpret the "signs of the times" we are to seek to interpret them as God has already interpreted them. We interpret history only by the light of the interpretation of God. The Christian philosophy of nature and the Christian philosophy of history are the diametrical opposites of the non-Christian philosophy of nature and the non-Christian philosophy of history.

In this first chapter we have only a very broad and general statement of what we are going to vindicate as being the truth of God. But even in this broad survey it is shown *first* that it is the Reformed Faith, not some common denominator "core" of Christianity, that must be defended. By the "Christian philosophy of life" I mean the truths of Scripture as set forth by the classical Reformed theologians under the *loci* enumerated.

We may therefore speak of classic Reformed theology as over against the dialectical theology of such modern theologians as Emil Brunner and Karl Barth.[3]

[3] Some recent Reformed writers have found the terminology used in this chapter "scholastic." The writer's main concern is that it shall be true to *biblical* meaning. Although it may appear "scholastic" in form, it is biblical in content.

Classic Reformed theology may be thought of as best expressing the genius of historic Protestantism: first as over against Romanism, second as over against the modern Protestantism of Friedrich Schleiermacher and his school, and third as over against the "theology of the word" of neo-orthodox or Barthian theology. These three movements are drawing ever more closely together in order to join forces against the fully biblical approach of classical Reformed thinking.

APPENDIX TO CHAPTER I

(a) In his *Church Dogmatics* Karl Barth has substituted a modern dialectical view of the relation of the two natures of Christ for that of the historic Christian church. Barth holds that in the incarnation God turns wholly into the opposite of himself and man participates in the being of God. Cf. the writer's *Karl Barth on Chalcedon.*

(b) Barth's idea of the work of Christ is again informed by his dialectical motif. According to Barth, the steps in Christ's exaltation do not follow in history upon the steps of his humiliation. Thus there is, on Barth's view, no transition from wrath to grace in history. The real transaction between man, Barth argues, takes place not in history but in *Geschichte.* Cf. the writer's *Christianity and Barthianism.*

Chapter II

THE CHRISTIAN PHILOSOPHY OF REALITY

After we answer, in preliminary fashion, the question as to *what* we believe as Reformed Christians, we face the problem how to get people interested in our faith. Men in general do not use or even know our theological terms. But, to the extent that they are educated, they have had some training in secular philosophy. They have a non-Christian familiarity with the categories of God, man and the universe. If we are to speak to them and win them, it is necessary for us to learn their language.

There is no possibility of avoiding this. We can make no contact with men unless we speak to them in their language.[1] Many men, in declaring that they believe in God, assume that God is identical with Reality. It must be demonstrated to them that when we speak of reality, we at once make a distinction within it, namely the reality of God as self-sufficient and of the universe as existing by his plan,

[1] I do not understand why my critics object when I use such terms as "concrete universal" or employ such terms as "the universal," "the particular," "the one and many." Especially do I not understand this on the part of those who are "experts in philosophy" and whose business it is to teach philosophy from the Christian point of view. The charge of "intellectual anabaptism" might well be lodged against me if, as a teacher of Christian apologetics, I failed to translate Christian truth in the language of the day. Is not the important thing that Christian meanings be contrasted with non-Christian meanings? The Apostles did not shun the usage of language borrowed from non-Christian sources. When they used the term *logos* must they be thought of as followers of Philo's non-Christian thought simply because he also used that term?

creation and providence. This distinction in being will have basic significance for our views of knowledge and behavior. Our view of reality or being involves a view of knowledge and of ethics even as our view of knowledge and ethics involves and is based on our view of being.

But we cannot set forth a complete system of being, of knowledge and of ethics.

We need do no more than take a few of the main concepts of the system of theology and state them in philosophical terms.[2] So we need to use the language of the philosophers. But most philosophers have not been Christians. At any rate philosophical language has to a great extent been formed under non-Christian influence. Is it not likely then that we shall, if we use the language of philosophers, also import into the Christian scheme of things the problems of philosophy as these have been formulated by non-Christian people? . . . The answer is that we shall be obliged, to a large extent, to use the language of the philosophers or we shall have no point of contact with them. But we shall have to be on our guard to put Christian content into this language that we borrow.[2]

The philosophers have sought for a unified outlook on human experience. Philosophers have sought for as comprehensive a picture of the nature of reality as a whole as man is able to attain. But the universe is composed of many things. Man's problem is to find unity in the midst of the plurality of things. He sometimes calls this the One-and-Many problem. To this formulation of the problem of philosophy we have no objection. We too formulate our conception of the nature of philosophy from our notion of the totality picture that we think we have. "It will be our business then to take the totality picture of Christianity, and compare it with the totality picture of non-Christian thought.

[2] *Apologetics,* p. 13. The material which follows (I and II) also appeared originally in the author's syllabus on *Christian Apologetics.*

I

Eternal Unity and Plurality

The difference between a Christian and a non-Christian philosophy will appear to be a basic difference so soon as we attempt to take the first step in answering the One-and-Many question from the Christian point of view. In answering this question of the One-and-Many we find it necessary to distinguish between the Eternal One-and-Many and the temporal one and many. Non-Christian philosophers on the other hand find it unnecessary to make this distinction. We find this necessary of course because our conception of God as the triune God stands at the center of our thinking. We may express this thought philosophically by saying that for us the eternal one and many form a self-complete unity. God is absolute personality and therefore absolute individuality. He exists necessarily. He has no non-being over against himself in comparison with which he defines himself; he is internally self-defined.

Using the language of the One-and-Many question we contend that in God the one and the many are equally ultimate. Unity in God is no more fundamental than diversity, and diversity in God is no more fundamental than unity. The persons of the Trinity are mutually exhaustive of one another. The Son and the Spirit are ontologically on a par with the Father. It is a well-known fact that all heresies in the history of the church have in some form or other taught subordinationism. Similarly, we believe, all "heresies" in apologetic methodology spring from some sort of subordinationism.

It may be profitable at this juncture to introduce the notion of a *concrete universal.* In seeking for an answer to the One-and-Many question, philosophers have admittedly experienced great difficulty. The *many* must be brought into contact with one another. But how do we know that they can be brought into contact with one another? How do we know that the many do not simply exist as unrelated particulars? The answer given is that in such a case we should know nothing of them; they would be abstracted from the body of knowledge that we have; they would be *abstract* particulars. On the other hand, how is it possible that we should obtain a unity that does not destroy the particulars? We seem to get our unity by generalizing, by abstracting from the particulars in order to include them into larger unities. If we keep up this process of generalization till we exclude all particulars, granted they can all be excluded, have we then not stripped these particulars of their particularity? Have we then obtained anything but an *abstract* universal?

As Christians we hold that there is no answer to these problems from a non-Christian point of view. We shall argue this point later; for the nonce we introduce this matter in order to set forth the meaning of the notion of the concrete universal. The notion of the concrete universal has been offered by idealist philosophy in order to escape the *reductio ad absurdum* of the abstract particular and the abstract universal. It is only in the Christian doctrine of the triune God, as we are bound to believe, that we really have a *concrete universal.*[3] In God's being there are no particulars not related to the universal and there is nothing universal that is not fully expressed in the particulars.

II

Temporal Unity and Plurality

It goes without saying that if we hold to the eternal one and many in the manner explained above we must hold the temporal one and many to be *created* by God. We said above that God needed no such thing as *non-being* over against himself in order to define himself in comparison with it. Christianity takes non-being seriously. In discussing the question of non-being we hasten to distinguish between God's relation to non-being and man's relation to non-being. For God non-being is nothing in itself; for man non-being is the field of God's possible operation. Since non-being is nothing in itself for God, God had to create, if he wished to create at all "out of nothing." It would perhaps be better to say that God created the universe *into* nothing. Creation, on Christian principles, must always mean fiat creation.

[3] The reader may note that the meaning I attribute to the phrase "concrete universal" is sharply contrasted with the meaning attributed to the same phrase by idealist philosophers.

If the creation doctrine is thus taken seriously, it follows that the various aspects of created reality must sustain such relations to one another as have been ordained between them by the Creator, as superiors, inferiors or equals. All aspects being equally created, no one aspect of reality may be regarded as more ultimate than another. Thus the created *one and many* may in this respect be said to be *equal* to one another; they are equally derived and equally dependent upon God who sustains them both. The particulars or facts of the universe do and must act in accord with universals or laws. Thus there is order in the created universe. On the other hand, the laws may not and can never reduce the particulars to abstract particulars or reduce their individuality in any manner. The laws are but generalizations of God's method of working with the particulars. God may at any time take one *fact* and set it into a new relation to created law. That is, there is no inherent reason in the facts or laws themselves why this should not be done. It is this sort of conception of the relation of facts and laws, of the temporal one and many, imbedded as it is in that idea of God in which we profess to believe, that we need in order to make room for miracles. And miracles are at the heart of the Christian position.

Thus there is a basic equality between the created one and the created many, or between the various aspects of created reality. On the other hand, there is a relation of subordination between them as ordained by God. The "mechanical" laws are lower than the "teleological" laws. Of course, both the "mechanical" and the "teleological" laws are teleological in the sense that both obey God's will. So also the facts of the physical aspect of the universe are lower than the facts of the will and intellect of man. It is this subordination of one fact and law to other facts and laws that is spoken of in Scripture as man's government over nature. According to Scripture man was set as king over nature. He was to subdue it. Yet he was to subdue it for God. He was priest under God as well as king under God. In order to subdue it under God man had to interpret it; he was therefore prophet as well as priest and king under God.[4]

[4] For a detailed analysis of the relation of the aspects of the God-created and redeemed universe to one another see Herman Dooyeweerd's *A New Critique of Theoretical Thought.*

The subordination of one fact and law under higher created facts and laws appears particularly in the notion of miracle. When Moses commanded the sea to stand aside so that Israel might go through dry-shod, the laws of the physical universe were set aside at the behest of the will of man. But the subordination of the laws of nature to the will of man was in order to the subordination of the will of man to God.

Using the current terminology of philosophy we may express what we have said about the subordination of one aspect of the created universe to other aspects of the created universe by saying that the lower *universes of discourse* anticipate the higher, and the higher universes of discourse look back to the lower universes of discourse. The mechanical universe of discourse is subject to and anticipates the organic, while the organic looks back to the mechanical. In turn the organic universe of discourse anticipates the intellectual and moral universes of discourse, while these look back to the organic.

III

Sin and Its Curse

To the theism set forth above, Christianity must now be added. Due to the sin of man the curse of God rests upon the whole creation. Man has joined Satan in his opposition to God. At the same time God has inserted a remedial influence against sin into the world. This remedial work centers in the Christ.

He came forth "To destroy the works of the evil one." He came to bring peace, to be sure, but the peace that he came to bring must be built upon the complete destruction of the power of darkness. "I came not to bring peace upon the earth but the sword." Such was the message of the Prince of Peace. To herald this message, he sent prophets before him and apostles after him. When most enveloped in this message, when most enthusiastic about this peace, the psalmist cries out: "Shall I not hate those that hate thee? I hate them with a perfect hatred." When he was on earth Christ entered the arena with Satan single-handed and triumphed. He is seen by John the Apostle, riding upon his white horse, conquering and to conquer. When he sees his armies languish, weary of the fight, his clarion voice bids them put on the whole armour of God. They may not waver, it is the church militant, this people of God. Only those who fight to the end receive the crown. And then there is peace indeed. In the "regeneration of all things" he that sits upon the throne is surrounded by the twenty-four elders and the four living creatures. The whole creation is there; the whole creation is redeemed. No discordant voice is heard. All sing the great song of the redeemed creation. Through redemption creation's purpose was accomplished. Where are the enemies? They are sealed in a soundproof exclusion chamber. Satan has lost the struggle; God is God.

Such then, in broad outline, is the Christian conception of being or the Christian conception of metaphysics. We may speak of it as a two-layer theory of reality. When men ask us, What is, according to your notion, the nature of reality or being?, we shall have to say that we cannot give an answer unless we are permitted to split the question. For us God's being is ultimate, while created being is, in the nature of the case, derivative.

Again, if we are asked, What do you think of the relation of the eternal to the temporal? we reply that the eternal for us does not exist as a principle but as a person, and that as an absolute person. Accordingly, we do not use the eternal as a correlative to the temporal; we use the notion of the eternal God as the personal creator of the temporal universe.

Once more, if men ask us as to which is first, *becoming* or *being*, we reply by saying first of all that the term becoming cannot be applied to God. God's being is not subject to becoming. He is eternal being. And as for created being, it is in the process of becoming by virtue of the plan of God. God's being, is therefore "before" the becoming of the created universe. The eternal One-and-Many are "prior to" the created one and many. We have put the words "before" and "prior to" in quotation marks. It will readily be seen that if our theory of reality is true, we cannot simply say that God is prior to the universe, meaning by "prior to" temporal priority. Inasmuch as God is not subject to time, we cannot enclose him in the calendar. God is the creator of time itself as a form of created being. On the other hand, if we say that God is "prior to" the created universe we do not simply mean what is usually meant by logical priority. God is, to be sure, logically "prior to" the created universe but he is logically prior by virtue of the fact that he has actually created the universe with its temporal form out of or into nothing. Without the notion of temporal creation, the notion of logical dependence cannot be maintained.

It will now be plain that our conception of the nature of reality goes counter to every theory of reality that the history of philosophy affords. That this is the case will appear more fully later. For the present we wish to emphasize the fact that we can do nothing less than take the conception of reality as we find it in a systematic theology that is based upon Scripture. And therewith we approach the problem of epistemology, our subject in the next chapter.

Chapter III

THE CHRISTIAN PHILOSOPHY OF KNOWLEDGE

Thus far we have asserted frankly that as Christians we find *what* we believe expressed in the Bible as the word of God. From the Bible we have taken our doctrines of God, man, Christ, salvation and the last things. As Reformed Christians we wish to show men that it is Reformed theology not Romanism, nor even some lower form of evangelical Protestantism, that they need.

When seeking to persuade men to accept the truth of the system of doctrine revealed in Scripture, we speak of our Christian view of Life. And we subdivide this Christian view of life into three main sections, the Christian theory of being, the Christian theory of knowledge and the Christian theory of ethics or behavior. We must set off the Christian view of life sharply from the non-Christian view of life. Basic to all the differences between the Christian and the non-Christian views of life is the fact that Christians worship and serve the Creator, while non-Christians worship and serve the creature. Through the fall of mankind in Adam, the first man, the representative of all men, all became creature-worshippers. But through the redemption wrought by Christ and applied to his people by the Holy Spirit, the chosen ones have learned, be it only in principle, to worship and serve the Creator more than the creature. They now believe the theory of reality offered in Scripture. They now believe in God as self-sufficient, in the creation of all things in this universe by God, in the fall of man at the beginning of history and in the "regeneration of all things" through Christ.

But it is just as important to have a Christian theory of knowledge as it is to have a Christian theory of being. One cannot well have the one without at the same time also having the other. Modern thought is largely preoccupied with the theory of knowledge. As Christians we shall therefore find it necessary to set the Christian theory of knowledge over against the modern form of the non-Christian theory of knowledge. Even so we shall have to make it plain that our theory of knowledge is what it is because our theory of being is what it is. As Christians we cannot begin speculating about knowledge by itself. We cannot ask *how* we know without at the same time asking what we know. We quote again from *Christian Apologetics.*

We have felt ourselves compelled to take our notions with respect to the nature of reality from the Bible. It will readily be conceded that such a notion of reality as we have presented could be received upon authority only. Such a notion of being as we have presented is to be found nowhere except in the Bible. The Bible is taken so seriously that we have not even left any area of known reality by which the revelation that comes to us in the Bible may be compared, or to which it may be referred as to a standard. We have taken the final standard of truth to be the Bible itself.

It is needless to say that this procedure will appear suicidal to most men who study philosophy. Is it not by the help of man's own reason that we are to think out the nature of reality and knowledge? To accept an interpretation of life upon authority is permissible only if we have looked into the foundations of the authority we accept. But if we must determine the foundations of the authority, we no longer accept authority on authority. Authority could be authority to us only if we already knew that it had the right to claim authority. Such could be the case only if we knew in advance the nature of that authority. Thus we would have a theory of being already taken for granted at the outset of our investigation. In this manner we could not give a fair hearing to opposing views.

A modern way of stating this objection to our position is found in the words of Dr. Edgar A. Singer's, *Notes on Experience and Reflection.*[1] Dr. Singer tells us it is the business of philosophy to ask, *How do we know?* In other words, according to Singer the epistemological question can and must be asked without saying anything with respect to the ontological question.

Is this position of Dr. Singer tenable? Suppose it is true, for argument's sake, that such a being as we have described God to be, does actually exist. Would not such a God have the right to speak to us with authority? Are we not, by saying that the question of knowledge is independent of the question of being, excluding one possible answer to the question of knowledge itself? If the Being of God is what on the basis of Scripture testimony we have found it to be, it follows that our knowledge will be true knowledge only to the extent that it corresponds to his knowledge. To say that we do not need to ask about the nature of reality when we ask about the nature of knowledge is not to be neutral but is in effect to exclude the Christian answer to the question of knowledge.

That Singer has in effect excluded from the outset the Christian answer to the question of knowledge appears from the fact that in his search for an answer to this question he affirms that we must go to *as many as possible* of those reputed to *have* knowledge (p. 5). The notion of going to One whose opinion may be more valuable than the opinion of others even to the extent of being authoritative over the opinion of others is not even considered. In paradise, Eve went to *as many as possible* of those who were reputed to have knowledge. God and Satan both had a reputation for knowledge. Apparently God did not think well of Satan's knowledge and Satan did not think well of God's knowledge but each thought well of his own knowledge. So Eve had to weigh these reputations. It was for her a question as to, How do we know?

The problem that Eve faced was a difficult one. God told her that she would surely die if she ate of the forbidden tree. Numerically there was only one in favor of one and only one in favor of the opposite point of view. Thus she could not settle the

[1] An unpublished class syllabus.

matter of reputation by numbers. She herself had to decide this matter of reputation by a motion and a vote. God claimed that he was the Creator. He claimed that his Being was ultimate while Satan's being was created and therefore dependent upon God's being. Satan said in effect that she should pay no attention to this problem of Being. He told her she should decide the question, *How do we know?* without asking the question, *What do we know?* He said she should be neutral with respect to his interpretation and God's interpretation of what would take place if she ate of the forbidden tree. Eve did ignore the question of being in answering the question of knowledge. She said she would gather the opinions of as many as she could find with a reputation for having knowledge and then give the various views presented a fair hearing.

We should observe particularly that in doing what she did Eve did not really avoid the question of *What do we know?* She gave by implication a very definite answer to that question. She made a negation with respect to God's Being. She denied God's Being as ultimate being. She affirmed therewith in effect that all being is essentially on one level.

At the same time she also gave a definite answer to the question *How do we know?* She said we know independently of God. She said that God's authority was to be tested by herself. Thus she came to take the place of ultimate authority. She was no doubt going to test God's authority by *experience* and *reflection* upon experience. Yet it would be *she,* herself, who should be the final authority.

It would appear then that the theory of being that we have presented fits in with the notion of the Bible as an authoritative revelation of God. Such a being as the Bible speaks of could not speak otherwise than with absolute authority. In the last analysis we shall have to choose between two theories of knowledge. According to one theory God is the final court of appeal; according to the other theory man is the final court of appeal.

To what we have said we must now add this further point. Sin has been most ruinous in the heart and mind of man. Man is "dead in trespasses and sins." If there is to be on man's part a recognition of God in his rightful place man must be *regenerated.* Without regeneration it is not possible for him to see the "kingdom of heaven."

Sin will reveal itself in the field of knowledge in the fact that man makes himself the ultimate court of appeal in the matter of all interpretation. He will refuse to recognize God's authority. We have already illustrated the sinful person's attitude by the narrative of Adam and Eve. Man has declared his autonomy as over against God.

This means that in the totality picture that man must seek for himself, he must go to Scripture as the final court of appeal. He learns form nature still, but what nature teaches him must be brought into relationship with what the Scriptures teach in order that it may be properly understood.

I

God's Knowledge of Himself

We have therefore a two-layer theory of knowledge as we have a two-layer theory of reality. The two stand or fall together. God, we have contended, is self-determinative. He has no non-being over against himself in terms of which he needs or can to any extent interpret himself. He is *omniscient.* He is omniscient because of what he is as a self-sufficient Being. On the other hand we must add that the nature of God's being requires complete exhaustive self-consciousness. *God's Being is coterminous with his self-consciousness.*

This point it is of importance to emphasize. There are those who say that God's being is absolute but God's consciousness is subject to succession of moments. This theory is introduced in order to help us understand how God can be aware of succession in our temporal world. The Arminian theologian, Watson, in his *Theological Institutes* reasons as follows with respect to the knowledge that God has of temporal events. "Duration then as applied to God, is no more than an extension of the idea as applied to ourselves; and to exhort us to conceive of it as something essentially different, is to require us to conceive what is inconceivable" (Vol. I, p. 357). In answer to the point made by Watson we observe the following: If we are to make the possibility of understanding the relation of time to eternity the test of a theory of eternity we shall soon have done with God's eternity entirely. An eternity, the relationship of which to time we should be able to comprehend, is destructive of the eternity of God as a self-determinative being. If we introduce time or succession of moments into the consciousness of God in order that we may understand how God is related to time we have to ask ourselves in turn how the consciousness of God is related to the being of God. Thus we should have to introduce succession of moments into the being of God for the same reason that we have introduced it into the consciousness of God.

In contrast with this, Scripture portrays God as omniscient, as being completely self-conscious. In God there can be no hidden depth of possibility unfathomed by his own consciousness. Neither can there be anything in non-being for which God must wait before he can be fully aware of himself. The limits of our thinking of God's relation to time should not be used as a standard for determining the nature of the knowledge of God.

It should be noted that it is only if we hold to the coterminеity of the being and the consciousness of God that we can avoid pantheism. If knowledge and being are not identical in God, as pertaining to himself, he is made dependent upon something that exists beside himself. In that case the consciousness of God is made to depend upon temporal reality and then the being of God in turn is made dependent upon temporal reality.

It is true that Spinoza, the pantheist, might also use the phrase that knowledge and being are identical in God. But what makes our position completely antithetical to that of Spinoza or any other non-theistic system of thought is the fact that when we identify knowledge and being in God we speak of the relation of God's own being to his knowledge only. We do not then speak of his knowledge of the things he has created. As we shall see later, it is upon the identity of knowledge and being in God that we pin our hopes and convictions that human predication is possible.

We do not hesitate to emphasize therefore that God has and is complete internal coherence. As far as God's own person is concerned the subject is the object of knowledge. His knowledge of himself is therefore entirely analytical. By that we do not suggest that God had to go through a process of looking into himself and finding information with respect to himself. It is impossible for us as creatures to get away from the temporal associations that come with all the words we use. But the term analytic has come to mean in the field of philosophy the idea of self-dependence. Analytical knowledge, in distinction from synthetic knowledge, means knowledge that is not gained by reference to something that exists without the knower. God knows himself not by comparing and contrasting himself with anything, not even non-being, outside himself. He knows himself by one simple eternal act of vision. In God therefore the real is the rational and the rational is the real.

II

God's Knowledge of the World

In the preceding paragraphs we spoke of God's knowledge of himself. We ask now as to the nature of God's knowledge of things beyond himself. Here we must turn to the creation doctrine. God had from all eternity a plan to create the universe. We may roughly and analogically compare this to the blueprint a contractor has of a house he is going to build. When the contractor has his blueprint he does not yet have his house. The idea of a thing and the reality of the thing are not identical for him. Similarly God had from all eternity the idea of a universe. Spinoza would conclude from this that therefore the universe has existed from all eternity. It is thus that he would apply his principle of identification of all Reality, including God and the universe, and all Rationality. In complete contradistinction from this we, as Christians, hold to the notion of creation into nothing. We distinctly affirm that God's eternal idea of the universe did not imply the eternal creation of the universe.

Quite obviously we have involved ourselves in difficulty here. We have maintained that God's knowledge of himself is analytical. We have said repeatedly that there was and can be no non-being over against God as in any sense determinative of God. Thus the rails would seem to be prepared for a run into the pantheistic switch. We have said that God's knowledge with respect to himself is identical with his being; would it not seem to follow that God's knowledge of the universe is to be identified with the being of the universe?

This argument is the converse of the argument which says that we must have succession of moments in the consciousness of God in order to think of God as appreciative of the passage of time in the universe. We have rejected this latter argument on the ground that it begins with a non-theistic assumption. It begins with the assumption that the temporal is the standard for our notions with respect to the eternal, while in reality the eternal should be our standard by which to understand the temporal. To be sure, we begin our human experience with awareness of ourselves as temporal beings. Yet if we think self-consciously we should see that our awareness of ourselves as temporal beings presupposes God's awareness of himself as an eternal being. We shall not now seek to develop this argument. We are at this juncture merely concerned to point out that as a matter of fact we deal here with the most basic contrast conceivable between a Christian and a non-Christian theory of knowledge. Christianity interprets reality in terms of the eternally self-conscious divine personality; non-Christian thought interprets reality in terms of an existence independent of God.

The argument that if we think of God's being and knowledge of himself as identical then we must also hold to eternal creation, must therefore be rejected as based upon an anti-theistic assumption. It is a finite created being who cannot understand how God can have completely comprehensive knowledge of all reality beside himself without determining the nature of that "outside" reality in such a way as to make it meaningless. It is a finite understanding which says that time is reduced to an absurdity if there is pre-interpretation of temporal reality. It is a finite understanding which would draw determinism from the statement that in God being and knowledge of his being are identical.

The finite mind cannot thus, if we are to reason theistically, be made the standard of what is possible and what is impossible. It is the divine mind that is determinative of the possible. We conclude then that God's knowledge of the universe is also analytical. God's knowledge of the universe depends upon God's knowledge of himself. God has made the universe in accordance with his eternal plan for that universe. Thus the very existence of the universe depends upon God's knowledge of or plan for the universe. God does, to be sure, behold the universe and the children of men as being "outside" himself. He beholds them now as actually existing beings engaged in actual work of their own, because he has from all eternity beheld them as going to exist. His knowledge of that which now takes place in the universe is logically dependent upon what he has from all eternity decided with respect to the universe.

III

Man's Knowledge of God

All of this may again be expressed from another point of view by saying that human knowledge is analogical of divine knowledge. We cannot avoid coming to a clear-cut decision with respect to the question as to whose knowledge, man's or God's, shall be made the standard of the other. The one must be original and the other analogical of the original. The one must be determinative and the other subordinate. Roman Catholic theology seeks to serve two masters here. It too speaks of created being and human knowledge as being analogical of divine being and divine knowledge but it does not really take this seriously. In its philosophy and apologetics Romanism reasons as though man can, by himself, determine the nature and possibility of knowledge without reference to God. On the other hand it refers to mysteries as being above the understanding of man. But as Protestants we should definitely choose to make God the original in the knowledge situation.

The first thing to note in the question of our knowledge of God is that it must be true or objective. That this is so is once more involved in our God-concept. God knows himself analytically and completely and therefore must know all things beyond him analytically and completely. God certainly must have true knowledge of us and of the universe in general. Our existence and our meaning, our denotation and our connotation are derived from God. We are already fully interpreted before we come into existence. God knows us before and behind; he knows the thoughts of our hearts. We could not have existence and meaning apart from the existence and meaning of God. All this is the road from God to us. But surely we can get back to God by the road that he has used to create us. If I lay a road in order to build a city somewhere the inhabitants of that city can come back to me by the road that I have built. Of course we might say that some one could destroy that road. In this case the city would still exist and yet its inhabitants could not get back to me. But this cannot be applied in the case of our relationship to God. It is not that we are merely brought into existence by God, but our meaning also depends upon God. Our meaning cannot be realized except through the course of history. God created man in order that man should realize a certain end, that is, the glory of God, and thus God should reach his own end. For that reason if we could think of the road between God and man as broken, it would mean also that we should no longer exist and thus the whole question would disappear.

We may safely conclude then that if God is what we say he is, namely a being who exists necessarily as a self-complete system of coherence, and we exist at all as self-conscious beings, we must have true knowledge of him. (We are not now speaking of the question of sin. That is an ethical and not a metaphysical question. Our metaphysical dependence upon God has not been wiped out by sin.) All this we express theologically when we say that man is created in God's image. This makes man like God and assures true knowledge of God. We are known of him and therefore we know him and know that we know him. God is light and therefore we have light.

Important as it is to insist that our knowledge of God must be true, because God is what he is, it is equally important to insist that our knowledge of God is not and cannot be comprehensive. We are God's creatures. We cannot know God comprehensively now nor can we hope to know God comprehensively hereafter. We may know much more in the future than we know now. Especially when we come to heaven will we know more than we know now, but we will not know comprehensively.

We are therefore like God so that our knowledge is true and we are unlike God and therefore our knowledge can never be comprehensive. When we say that God is a mystery for us we do not mean that our knowledge of him is not true as far as it goes. When we say that God is transcendent above us or when we say that God is "the absolutely Other" we do not mean that there is not a rational relation between God and us. As God created us in accordance with his plan, that is, as God created us in accordance with his absolute rationality, so there must be a rational relationship from us to God. Christianity is, in the last analysis, not an absolute irrationalism but an absolute "rationalism." In fact we may contrast every non-Christian epistemology with Christian epistemology by saying that Christian epistemology believes in an ultimate rationalism while all other systems of epistemology believe in an ultimate irrationalism.

When we say that as Christians we believe in an ultimate rationalism we are, naturally, not intending anything like the idea that we as human beings have or may at some time expect to have a comprehensive rational understanding of God. We have just asserted the contrary. Here too every non-Christian epistemology may be distinguished from Christian epistemology in that it is only Christian epistemology that does not set before itself the ideal of comprehensive knowledge for man. The reason for this is that it holds that comprehensive knowledge is found only in God. It is true that there must be comprehensive knowledge somewhere if there is to be any true knowledge anywhere but this comprehensive knowledge need not and cannot be in us; it must be in God.

IV

Man's Knowledge of the Universe

What we have said about man's knowledge of God is really determinative for what we have to say about man's knowledge of the universe. By the term universe we now mean the whole of the created world including man himself and his environment.

The first question we must ask with respect to the relation of our knowledge of God to our knowledge of the universe is, which of these two is prior?

Man cannot help but know himself at once in relation to his environment. The subject of knowledge must know itself in relation to and in contrast with the object of knowledge.

This contention that man must know himself in relation to his environment is not merely a general consideration obtained by observation of experience. It is implied in the very bedrock of Christian-theism. This may be seen by again referring to our idea of God and of God's relation to the created universe. Man exists by virtue of God's existence. Man's environment precedes man. God is man's ultimate environment and this environment is completely interpretative of man who is to know himself.

In other words man's environment is not impersonal. It is, moreover, not merely personal in the sense that simultaneous with his own appearance there are also other finite persons in relation to which he knows himself to be a person. Back of this relationship of finite persons to other finite persons and to other finite but impersonal things is the absolute personality of God. Back of the question as to whether man needs other finite persons or needs a finite non-personal environment is the question of the environment of man's immediate environment. God is man's ultimate environment and this ultimate environment controls the whole of man's immediate environment as well as man himself. The whole of man's own immediate environment as well as man himself is already interpreted by God. Even the denotation of the whole universe exists by virtue of the connotation or plan of God. Thus we have answered our question about temporal priority by answering the question of logical priority. Because man's knowledge of God is logically more fundamental than man's knowledge of the universe, we may be indifferent to the question of temporal priority. Even if in our psychological experience we know ourselves and the universe about us before we speak self-consciously of God, we have all the while known God if we have truly known anything else.

We have constantly emphasized the concept of God as being

basic to everything else which a Christian believes. This is so because God exists, as he exists, necessarily. For that reason we cannot know ourselves in any true sense unless we know God. He is our most ultimate and therefore absolutely indispensable environment. For that reason if we know him we know him truly though not comprehensively.

It follows from all this that we know the world truly too though not comprehensively.

Our argument for the objectivity of knowledge with respect to the universe can never be complete and satisfactory unless we bring in the relation of both the object and the subject of knowledge to God. We may debate endlessly about psychological problems without fruitage if we refuse to bring in the metaphysical question of the nature of reality. If the Christian position with respect to creation, that is, with respect to the idea of the origin of both the subject and the object of human knowledge is true, there is and must be objective knowledge. In that case the world of objects was made in order that the subject of knowledge, namely man, should interpret it under God. Without the interpretation of the universe by man to the glory of God the whole world would be meaningless. The subject and the object are therefore adapted to one another. On the other hand if the Christian theory of creation by God is not true then we hold that there cannot be objective knowledge of anything. In that case all things in this universe are unrelated and cannot be in fruitful contact with one another. This we believe to be the simple alternative on the question of the objectivity of knowledge as far as the things of this universe are concerned.

One of the points about which there has been much confusion when we speak of the objectivity of human knowledge is whether human knowledge of the world must be comprehensive to be true. Sometimes it is said that though we cannot hope to obtain comprehensive knowledge of God we may hope eventually if not now to have comprehensive knowledge of the things of this universe. But we believe that just for the reason that we cannot hope to obtain comprehensive knowledge of God we cannot hope to obtain comprehensive knowledge of anything in this world.

Not as though anything in this world is infinite as God is infinite and for that reason not fully comprehensible, for it is not the infinity of things in themselves but once more the infinity of God that makes it impossible for us comprehensively to understand things in the created universe. The reason for this is not far to seek. The things of this universe must be interpreted in relation to God. The object of knowledge is not interpreted truly if though brought into relation with the human mind, it is not also brought into relation with the divine mind. God is the ultimate category of interpretation. Now we cannot fully understand God's plan for created things and so we cannot fully understand things.

We see then that our knowledge of the universe must be true since we are creatures of God who has made both us and the universe. Then too our knowledge of the universe cannot be comprehensive because our knowledge of God cannot be comprehensive.

A word must here be said about the question of antinomies. It will readily be inferred what as Christians we mean by antinomies.[2] They are involved in the fact that human knowledge can never be completely comprehensive knowledge. Every knowledge transaction has in it somewhere a reference point to God. Now since God is not fully comprehensible to us we are bound to come into what seems to be contradiction in all our knowledge. Our knowledge is analogical and therefore must be paradoxical. We say that if there is to be any true knowledge at all there must be in God an absolute system of knowledge. We therefore insist that everything must be related to that absolute system of God. Yet we ourselves cannot fully understand that system.

We may, in order to illustrate our meaning here, take one of the outstanding paradoxes of the Christian interpretation of things, namely, that of the relation of the counsel of God to our prayers. To put it pointedly: We say on the one hand that prayer changes things and on the other hand we say that everything happens in accordance with God's plan and God's plan is immutable.

The thing we are concerned about here is to point out that in the nature of the case there would have to be such a paradox

[2] Cf. *Common Grace*, p. 9.

or seeming contradiction in human knowledge. God exists as self-complete apart from us; he is all-glorious. Yet he created the universe that it might glorify him. This point lies at the bottom of every paradox or antinomy. We were in the nature of the case completely interpreted before we came into existence; the universal plan of God needed not to be supplemented by historical particulars and could not be supplemented in this way. The historical could not produce anything wholly new. This much we see clearly. God being what he is, it must be his counsel which acts as the indispensable and self-complete unity back of the finite one and many. The only alternative to saying this is to say that the historical produces the wholly new, and this would be to give up the basic idea of the Christian-theistic scheme, namely, the idea of God and of his creation and control of the universe. On the other hand the historical must have genuine significance. Or else why should God have created it? Prayer must be answered or God would not be God. The universe must really glorify God; that is the purpose of its existence. So we seem to have on the one hand a bucket that is full of water and on the other hand we seem to add water to this bucket which we claim to be already full.

It appears that there must seem to be contradiction in human knowledge. To this we must now add that the contradiction that seems to be there can in the nature of the case be no more than a *seeming* contradiction. If we said that there is real contradiction in our knowledge we would once more be denying the basic concept of Christian-theism, i.e., the concept of the self-complete universal in God. We should then not merely be saying that there is no complete coherence in our thinking but we should also be saying that there is no complete coherence in God's thinking. And this would be the same as saying that there is no coherence or truth in our thinking at all. If we say that the idea of paradox or antinomy is that of real contradiction, we have destroyed all human and all divine knowledge; if we say that the idea of paradox or antinomy is that of seeming contradiction we have saved God's knowledge and therewith also our own.

We must note here again how impossible it is in an apologetic argument to close one's eyes to differences between various theological schools. That fact comes out here more strikingly than anywhere else. Arminianism has not been true to its own belief in creation. With belief in creation it stands committed to that view of God and of God's counsel and that view of man's relation to that counsel which we have outlined. Yet it has been untrue to all this in its insistence that the historical does produce the absolutely new. For that reason it has to think of the relation of God's counsel to man's activity as one of real contradiction. In order to avoid this "contradiction" it has simply thrown overboard the idea of the counsel of God, as controlling all things. Therewith it has in effect sought to destroy both divine and human knowledge and therewith it has destroyed the very meaning of history which it was so anxious to preserve. God cannot answer our prayers for the salvation of people if those people can reject that salvation when they wish.

V

Sin and Its Curse

What we have said thus far in this chapter about man's knowledge has not taken sin into consideration. We have spoken only of the normal situation as it existed when man was first created perfect by God. We must now ask what happened to the knowledge situation when sin entered into the heart of man.

We know that sin is an attempt on the part of man to cut himself loose from God. But this breaking loose from God could, in the nature of the case, not be metaphysical; if it were, man himself would be destroyed and God's purpose with man would be frustrated. Sin is therefore a breaking loose from God ethically and not metaphysically. Sin is the creature's enmity and rebellion against God but is not an escape from creaturehood.

When we say that sin is ethical we do not mean, however, that sin involved only the will of man and not also his intellect. Sin involved every aspect of man's personality. All of man's reactions in every relation in which God had set him were ethical and not merely intellectual; the intellectual itself is ethical.

What then was the result as far as the question of knowledge is concerned of man's rebellion against God? The result was that man tried to interpret everything with which he came into contact without reference to God. The assumption of all his future interpretation was the self-sufficiency of intra-cosmical relationships. This does not signify that man would immediately and openly deny that there is a God. Nor does it mean that man would always and everywhere deny that God is in some sense transcendent. What he would always deny, by implication at least, would be that God is self-sufficient or self-complete. At best he would allow that God is a correlative to man. He might say that we need God to interpret man but he would at the same time say that in the same sense we need man to interpret God. He might say that the temporal cannot be interpreted without reference to the eternal but he would at the same time say that the eternal cannot be interpreted without reference to the temporal. He might say that we need God in order to obtain unity in our experience, but he would at the same time say that God needs the historical many in order to get diversity into his experience. All these forms of correlativity amount in the end to the same thing as saying that the finite categories are self-sufficient. For that reason we can make a very simple and all comprehensive antithesis between the knowledge concept of all non-Christian philosophies and the Christian view. Scripture says that some men worship and serve the Creator; they are the Christians. All other men worship and serve the creature rather than the Creator.

Christian-theism says that there are two levels of thought, the absolute and the derivative. Christian theism says that there are two levels of interpreters, God who interprets absolutely and man who must be the re-interpreter of God's interpretation. Christian-theism says that human thought is therefore analogical of God's thought. In opposition to all this, non-Christian thought holds in effect that the distinction between absolute and derivative thought must be wiped out. To be sure, God's thoughts may be more comprehensive than ours but it is not self-complete without ours. This means that as all being was thought of as equally ultimate, so now all thought is thought of as equally ultimate. There is only one level of interpreters; if God comes into the picture at all, it is as a collaborator with man. We do not think God's thoughts after him, but together with God we think out thoughts that have never been thought either by God or by man. Non-Christian philosophies hold that human thought is univocal instead of analogical.

Thus the Christian concept of analogical thought and the non-Christian concept of univocal thought stand over against one another as diametrical opposites.

Non-Christian thought holds to the ultimacy of the created universe. It holds therefore to the ultimacy of the mind of man itself and must in consequence deny the necessity of analogical thought. It holds to the normalcy of the human mind as well as to its ultimacy. It holds to the normalcy of the human mind as it holds to the normalcy of everything else in the world.

Naturally this conception of the normalcy of the human mind does not imply that the human mind never makes mistakes. It only means that mistakes are thought of as natural and to be expected and have nothing to do with sin.

We can readily see from this that the non-theistic mind must set for itself the ideal of absolutely comprehensive knowledge as long as it has not become fully conscious of the implications of its own thought. However, it will maintain that it is unnecessary for man to have any comprehensive universal in order to live. As long as non-theistic thought still thinks it necessary for man to have an absolute universal it naturally has to set for itself the task of finding this universal, inasmuch as God has been put out of the picture. Then when it appears impossible for man ever to find a universal, inasmuch as the particulars of the time are by definition always ahead of any time-generated universal, man says that he does not need any absolute universal anyway except as a limiting concept.

It may be useful in this connection to point out that in the whole situation we have therefore to deal with three types of consciousness.

In the first place there is the Adamic consciousness. When man was first created he was perfect. He recognized the fact that he was a creature; he was actually normal. He wanted to be nothing but a re-interpreter of the interpretation of God. He was receptive to God's revelation which appeared within him and round about him; he would reconstruct this revelation. He was receptively reconstructive. For that reason he had real though not comprehensive unity in his experience.[8]

In the second place we deal with the fallen or non-regenerate consciousness. It builds upon the non-theistic assumption. It in effect denies its creaturehood. It claims to be normal. It will not be receptive of God's interpretation; it wants to create its own interpretation without reference to God. It will not reconstruct God's interpretation. It will construct only its own interpretation. It seeks to be creatively constructive. It thus tries to do the impossible with the result that self-frustration is written over all its efforts. There is no unity and never will be unity in non-theistic thought; it has cut itself loose from the only existing source of unity. Yet since it could not cut itself loose from God metaphysically and since God, for the purpose of realizing his plan of redemption, *rudera* or *scintillae* of the knowledge of God and of the universe remain in man. Non-Christians know after a fashion, as Paul tells us in Romans. Thus also there is a relative good in those who are ethically totally evil. The unity that they have in experience is a shadow unity, a unity that prevents them from falling into complete disintegration in this world. Hereafter complete disintegration will follow, though even hereafter the disintegration can only be ethical and not metaphysical; there must be a kingdom or mock-unity even in hell.

In the third place there is the regenerate consciousness. This regenerate consciousness has *in principle* been restored to the position of the Adamic consciousness. It recognizes anew that man is God's creature and that he has fallen into sin. It recognizes the fact that it has been saved by grace. It therefore wants to be receptively reconstructive once more. It wants to interpret reality in terms of the eternal one and many. It therefore does have unity in its experience, though not comprehensive unity.

Yet this regenerate consciousness is restored *in principle* only. It does not and cannot, because of the remnants of sin that remain in man, even after regeneration, live up to its own principle fully. For this reason there is the relatively evil in those who are absolutely good in principle. This relative evil in the

[8] The reader may observe again how basically important Adam's place in history is said to be.

absolutely good has a very great detrimental effect on the consistency of presentation of the theistic position on the part of the Christian. And this inconsistency appears both in word and in deed, in the compromising presentation of the intellectual argument for Christianity and in the un-Christian life that Christians live. Hence non-Christians frequently do not have the full Christian position placed before them.

All this makes the matter of apologetical argument very complicated. Only a clear recognition of the three types of consciousness, of the total inability of the non-regenerate consciousness of itself to accept the truth of Christianity, of the necessity of a consistent presentation of the Christian position together with firm reliance on the grace of God, can help us to reason fruitfully with men.[4]

[4] The absolute contrast between the Christian and the non-Christian in the field of knowledge is said to be that of principle. Full recognition is made of the fact that in spite of this absolute contrast of principle, there is relative good in those who are evil in principle and relative evil in those who are good in principle. Is it possible to set forth the fully Biblical or Reformed position without maintaining both of these points? Some of my critics deny the necessity of maintaining both points at all times. In this, I feel, they depart from generic Calvinism.

CHAPTER IV

THE CHRISTIAN PHILOSOPHY OF BEHAVIOR

Having now briefly set forth the Christian view of being and the Christian view of knowledge a brief exposition of the Christian view of human action or behavior must be given.

In setting forth the Christian view of Ethics we take from the Reformed confessions the simple statement to the effect that good works must be done to the glory of God.

We speak therefore of the highest good of man as the goal he must seek to reach if as a redeemed creature he is to live to the glory of God. He does this concretely on earth by seeking to establish the kingdom of God.

Secondly, man cannot set his own standard or criterion by which he will seek to realize the kingdom of God. His standard must be the revealed will of God in Scripture.

Thirdly, as a sinner man can have no power with which to work toward the realization of the kingdom of God. Without faith it is impossible to please God. And faith comes from God through regeneration by the Holy Spirit.

This confessional scheme of ethics is very simple. It enables us to find our way through the labyrinth of ethical literature. All writers must, in one way or another, deal with man's (a) *summum bonum*, (b) his criterion, and (c) his motivation.

I

Ethics and the Christian Philosophy of Knowledge

In order to deal with the Christian *summum bonum*, the Christian standard and Christian motivation, we may first intimate how directly the whole of Christian ethics is related to the Christian view of knowledge. I quote from the syllabus on *Christian Ethics*.

God, as absolute personality, is the ultimate category of interpretation for man in every aspect of his being. Every attribute of God will, in the nature of the case, be reflected primarily in every other attribute of God. There will be mutual and complete exhaustiveness in the relationship of the three persons of the trinity. Consequently no one of the persons of the trinity can be said to be correlative in its being, to anything that exists beyond the Godhead. If then man is created it must be that he is absolutely dependent upon his relationship to God for the meaning of his existence in its every aspect. If this is true it means that the good is good for man because it has been set as good for man by God. This is usually expressed by saying that the good is good because God says it is good. As such it is contrasted with non-Christian thought which says that the good exists in its own right and that God strives for that which is good in itself. We do not artificially separate the will of God from the nature of God. It is the nature as well as the will of God that is ultimately good. Yet since this nature of God is personal there is no sense in which we can say that the good exists in its own right.

a. *Man as Made in God's Image*

With these considerations as a background we can think of man as he first appeared on the face of the earth. It follows logically that he appeared upon the earth as a perfect though finite replica of the Godhead. The original perfection of man in every respect, and in particular in the moral respect, is implied in the conception of God which lies at the foundation of the whole structure of Christian thought.

Now if there cannot be any evil in God it would be quite

impossible to think that he should create man as evil. Again this is true not only because we abhor the idea of attributing such a deed to God but because it would be a contradiction of his being so to do. Thus we hold that man appeared *originally with a perfect moral consciousness.* It is this that the Genesis narrative tells us.

The difference between Christian ethics and non-Christian ethics has not been made perfectly clear at this point unless we dwell on the fact that even in its original perfect condition the moral consciousness of man was derivative and not the ultimate source of information as to what is good. Man was in the nature of the case finite. Hence his moral consciousness too was finite and as such had to live by revelation. Man's moral thought as well as the other aspects of his thought had to be receptively reconstructive.

This then is the most basic and fundamental difference between Christian and non-Christian epistemology, as far as it has a direct bearing upon questions of ethics, that in the case of non-Christian thought man's moral activity is thought of as *creatively constructive* while in Christian thought man's moral activity is thought of as being *receptively reconstructive.* According to non-Christian thought, there is no absolute moral personality to whom man is responsible and from whom he has received his conception of the good, while according to Christian thought God is the infinite moral personality who reveals to man the true nature of morality.

It is necessary, however, to think of this revelation of God to man as originally internal as well as external. Man found in his own makeup, in his own moral nature, an understanding of and a love for that which is good. His own nature was revelational of the will of God. But while thus revelational of the will of God, man's nature, even in paradise, was never meant to function by itself. It was at once supplemented by the supernatural, external and positive expression of God's will as its correlative. Only thus can we see how basic is the difference between the Christian and the non-Christian view of the moral nature of man in relation to ethical questions.

b. *Sin and Its Curse*

The second point of difference that must be included in our general antithesis stated above concerns the question of the influence of sin on the moral consciousness of man. We cannot begin to give a survey here of all the Biblical material that bears on this question. Nor is this necessary. The main point is clear enough. Just as sin has blinded the intellect of man, so it has corrupted the will of man. This is often spoken of as the hardening of man's heart. Paul says that the natural man is at enmity against God. The natural man cannot will to do God's will. He cannot even know what the good is. The sinner worships the creature rather than the Creator. He has set all the moral standards topsy-turvy.

This doctrine of the *total depravity* of man makes it plain that the moral consciousness of man as he is today cannot be the source of information about what is ideal good or about what is the standard of the good or about what is the true nature of the will which is to strive for the good. It would seem plain enough that men have to choose on this point between the Christian and the non-Christian position.

It is this point particularly that makes it necessary for the Christian to maintain without any apology and without any concession that it *is Scripture, and Scripture alone,* in the light of which all moral questions must be answered. Scripture as an external revelation became necessary because of the sin of man. No man living can even put the moral problem as he ought to put it, or ask the moral questions as he ought to ask them, unless he does so in the light of Scripture. Man cannot of himself truly face the moral question, let alone answer it.

Man's moral consciousness then as it is today is (a) finite and (b) sinful. If it were only finite and not sinful we could go to the moral consciousness of man for our information. Even then, however, we should have to remember that we could go there not because the moral consciousness would be able either to ask or to answer the moral question correctly in its own power alone, but because its own activity would be in fruitful contact with

God from whom the questions and the answers would ultimately come.

It is true that the non-regenerate consciousness of man cannot entirely keep under the requirements of God that speak to it through its own constitution. Thus God's will is heard through it in spite of it. Hence the natural man excuses or accuses himself for his ethical action. But for the main point now under consideration this point may be ignored. For to the extent that man is not restrained *by God's common grace from living out his sinful principle,* the natural man makes his own moral consciousness the ultimate standard of moral action.

c. *The Regenerated Consciousness*

But what then of the regenerated moral consciousness? In the first place the regenerated consciousness is once more *in principle* restated to its former place. This implies that we can go to it because we could originally go to it for our answers. This is of basic importance for it furnishes the point of contact between Christian and non-Christian ethics. As Christians we do not maintain that man's moral consciousness cannot under any circumstances and in any sense serve as a point of reference. But man's moral consciousness must be regenerated in order to serve as a reference point. Moreover the regenerated consciousness is still finite. It must still live by revelation as it originally lived by revelation. It can never become an ultimate information bureau. Finally, the regenerated moral consciousness is changed *in principle* only, and therefore often errs. Consequently it must constantly seek to test itself by Scripture. More than that, the regenerated consciousness does not in itself fabricate any answers to the moral questions. It receives them and reworks them. Now if this receiving, in so far as it implies an activity of the mind, be called the function of the moral consciousness, we may speak of it as a source of information. The regenerated moral consciousness which constantly nourishes itself upon the Scripture is as the plenipotentiary who knows fairly well what his authority desires.

So then we have before us the Christian and the non-Christian conception of the moral consciousness of man. Summing up the matter we may say (a) that there once was a moral consciousness that was perfect and could act as a source, but only as a proximate source, of information on moral questions; (b) that there now are two types of moral consciousness which to the extent that they work from their respective principles agree on no ethical answer and on no ethical question, namely the non-regenerate and the regenerate consciousness; (c) that the non-regenerate consciousness denies while the regenerate consciousness affirms that the moral verdict of any man must be tested by Scripture because of the sin of man.

d. *Roman Catholicism*

On the question discussed in this chapter Roman Catholicism takes a position half way between that of Christianity and that of paganism. The notion of the human consciousness set forth in the works of Thomas Aquinas is worked out, to a great extent, by the form-matter scheme of Aristotle. In consequence a large measure of autonomy is assigned to the human consciousness as over against the consciousness of God. This is true in the field of knowledge and it is no less true in the field of ethics.

In the field of ethics this means that even in paradise, before the fall, man is not thought of as being receptively constructive in his attitude toward God. In order to maintain man's autonomy —or, as Thomas thinks, his very manhood as a self-conscious and responsible being—man must, from one point of view at least, be wholly independent of the counsel of God. This is implied in the so-called "free-will" idea. Thomas cannot think of man as responsible and free if all his actions have their ultimate and final reference point exclusively in God and his will. Thus there is no really Scriptural idea of authority in Romanism.

It follows that Rome has too high a notion of the moral consciousness of fallen man. According to Thomas, fallen man is not very dissimilar from Adam in paradise. He says that while the sinner needs grace for more things than did Adam he does not need grace more.[1] Putting the matter somewhat differently, Thomas says, "And thus in the state of perfect nature man needs a gratuitous strength superadded to natural strength for one reason, viz., in order to do and wish supernatural good; but for two

[1] *Summa Theologica,* trans. by Fathers of the English Dominican Province, Vol. 4, p. 324.

reasons, in the state of corrupt nature, viz., in order to be healed, and furthermore in order to carry out works of supernatural virtue, which are meritorious. Beyond this, in both states man needs the Divine help, that he may be moved to act well."[2] In any case, for Thomas the ethical problem for man is as much one of finitude as it is one of ethical obedience. Man is naturally finite. As such he tends naturally to evil. He needs grace because he is a creature even though he is not a sinner. Hence God really owes grace to man at least to some extent. And man does not become totally depraved when he does not make such use of the grace given him as to keep himself from sin entirely. For in any case the act of his free will puts him naturally in grave danger. Fallen man is therefore only partly guilty and only partly to blame. And he retains much of the same ethical power that man had in paradise. For ethical ability is virtually said to be implied in metaphysical ability or free will.

It follows still further that even the regenerate consciousness need not and cannot subject itself fully to Scripture. Thomas is unable to do justice to St. Paul's position that whatever is not of faith is sin. The entire discussion by Thomas of the cardinal virtues and their relation to the theological virtues proves this point. He distinguishes sharply between them. "Now the object of the theological virtues is God Himself, Who is the last end of all, as surpassing the knowledge of our reason. On the other hand, the object of the intellectual and moral virtues is something comprehensible to human reason. Wherefore the theological virtues are specifically distinct from the moral and intellectual virtues."[3] In respect to the things that are said to be knowable by reason apart from supernatural revelation, then, the Christian acts, and should act, from what amounts to the same motive as the non-Christian. Faith is not required for a Christian to act virtuously in the natural relationships of life. Or if the theological virtues do have some influence over the daily activities of the Christian, this influence is of an accidental and subsidiary nature.

All in all then it is clear that Romanism cannot ask its adherents to submit their moral consciousness to Scripture in any thorough way. And accordingly Rome cannot challenge the non-Christian position in any thorough way.

[2] *Ibid.* Vol. 8, p. 327.
[3] *Ibid.* Vol. 7, p. 150.

e. *Evangelicalism*

A position similar to that of Romanism is frequently maintained by evangelical Protestants. As a recent illustration we mention the case of C. S. Lewis.

Like Romanism, Lewis, in the first place, confuses things metaphysical and ethical. In his book *Beyond Personality* he discusses the nature of the divine trinity. To show the practical significance of the doctrine of the trinity he says: "The whole dance, or drama, or pattern of this three-Personal life is to be played out in each one of us: or (putting it the other way 'round) each one of us has got to enter that pattern, take his place in that dance."[4] The purpose of Christianity is to lift the *Bios* or natural life of man up into the Zoe, the uncreated life.[5] In the incarnation there is given one example of how this may be done. In him there is "one man in whom the created life, derived from his mother, allowed itself to be completely and perfectly turned into the begotten life." Then he adds: "Now what *is* the difference which he has made to the whole human mass? It is just this; that the business of becoming a son of God, of being turned from a created thing into a begotten thing, of passing over from the temporary biological life into timeless 'spiritual' life, has been done for us."[6]

All this is similar in import to the position of Aquinas which stresses the idea that man is, through grace, to participate in the divine nature.

It is a foregone conclusion that the ethical problem cannot be fairly put on such a basis. Perhaps the most fundamental difference between all forms of non-Christian ethics and Christian ethics lies in the fact that according to the former it is man's finitude as such that causes his ethical strife while according to the latter it is not finitude as such but created man's disobedience of God that causes all the trouble. C. S. Lewis cannot signalize this difference clearly. Lewis does not call men back with clarion voice to the obedience of the God of the Bible. He asks men to "dress up as Christ" in order that while they have the Christ ideal before them and see how far they are from realizing it, Christ,

[4] *Beyond Personality*, p. 27.
[5] *Ibid.*, p. 28.
[6] *Ibid.*, p. 31.

who is then at their side, may turn them "into the same kind of thing as Himself," injecting "His kind of life and thought, His Zoe" into them.[7]

Lewis argues that "a recovery of the old sense of sin is essential to Christianity."[8] Why does he then encourage men to hold that man is embroiled in a metaphysical tension over which not even God has any control? Lewis says that men are not likely to recover the old sense of sin because they do not penetrate to the motives behind moral actions.[9] But how shall men ever be challenged to look inside themselves and find that all that is not of faith is sin if they are encouraged to think that without the light of Scripture and without the regenerating power of the Holy Spirit they can, at least in the natural sphere, do what is right? Can men really practice the "cardinal virtues" of prudence, temperance, justice and fortitude in the way that they should, even though they have no faith? No Protestant ought to admit such a possibility.

Lewis seeks for objective standards in ethics, in literature, and in life everywhere. But he holds that objectivity may be found in many places. He speaks of a general objectivity that is common between Christians and non-Christians and argues as though it is mostly or almost exclusively in modern times that men have forsaken it. Speaking of this general objectivity he says: "This conception in all its forms, Platonic, Aristotelian, Stoic, Christian, and Oriental alike, I shall henceforth refer to for brevity simply as 'the *Tao*.' Some of the accounts of it which I have quoted will seem, perhaps, to many of you merely quaint or even magical. But what is common to them all is something we cannot neglect. It is the doctrine of objective value, the belief that certain attitudes are really true, and others really false, to the kind of thing the universe is and the kind of things we are."[10] But surely this general objectivity is common to Christians and non-Christians in a formal sense only. To say that there is or must be an objective standard is not the same as to say what that standard is. And it is the *what* that is all important. Granted

[7] *Ibid.*, p. 37.
[8] *The Problem of Pain*, p. 45.
[9] *Ibid.*, p. 47.
[10] *The Abolition of Man*, London, 1947, p. 17.

that non-Christians who hold to some sort of something somewhere above men are better than non-Christians who hold to nothing whatsoever above man, it remains true that in the main issue the non-Christian *objectivists* are no less subjective than are the non-Christian *subjectivists*. There is but one alternative that is ultimate; it is that between those who obey God and those who please themselves. Only those who believe in God through Christ seek to obey God; only they have the true principle in ethics. One can only rejoice in the fact that Lewis is heard the world around, but one can only grieve over the fact that he so largely follows the method of Thomas Aquinas in calling men back to the gospel. The "gospel according to St. Lewis" is too much of a compromise with the ideas of the natural man to constitute a clear challenge in our day.

II

Ethics and the Christian Philosophy of Reality

As God is absolute rationality so God is also absolute will. By this we mean primarily that God did not have to become good, but has from everlasting to everlasting been good. In God there is no problem of activity and passivity. In God there is *eternal accomplishment*. God is finally and *ultimately self-determinative*. God is finally and absolutely necessary and *therefore* absolutely free.

It should be especially noted that Christians put forth this concept of God, not as something that may possibly be true and may also possibly be untrue. From the non-theistic point of view our God will have to appear as the dumping ground of all difficulties. For the moment we waive this objection in order to call attention to the fact that all the differences between the Christian and the non-Christian point of view, in the field of ethics, must be ultimately traced to their different God-concepts. Christians hold that the conception of God is the necessary presupposition of all human activity. Non-Christian thought holds that the Christian conception of God is the death of all ethical activity. All non-Christian ethics takes for granted that such a God as Christians believe in does not exist. Non-Christian thought takes for granted that the *will of God, as well as the will of man, has an environment.* Non-Christian ethics assumes an ultimate activism. For it God has to become good. *Character is an achievement through a process for God as well as for man.* God is thought of as determined as well as determinated and determinative.

Non-theism starts with the assumption of an *ultimately indeterminate Reality.* For it all determinate existence, all personality is therefore derivative.

Idealists may object that in the eternally Good of Plato, and in the modern idealist idea of the Absolute, there is no mention made of achievement. In those concepts, it will be said, you have absolutely self-determinative experience. In answer to this we only point out that the God of Plato was not really ultimate. The Good rather than God was Plato's most ultimate concept. His god, to the extent that he was personal was metaphorical and, in any case, dependent upon an environment more ultimate than himself. The element of Chance is absolutely ultimate in the philosophy of Plato. And it is this ultimacy of Chance that either makes the determinate good an achievement, or it sets the Good out of relation to its environment, and therewith destroys its value.

Then as to the modern idealist conception of the Absolute, it is to be noted that it is the result of a definite and prolonged effort to find the conception of an absolutely self-determinative Experience. The idealists have been basically convinced, it seems, that unless an absolutely self-determinative Experience can be presupposed, all human experience in general, and ethical experience in particular, would be meaningless. Modern idealism has definitely attempted to set the Good of Plato into a fruitful relation to its environment. Yet it has not overcome the difficulties inherent in Plato's ethics. It has ended with a *determined* instead of with a *self-determinative* God. It has taken for granted that the space-time universe is a part or aspect of ultimate existence. With this assumption it made time as ultimate as eternity and made God dependent upon whatever might come out of the space-time matrix.

The basic difference then that distinguishes Christian from non-Christian ethics, is the acceptance, or denial, of the ultimately *self-determinative* will of God. As Christians we hold that determinate human experience could work to no end, could work in accordance with no plan, and could not even get under way, if it were not for the existence of the absolute will of God.

It is on this ground then that we hold to the absolute will of God as the presupposition of the will of man. Looked at in this way, that which to many seems at first glance to be the greatest hindrance to human responsibility, namely the conception of an absolutely sovereign God, becomes the very foundation of its possibility.

In order to avoid misunderstanding, however, we should distinguish the concept of an absolutely personalist environment from philosophical determinism. It is all too common for men hastily to identify consistent Christianity with philosophical necessitarianism. Yet they are as the poles apart. Philosophical necessitarianism stands for an ultimate impersonalism; consistent Christianity stands for an ultimate personalism. What this implies for the activity of the will of man itself we may now briefly examine.

III

The Kingdom of God as Man's Highest Good

a. *The Non-Christian Summum Bonum*

What is the ideal of human behavior that non-Christian writers on ethics set for themselves? The main difference between all non-Christian theories and the Christian theory of the *summum bonum* is due to the fact that all non-Christian ethics takes existence, as it now is, for granted *as being normal*. Our idea of the original state of man does not only appear to them as a sad delusion, but also as a piece of *unpardonable arrogance*. Men are glad to read the utopias that dreamers have dreamed; they are glad even to include the story of Genesis in their repertoire of light reading for leisure hours, but men rebel against being told that their ethical ideals must be judged by the ethical ideals of Adam.[11]

The real meaning of this opposition to the original perfect ethical ideal is nothing short of hatred of the living God. If God does exist as man's Creator, it is as we have seen, impossible that evil should be inherent in the temporal universe. If God exists, man himself must have brought in sin by an act of wilful transgression. Hence, existence, as it now is, is not normal but abnormal. Accordingly, to maintain that existence, as it now is, is normal, is tantamount to a denial of man's responsibility for sin, and this in turn makes God responsible for sin, and this simply means that there is no absolute God.

In addition to assuming that man's moral consciousness is *normal*, the non-Christian view assumes that it is non-created or ultimate. Even when the absolute idealists speak of God as absolute, this God is not the creator of man. The difference between a truly Christian theory of self-development and the idealist theory of self-development can best be observed if we see that *the idealist notion is based upon the non-Christian conception* of the self that is to be realized. That self is not thought of as a creature of God, but as an aspect of rationality somehow here in the midst of a universe among other specks of rationality also somehow here.

We have said enough, we trust, to bring out the chief points of contrast by which one can distinguish the Christian from the non-Christian *summum bonum*. We have indicated that all the contrasts between various schools of non-Christian ethics, such as those between intellectualistic and voluntaristic, between national and international, between individual and social, between selfish and altruistic, between happiness and goodness, between

[11] The Genesis narrative, taken as historical, is again made basic to the Christian view of ethics.

usefulness and virtue are *all due to the assumed correlativity of God and man.* This assumed correlativity of God and man, this assumed denial of the creation doctrine, this assumed ultimacy of evil allows for no ethical ideal other than that of a give-and-take, of a "claims and counter-claims" *between individuals who must live together and who yet must live at the expense of one another.* It is marvelous that out of such a soil the lofty ethics of idealism in all its forms has sprung. It can only be the common grace of God that accounts for it.

b. *The Biblical Summum Bonum*

Over against this non-Christian view of man's *summum bonum* as it centers in man assumed to be normal and ultimate, is that of Scripture.

1. The absolute ideal is maintained. The Old and New Testaments as a unit maintain that God, as man's creator and judge, must naturally set the ideal for man's life. Both Old and New Testament ethics thinks of man as created in the image of God with ability to do the will of God perfectly. This conception of man is involved in the notion of an absolute ideal. The very fact that nowhere but in the Old and the New Testaments is found any such idea as the original perfection of man, in turn proves that man was given an absolute ideal.

Even after the fall God set the ideal of the absolute perfection, individually and racially, before man as something that man must not merely strive after but actually accomplish.

2. But since as a sinner he cannot take even the first step in the direction of accomplishing this ideal, the kingdom of God, as man's *summum bonum* is presented as being a *gift of God.* The *Aufgabe* has become a *Gabe* even as the *Gabe* is also the *Aufgabe* for men.

3. Thirdly the Biblical *summum bonum* requires the absolute destruction of sin and evil in the individual and in society. In the Old Testament times this goal had to be

reached in an externalistic fashion, while in New Testament times this goal is to be reached in more spiritual or internalistic ways. But the goal was the same in both instances.

Our task with respect to the destruction of evil is not ended when we have sought to fight sin itself everywhere we see it. We have the further obligation to destroy the consequences of sin in this world as far as we can. We must do good to all men, especially to those of the household of faith. To help relieve something of the sufferings of the creatures of God is our privilege and our task.

Such then is the third aspect of the *summum bonum*. We have an absolute ethical ideal to offer men. This absolute ideal is a gift of God. This gives us courage to start with the program of the eradication of evil from God's universe. We cannot carry on from the place where God first placed man. A great deal of our time will have to be taken up with the destruction of evil. We may not even seem to see much progress in ourselves or 'round about us, during our lifetime. We shall have to build with the trowel in one hand and the sword in the other. It may seem to us to be but a hopeless task of sweeping the ocean dry. Yet we know that this is exactly what our ethical ideal would be if we were not Christians. We know that for non-Christians their ethical ideal can never be realized either for themselves or for society. They do not even know the true ethical ideal. And as to our own efforts, we know that though much of our time may have to be taken up with pumping out the water of sin, we are nevertheless laying the foundation of our bridge on solid rock, and we are making progress toward our goal. Our victory is certain. The devil and all his servants will be put out of the habitable universe of God. There will be a new heaven and a new earth on which righteousness will dwell.

4. Finally we must note the fourth characteristic of Biblical ethics, namely, that it is an ethics of hope. It is to live in the daily assurance that the universe can and will be renovated completely in God's own time. It is to look for the new heaven and the new earth.

Such then is the ethical ideal of the Scriptures. It presents to us an absolute ideal such as no other ethical literature presents. This ethical ideal is a gift of God to man, and the power to set out upon the way to that ethical ideal is also a gift of God to man. It is this that assures us that the ideal will be reached without a doubt. Then this ethical ideal, just because it is absolute, demands that all evil be destroyed. Hence both in the Old Testament and in the New it is a part of the task of the people of God to destroy evil. Finally, because this ethical ideal is an absolute ideal and demands the complete destruction of evil, its full realization lies in the life hereafter; Biblical ethics is an ethics of hope.

That this ethical ideal of Scripture is unique ought to be abundantly plain from this description. There is no other ethical ideal that is even remotely similar to it. All other ideals visualize a relative end. None of them think of the ideal as a gift to man. None of them demand the absolute destruction of evil. None of them look to the hereafter for the full realization of their ideal. The Old Testament is in all these respects just as unique as is the New Testament. They are in perfect agreement on these points. Together they are in perfect disagreement with all other ethical ideals.

A fuller discussion of Christian ethics as distinguished from non-Christian ethics on the point of criterion and motivation would take us too far afield. In both cases the Christian position as maintained in the Reformed faith centers about the doctrines of God, of creation, of the fall and of redemption through Christ. The Christian has his standard in the revealed will of God. This standard is *absolute*. He, the non-Christian, finds his standard in human experience. So also the Christian seeks to realize his ideal by following his standard through the power of faith given him by God. The non-Christian, be he realist, idealist or pragmatist, seeks to realize his ideal in his own power.

Chapter V

CHRISTIAN APOLOGETICS (POINT OF CONTACT)

In the preceding chapters we have dealt with the question *what* the Reformed Christian believes. In this and the next chapter our concern will be how he is to defend and propagate what he believes.

In the present chapter the subject will be that of the point of contact and in the next it will be that of method.

On both questions there is considerable difference between Reformed theologians. The nature of this difference will appear as the discussion proceeds.

What point of contact is there in the mind and heart of the unbeliever to which the believer may appeal when he presents to him the Christian view of life?[1]

Is there an area known by both from which, as a starting point, we may go on to that which is known to believers but unknown to unbelievers? And is there a common method of knowing this "known area" which need only to be applied to that which the unbeliever does not know in order to convince him of its existence and its truth? It will not do to assume at the outset that these questions must be answered in the affirmative. For the knower himself needs interpretation as well as the things he knows. The human mind as the knowing subject, makes its contribution to the knowledge it obtains. It will be quite impossible then to find a common area of knowledge between believers and unbelievers unless there is agreement between them as to the nature of man himself. But there is no such agreement. In his

[1] The rest of the material of this chapter is taken from the Syllabus on *Christian Apologetics*.

recent work, *An Essay on Man,* Ernest Cassirer traces the various theories of man that have been offered by philosophers in the course of the ages. Our modern theory of man, Cassirer asserts, has lost its intellectual center. "We acquired instead a complete anarchy of thought. Even in former times to be sure there was a great discrepancy of opinions and theories relating to this problem. But there remained at least a general orientation, a frame of reference, to which all individual differences might be referred. Metaphysics, theology, mathematics, and biology successively assumed the guidance for thought on the problem of man and determined the line of investigation. The real crisis of this problem manifested itself when such a central power capable of directing all individual efforts ceased to exist. The paramount importance of the problem was still felt in all the different branches of knowledge and inquiry. But an established authority to which one might appeal no longer existed. Theologians, scientists, politicians, sociologists, biologists, psychologists, ethnologists, economists, all approached the problem from their own viewpoints. To combine or unify all these particular aspects and perspectives was impossible. And even within the special fields there was no generally accepted scientific principle. The personal factor became more and more prevalent, and the temperament of the individual writer tended to play a decisive role. *Trahit sua quemque voluptas;* every author seems in the last count to be led by his own conception and evaluation of human life."[2]

The confusion of modern anthropology as here portrayed by Cassirer is in itself distressing enough. But one point, at least, is clear. The conception of man as entertained by modern thought in general cannot be assumed to be the same as that set forth in Scripture. It is therefore imperative that the Christian apologist be alert to the fact that the average person to whom he must present the Christian religion for acceptance is a quite different sort of being than he himself thinks he is. A good doctor will not prescribe medicines according to the diagnosis that his patient has made of himself. The patient may think that he needs nothing more than a bottle of medicine while the doctor knows that an immediate operation is required.

[2] Yale University Press, New Haven, 1944, p. 21.

Christianity then must present itself as the light that makes the facts of human experience, and above all the nature of man himself, to appear for what they really are. Christianity is the source from which both life and light derive for men.

I

Roman Catholicism

It is of the utmost importance to stress the point just made. If a Protestant finds it necessary to dispute with the Roman Catholic on the nature of Christianity itself he will find it equally necessary to dispute with him on the problem of the point of contact. A Protestant theology requires a Protestant apologetic.

The difference between a Protestant and a Roman Catholic conception of the point of contact will naturally have to be formulated in a way similar to that in which we state the difference between a Protestant and a Roman Catholic theology. There are two ways of stating this difference. One very common way is to indicate first an area of doctrine that the two types of theology have in common, in order afterwards to enumerate the differences between them. This is the course followed in B. B. Warfield's justly famous little book, *The Plan of Salvation.* Between those holding to a plan of salvation, says Warfield, there are those who think of this plan along naturalist and there are others who think of this plan along supernaturalist lines. As against the Pelagians who hold to a naturalist view " . . . the entire organized Church —Orthodox Greek, Roman Catholic, Latin, and Protestant in all its great historical forms, Lutheran and Reformed, Calvinistic and Arminian—bears its consentient, firm and emphatic testimony to the supernaturalistic conception of salvation." [3]

Continuing from this point Warfield then divides the supernaturalists into sacerdotalists and evangelicals. The issue between them concerns "the immediacy of the saving operations of God." The church of Rome, holding the sacerdotal point of view, teaches that "grace is communicated by and through the ministrations of the church, otherwise not" (p. 18). On the other hand, Evangelicalism "seeking to conserve what it conceives to

[3] Warfield: *Plan of Salvation,* Grand Rapids, 1935, p. 111.

be the only consistent supernaturalism, sweeps away every intermediary between the soul and its God, and leaves the soul dependent for its salvation on God alone, operating upon it by his immediate grace" (p. 19). Now Protestantism and Evangelicalism are "coterminous, if not exactly synonymous designations" (p. 20).

At this point Warfield goes on to mark the main variations within Protestantism. Among Protestants or evangelicals there are those who hold to a universalistic and there are those who hold to a particularistic conception of the plan of salvation. "All evangelicals agree that all the power exerted in saving the soul is from God and that this saving power is exerted immediately upon the soul. But they differ as to whether God exerts this saving power equally, or at least indiscriminately, upon all men, be they actually saved or not, or rather only upon particular men, namely upon those who are actually saved" (p. 22). Signalizing the difference between universalistic and particularistic evangelicals again, Warfield uses these words, "The precise issue which divides the universalists and the particularists is, accordingly, just whether the saving grace of God, in which alone is salvation, actually saves" (p. 24).

It is not germane to our purpose to follow Warfield further as he differentiates once more between various forms of particularists. The "differences of large moment" (p. 27) are now before us. Warfield defends particularism or Calvinism. And it has become customary to use the term evangelical with reference to non-Calvinistic Protestants.

What interests us now is the fact that, though beginning from the common denominator point of view, Warfield is compelled, each time he signalizes a new difference, to indicate that it is made in the interest of consistency. Protestants are Protestants in the interest of being more consistently supernaturalist than are the Roman Catholics. Calvinists are particularists in the interest of being more consistently evangelical than are the other Protestants. Calvinists aim at holding a position, according to Warfield, that shall be "uncolored by intruding elements from without" (p. 21). Accordingly the several conceptions of salvation "do not stand simply side by side as varying conceptions of that plan, each making its appeal in opposition to all the rest.

They are related to one another rather as a progressive series of corrections of a primal error, attaining ever more and more consistency in the embodiment of the one fundamental idea of salvation" (p. 31).

It appears then that Warfield himself really suggests a better way of expressing such differences as obtain between Romanism and Protestantism, or between universalistic and particularistic Protestantism than he has himself employed. That better way is pointed out by Professor John Murray when he says, "It would appear, therefore, that the truer, more effective and, on all accounts, more secure defense of Christianity and exposition of its essential content is not to take our starting point from those terms that will express the essential creedal confession of some of its most widely known historical deformations but rather from those terms that most fully express and give character to that redemptive religion which Christianity is. In other words, Christianity cannot receive proper understanding or its exposition proper orientation unless it is viewed as that which issues from, and is consummated in the accomplishment of, the covenant counsel and purpose of Father, Son and Holy Spirit."[4] We are not to define the essence of Christianity in terms of its lowest but rather in terms of its highest forms. Calvinism is "Christianity come to its own." Beginning from Calvinism we should descend to universalistic Protestantism and thence to Romanism as deviations from the true view of Christianity.

It is Romanism with which we are now primarily concerned. Romanism should be regarded as a *deformation* of Christianity, in fact as its lowest deformation. And this deformation expresses itself not merely at some but at every point of doctrine. The differences between Protestantism and Romanism are not adequately indicated if we say that Luther restored to the church the true doctrines of the Bible, of justification by faith and of the priesthood of all believers. The difference is rather that Protestantism is more consistently and Rome is less consistently Christian at every point of doctrine. It could not well be otherwise. Having inconsistency at one point of doctrine is bound to result in inconsistency at all points of doctrine. Rome has been consistently inconsistent in the confusion of non-Christian with

[4] *The Westminster Theological Journal,* Vol. IX, p. 90.

Christian elements of teaching along the entire gamut of doctrinal expression.

The bearing of all this on the question of starting point may now be briefly suggested. In the question of starting point it is all-important that we have a truly Christian doctrine of man. But this Rome does not have. Without going into details it may be asserted that Rome has a defective doctrine (a) with respect to the nature of man as he was created and (b) with respect to the effect of the entrance of sin upon the nature of man. "The important point of difference is," says Charles Hodge, "that Protestants hold that original righteousness, so far as it consisted in the moral excellence of Adam, was natural, while the Romanists maintain that it was supernatural. According to their theory, God created man soul and body. These two constituents of his nature are naturally in conflict. To preserve the harmony between them, and the due subjection of the flesh to the spirit, God gave man the supernatural gift of original righteousness. It was this gift that man lost by his fall; so that since the apostacy he is in the state in which Adam was before he was invested with this supernatural endowment. In opposition to this doctrine, Protestants maintain that original righteousness was concreated and natural."[5] The objections to this view, as Hodge enumerates them, are, (1) "That it supposes a degrading view of the original constitution of our nature. According to this doctrine the seeds of evil were implanted in the nature of man as it came from the hands of God. It was disordered or diseased, there was about it what Bellarmin calls a *morbus* or *languor*, which needed a remedy. . . . " (2) "This doctrine as to original righteousness arose out of the Semi-Pelagianism of the Church of Rome, and was designed to sustain it."[6]

Suppose then that a Romanist approaches an unbeliever and asks him to accept Christianity. The unbeliever, in his eyes, is merely such a one as has lost original righteousness. The image of God in him which, according to Romanism consists as Hodge says, "only of the rational, and especially the voluntary nature of man, or the freedom of the will" (p. 103) is thought of as still intact. That is to say, the unbeliever is, perhaps barring ex-

[5] *Systematic Theology*, II, 103.
[6] *Idem*, p. 105.

tremes, correct in what he himself thinks of the powers of his intellect and will. There is not necessarily any sin involved in what the unbeliever, or natural man, does by way of exercising his capacities for knowledge and action. On this view the natural man does not need the light of Christianity to enable him to understand the world and himself aright. He does not need the revelation of Scripture or the illumination of the Holy Spirit in order that by means of them he may learn what his own true nature is.

Christianity therefore needs, on this basis, to be presented to the natural man as something that is merely information additional to what he already possesses. The knowledge of Christianity is to be related to the knowledge derived from the exercise of man's powers of reason and observation in a way similar to that in which at the beginning original righteousness was added to the image of God in man.

But without the light of Christianity it is as little possible for man to have the correct view about himself and the world as it is to have the true view about God. On account of the fact of sin man is blind with respect to the truth wherever the truth appears. And truth is one. Man cannot truly know himself unless he truly knows God. Not recognizing the fact of the fall, the philosophers, says Calvin, throw everything into confusion. They do not reckon with the fact that "at first every part of the soul was formed to rectitude" but that after the fall man is equally corrupt in all aspects of his being.[7] "They tell us," says Calvin, "there is great repugnance between the organic movements and the rational part of the soul. As if reason also were not at variance with herself, and her counsels sometimes conflicting with each other like hostile armies. But since this disorder results from the depravity of nature, it is erroneous to infer that there are two souls, because the faculties do not accord harmoniously as they ought."[8]

It appears then that there is a fundamental difference of opinion between Romanism and Calvin on the origin and nature of the "disturbance" in human nature. The view of Rome is essentially the same as that of the Greek philosophers: in par-

[7] *Institutes,* Bk. I, Chap. XV, Sec. 8.
[8] *Idem,* I, XV, 6.

ticular, that of Aristotle. According to this view the disturbance is endemic to human nature because man is made up, in part, of non-rational elements. To the extent that man consists of intellect he does not and cannot sin. The "disturbance" in man's make-up is not due primarily to any fault of his own. It is basically due to "God" who "made" him. On the other hand, according to Calvin, there is no "disturbance" in the nature of man as he comes forth from the hands of God. The "disturbance" has come in as the result of sin. Accordingly every one of fallen man's functions operates wrongly. The set of the whole human personality has changed. The intellect of fallen man may, as such, be keen enough. It can therefore formally understand the Christian position. It may be compared to a buzz-saw that is sharp and shining, ready to cut the boards that come to it. Let us say that a carpenter wishes to cut fifty boards for the purpose of laying the floor of a house. He has marked his boards. He has set his saw. He begins at one end of the mark on the board. But he does not know that his seven-year-old son has tampered with the saw and changed its set. The result is that every board he saws is cut slantwise and thus unusable because too short except at the point where the saw first made its contact with the wood. As long as the set of the saw is not changed the result will always be the same. So also whenever the teachings of Christianity are presented to the natural man they will be cut according to the set of sinful human personality. The keener the intellect the more consistently will the truths of Christianity be cut according to an exclusively immanentistic pattern. The result is that however much they may formally understand the truth of Christianity, men still worship "the dream and figment of their own heart."[9] They have what Hodge calls "mere cognition," but no true knowledge of God.

Still further as the "philosophers" and Calvin differ on the source and nature of the "disturbance" in human nature so they also differ on the remedy to be employed for the removal of that disturbance. According to the philosophers man does not need supernatural help for the removal of the disturbance within his being. According to the Greek view, so largely followed by Rome, man's intellect has within itself the proper set. The fall

[9] *Idem,* I, IV, 1.

has not disturbed the set of the saw and therefore there is no need of the supernatural power of the Holy Spirit to reset it. The nature of the intellect and its activity is almost unaffected by what happens to man in the course of history.

In opposition to this view, Hodge, following the lead of Calvin, stresses the fact that the whole set of sinful man needs to be renewed by the power of the Holy Spirit. The natural man must be "renewed in knowledge after the image of him that created him" (Col. 3:10). "*New* man (νέον)," says Hodge, in exposition of St. Paul, "agreeably to the ordinary distinction between νέος and καινός means recent, newly made, as opposed to (παλαίος) old. The moral quality or excellence of this recently formed man is expressed in the word ἀνακαινούμενον; as in Scriptural usage what is καινός is pure. This renovation is said to be εις ἐπίγνωσιν, not *in* knowledge, much less *by* knowledge, but *unto* knowledge, so that he knows. Knowledge is the effect of the renovation spoken of."[10] A little further Hodge adds: "The knowledge here intended is not mere cognition. It is full, accurate, living, or practical knowledge; such knowledge as is eternal life, so that this word here includes what in Eph. 4:24 is expressed by righteousness and holiness."[11]

Hodge also exegetes Ephesians 4:24, "Put on the new man, which after God is created in righteousness and true holiness." "These words," says Hodge, "when used in combination are intended to be exhaustive; i.e., to include all moral excellence. Either term may be used in this comprehensive sense, but, when distinguished, δικαιοσύνη means rectitude, the being and doing right, what justice demands; ὁσιότης, purity, holiness, the state of mind produced when the soul is full of God. Instead of *true* holiness, the words of the Apostle should be rendered 'righteousness and holiness of the truth'; that is, the righteousness and holiness which are the effects or manifestations of the truth. By truth here as opposed to the *deceit* (ἀπάτη) mentioned in the twenty-second verse, is meant what in Col. 3:10 is called knowledge. It is the divine light in the understanding, of which the Spirit of truth is the author, and from which, as their proximate

[10] *Systematic Theology*, II, 99.
[11] *Idem*, p. 100.

cause, all right affections and holy acts proceed."[12] Repeatedly Hodge stresses the fact that according to Scripture the natural man is incapable of himself to understand and accept the truth of Christianity. "The natural man, man as he is by nature, is destitute of the life of God, i.e., of spiritual life. His understanding is darkness, so that he does not know or receive the things of God. He is not susceptible of impression from the realities of the spiritual world. He is as insensible to them as a dead man to the things of this world."[13] In discussing regeneration Hodge asserts, "The Bible makes eternal life to consist in knowledge, sinfulness is blindness, or darkness; the transition from a state of sin to a state of holiness is a translation from darkness into light; men are said to be renewed unto knowledge, i.e., knowledge is the effect of regeneration, conversion is said to be effected by the revelation of Christ; the rejection of Him as the Son of God and Saviour of men is referred to the fact that the eyes of those who believe not are blinded by the god of this world."[14] Or again, "The heart in Scripture is that which thinks, feels, wills, and acts. It is the soul, the self. A new heart is, therefore, a new self, a new man. It implies a change of the whole character. It is a new nature. Out of the heart proceed all conscious, voluntary, moral exercises. A change of heart, therefore, is a change which precedes these exercises and determines their character."[15] "According to the evangelical doctrine the whole soul is the subject of regeneration. It is neither the intellect to the exclusion of the feelings, nor the feelings to the exclusion of the intellect; nor is it the will alone, either in its wider or in its more limited sense, that is the subject of the change in question. . . ."[16] "Regeneration secures right knowledge as well as right feeling; and right feeling is not the effect of right knowledge, nor is right knowledge the effect of right feeling. The two are the inseparable effects of a work which affects the whole soul."[17]

We conclude then that it is natural and consistent for Roman

[12] *Idem,* p. 101.
[13] *Idem,* p. 244.
[14] Vol. III, p. 16.
[15] *Idem,* p. 35.
[16] *Idem,* p. 36.
[17] *Ibid.*

Catholic apologetics to seek its point of contact with the unbeliever in a "common area" of knowledge. Roman Catholic theology agrees with the essential contention of those it seeks to win to the Christian faith that man's consciousness of himself and of the objects of the world is intelligible without reference to God.

But herein precisely lies the fundamental point of difference between Romanism and Protestantism. According to the principle of Protestantism, man's consciousness of self and of objects presuppose for their intelligibility the self-consciousness of God. In asserting this we are not thinking of psychological and temporal priority. We are thinking only of the question as to what is the final reference point in interpretation. The Protestant principle finds this in the self-contained ontological trinity. By his counsel the triune God controls whatsoever comes to pass. If then the human consciousness must, in the nature of the case, always be the proximate starting-point, it remains true that God is always the most basic and therefore the ultimate or final reference point in human interpretation.

This is, in the last analysis, the question as to what are one's ultimate presuppositions. When man became a sinner he made of himself instead of God the ultimate or final reference point. And it is precisely this presupposition, as it controls without exception all forms of non-Christian philosophy, that must be brought into question. If this presupposition is left unquestioned in any field all the facts and arguments presented to the unbeliever will be made over by him according to his pattern. The sinner has cemented colored glasses to his eyes which he cannot remove. And all is yellow to the jaundiced eye. There can be no intelligible reasoning unless those who reason together understand what they mean by their words.

In not challenging this basic presupposition with respect to himself as the final reference point in predication the natural man may accept the "theistic proofs" as fully valid. He may construct such proofs. He has constructed such proofs. But the god whose existence he proves to himself in this way is always a god who is something other than the self-contained ontological trinity of Scripture. The Roman Catholic apologete does not want to prove the existence of this sort of God. He wants to prove the existence of such a God as will leave intact the autonomy of man to at least some extent. Rome's theology does not want a God whose counsel controls whatsoever comes to pass.

It is natural then that Rome's view of the point of contact with the unbeliever is what it is.

II

Evangelicalism

We have spoken of the basic difference between Romanism and Protestantism on this question of the point of contact. But not all Protestantism has been fully true to the Protestant principle. Warfield has pointed this out admirably in the book discussed. It was only in Calvinism that the Protestant principle that salvation is of God alone has come to its consistent expression. Non-Calvinistic Protestants, frequently spoken of as Evangelicals, have conceived of "the operations of God looking to salvation universalistically" in order to leave room for an ultimate decision on the part of the individual human being.[18] God, as it were, through Christ deposits a large sum of money in a bank and announces this fact in the daily papers, offering to each one who comes sufficient for all his needs. It is then, in the last analysis, up to the individual whether he wants to be and remain in the class of those who live by the generosity of this bank. God approaches man by means of universals. There are differences among evangelicals, but, in the last analysis, these differences are merely as to whether God approaches the individuals by means of a wider or a narrower species. The final issue is always left up to the individual. "Particularism in the processes of salvation becomes thus the mark of Calvinism."[19] Warfield speaks therefore of Calvinism as being the only form of Protestantism "uncolored by intruding elements from without." God's action is the ultimate source of all determinate being.

For our purposes then the point of importance is that Evangelicalism has retained something of Roman Catholicism both in its view of man and in its view of God. Like Romanism, Evan-

[18] Warfield: *Plan of Salvation,* Grand Rapids, 1935, p. 111.
[19] *Ibid.*

gelicalism thinks of human self-consciousness and consciousness of objects as to some extent intelligible without the consciousness of God. It is to be expected that Evangelicalism will be in agreement with Rome on the question of the point of contact. Both forms of theology are colored by elements of an underlying naturalism. Both are therefore unwilling to challenge the natural man's basic presupposition with respect to himself as the ultimate reference point in interpretation. Both are unwilling to prove the existence of such a God as controls whatsoever comes to pass.

The great textbook of Evangelical apologetics is Bishop Butler's famous *Analogy*. It is not our purpose here to deal with its argument fully. Suffice it to point out that its argument is closely similar to that which is found, for instance, in the *Summa Contra Gentiles* of Thomas Aquinas. Butler holds to an Arminian view in theology. He therefore assumes that the natural man by "a reasonable use of reason" can interpret aright "the course and constitution of nature." If only the natural man will continue to employ the same "reasonable use of reason" with respect to the facts presented to him in Scripture about Christ and his work there is every likelihood that he will become a Christian.[20]

III

Less Consistent Calvinism

The question of starting-point then is largely determined by one's theology. In the first chapters it has been our aim to set forth the salient features of Christianity according to the principles of the Reformed faith. In particular it has been the aim to indicate the main features of Christianity after the fashion indicated by the great Reformed theologians of recent times. It is on the basis of the work of such men as Charles Hodge, Herman Bavinck, and B. B. Warfield, to mention no others, that we have formulated the broad outline of the Reformed life and world view. It is only by the help of such men that we have been enabled to attain to anything like a consistent Protestantism.

It is only to follow out their suggestion then if we follow

[20] The Syllabus on *Evidences* takes up the position of Butler in detail.

their principles in apologetics as well as in theology proper. We are to defend, as Warfield himself so well expresses it, not some minimal essence of Christianity, nor every detail included in the doctrines of Christianity, but "just Christianity itself . . . including all its 'details' and involving its 'essence'—in its unexplicated and uncompressed entirety. . . ."[21]

And this Christianity we must bring to those who are dead in trespasses and sins. "It is," says Warfield, "upon a field of the dead that the Sun of righteousness has risen, and the shouts that announce His advent fall on deaf ears; yea, even though the morning stars should again sing for joy and the air be palpitant with the echo of the great proclamation, their voice could not penetrate the ears of the dead. As we sweep our eyes over the world lying in its wickedness, it is the valley of the prophet's vision which we see before us: a valley that is filled with bones, and lo! they are very dry. What benefit is there in proclaiming to dry dones even the greatest of redemptions? How shall we stand and cry, O, ye dry bones, hear ye the word of the Lord!' In vain the redemption, in vain its proclamation, unless there come a breath from heaven to breathe upon these slain that they may live."[22] "The Christian lives by virtue of the life that has been given him, and prior to the inception of that life, of course, he has no power of action; and it is of the utmost importance that as Christian men we should not lower our testimony to this supernaturalness of our salvation."[23] Regeneration, we have seen Hodge argue, is *unto* knowledge, righteousness and holiness.

It would seem that we have dropped from this high plane to the level of evangelicalism when Hodge speaks of the office of reason in matters of religion. Under this heading he takes up three points. First he shows that reason is necessary as a tool for the reception of revelation. About this point there can be little cause for dispute. "Revelations cannot be made to brutes or to idiots."[24] Second, Hodge argues that "Reason must judge of the credibility of a revelation."[25] And "the credible is that which can

[21] *Studies in Theology,* New York, 1932, p. 9.

[22] *Idem,* p. 43.

[23] *Idem,* p. 45.

[24] *Systematic Theology,* I, 49.

[25] *Idem,* p. 50-53.

be believed. Nothing is incredible but the impossible. What may be, may be rationally (i.e., on adequate grounds) believed." What then is impossible? Hodge replies: "(1) That is impossible which involves a contradiction; as, that a thing is and is not; that right is wrong, and wrong right. (2) It is impossible that God should do, approve, or command what is morally wrong. (3) It is impossible that He should require us to believe what contradicts any of the laws of belief which He has impressed upon our nature. (4) It is impossible that one truth should contradict another. It is impossible, therefore, that God should reveal anything as true which contradicts any well authenticated truth, whether of intuition, experience, or previous revelation." Third, Hodge continues, "Reason must judge of the evidences of a revelation." As "faith involves assent, and assent is conviction produced by evidence, it follows that faith without evidence is either irrational or impossible." The second and third prerogatives of reason, says Hodge, are approved by Scripture itself. Paul "recognized the paramount authority of the intuitive judgments of the mind" and "Jesus appealed to his works as evidence of the truth of his claims."

It is not our purpose here to deal fully with the question of reason and revelation. Suffice it to note the ambiguity that underlies this approach to the question of the point of contact. When Hodge speaks of *reason* he means "those laws of belief which God has implanted in our nature." Now it is true, of course, that God has planted such laws of belief into our very being. It is this point on which Calvin lays such great stress when he says that all men have a sense of deity. But the unbeliever does not accept the doctrine of his creation in the image of God. It is therefore impossible to appeal to the intellectual and moral nature of men, as *men themselves interpret this nature,* and say that it must judge of the credibility and evidence of revelation. For if this is done, we are virtually telling the natural man to accept just so much and no more of Christianity as, with his perverted concept of human nature, he cares to accept.

To use once again the illustration of the saw: the saw is in itself but a tool. Whether it will move at all and whether it will cut in the right direction depends upon the man operating it. So also reason, or intellect, is always the instrument of a person. And the person employing it is always either a believer or an unbeliever. If he is a believer, his reason has already been changed in its set, as Hodge has told us, by regeneration. It cannot then be the judge; it is now a part of the regenerated person, gladly subject to the authority of God. It has by God's grace permitted itself to be interpreted by God's revelation. If, on the other hand, the person using his reason is an unbeliever, then this person, using his reason, will certainly assume the position of judge with respect to the credibility and evidence of revelation, but he will also certainly find the Christian religion incredible because impossible and the evidence for it is always inadequate. Hodge's own teaching on the blindness and hardness of the natural man corroborates this fact. To attribute to the natural man the right to judge by means of his reason of what is possible or impossible, or to judge by means of his moral nature of what is good or evil, is virtually to deny the "particularism" which, as Hodge no less than Warfield, believes to be the very hall-mark of a truly Biblical theology. In such a case Christianity would not claim to interpret the reasoner himself. That reasoner would be taken as already having within himself, previous to his acceptance of Christianity, the ability rightly to interpret and rightly to employ the powers of his own nature. And this is the exact equivalent of the Arminian position when it claims that God made salvation objectively possible but did not actually save individual men.

The main difficulty with the position of Hodge on this matter of the point of contact, then, is that it does not clearly distinguish between the original and the fallen nature of man. Basically, of course, it is Hodge's intention to appeal to the original nature of man as it came forth from the hands of its Creator. But he frequently argues as though that original nature can still be found as active in the "common consciousness" of men. Now there is a large element of truth in the contention that the common sense of man has not strayed so far from the truth as have the sophistications of the philosophers. Outspoken, blasphemous atheism is not usually found among the masses of men. But this does not take away the fact that all men are sinful in all the manifestations of their personality.

A comparison may tend to clarify this point. In the seventh

chapter of Romans, Paul speaks of himself, though a believer, as having a law of sin within his members which often controls him against his will. His "new man" is the real man, the man in Christ Jesus. But his "old man" is the remnant of his sinful nature that has not been fully destroyed. Applying this analogy to the natural man we have the following. The sinner is the one whose "new man" is the man in alliance with Satan. But his "old man" is that which wars within his members against his will; it is his nature as he came forth from the hands of his Creator. When the prodigal has left his father's house he is on the way to the swine-trough. But while on his way he has his misgivings. He seeks to make himself believe that his true nature consists in his self-assertion away from the father's house. But he kicks against the pricks. He sins against better knowledge.

It is quite in accord with the genius of Hodge's theology to appeal to the "old man" in the sinner and altogether out of accord with his theology to appeal to the "new man" in the sinner as though he would form a basically proper judgment on any question. Yet Hodge has failed to distinguish clearly between these two. Accordingly he does not clearly distinguish the Reformed from the Evangelical and Roman Catholic views of the point of contact. Accordingly he also speaks about "reason" as something that seems to operate rightly wherever it is found. But the "reason" of sinful men will invariably act wrongly. Particularly is this true when they are confronted with the specific contents of Scripture. The natural man will invariably employ the tool of his reason to reduce these contents to a naturalistic level. He must do so even in the interest of the principle of contradiction. For his own ultimacy is the most basic presupposition of his entire philosophy. It is upon this presupposition as its fulcrum that he uses the law of contradiction. If he is asked to use his reason as the judge of the credibility of the Christian revelation without at the same time being asked to renounce his view of himself as ultimate, then he is virtually asked to believe and to disbelieve in his own ultimacy at the same time and in the same sense. Moreover this same man, in addition to rejecting Christianity in the name of the law of contradiction, will also reject it in the name of what he calls his intuition of freedom. By this he means virtually the same thing as his ultimacy. Speaking of the "philosophers" Calvin says, "The principle they set out with was that man could not be a rational animal unless he had a free choice of good and evil. . . . They also imagined that that distinction between virtue and vice was destroyed, if man did not of his own counsel arrange his life."[26] If such a one is asked to accept the position of Christianity, according to which his destiny is ultimately determined by the counsel of God, he is asked to accept what to him makes right wrong and wrong right.

It is only to follow out the lead which Hodge in his theology, following Calvin, has given, if we seek our point of contact not in any abstraction whatsoever, whether it be reason or intuition. No such abstraction exists in the universe of men. We always deal with concrete individual men. These men are sinners. They have "an axe to grind." They want to suppress the truth in unrighteousness. They will employ their reason for that purpose. And they are not formally illogical if, granted the assumption of man's ultimacy, they reject the teachings of Christianity. On the contrary, to be logically consistent they are bound to do so. This point will engage us more fully in the sequel. For the moment it must suffice to have shown how the apologist is not only untrue to his own doctrine of man as the creature of God, but also defeats his own purpose if he appeals to some form of the "common consciousness of man."

Before going on to discuss what appears to us to be a more truly Biblical view of the problem of the point of contact, we would call attention to one other form of inconsistent Calvinism on this matter. In his book, *Het Testimonium Spiritus Sancti,* D. Valentine Hepp speaks about *prima principia* with respect to God, man and the world which, he says, men in general accept. With respect to the central truths which speak to us from creation as such, there is little doubt among men. A few mistaken scientists, who insist on maintaining their mistaken starting-point, insist that they doubt whether God or man or world exist. They owe such statements, not to experience, but to their systems. But their number, though we hear much of them, is very small. Taken as a whole mankind does not deny the central truths. The great majority of men recognize a higher power above them, and do

[26] *Institutes,* I, XV, 8.

not hesitate to accept the reality of the world and of man.[27] The position of Hepp, as appears even from this one quotation, is similar to that of Hodge. Like Hodge, Hepp wants to appeal to a general faith in "central truths" that all men, when not too sophisticated, accept. There seems to be for Hepp, as for Hodge, something in the way of a common sense philosophy which the natural man has and which, because intuitive or spontaneous, is, so far forth, not tainted by sin. It appears, however, even from the brief quotation given, that the "common notions" of men are sinful notions. For man to reflect on his own awareness of meaning and then merely to say that a higher power, *a* god, exists, is in effect to say that God does not exist. It is as though a child, reflecting upon his home environment would conclude that *a* father or *a* mother exist. And to "recognize the reality of the world and of man" is in itself not even to recognize the elemental truths of creation and providence. It is not enough to appeal from the more highly articulated systems of non-Christian thinkers to the philosophy of the common consciousness, of common sense, of intuition, that is to something that is more immediately related to the revelational pressure that rests upon men. Both Hepp and Hodge seem to be desirous of doing no more than Calvin does when he appeals to the sense of deity present in all men. But this notion, seeking to set forth as it does the teaching of Paul, that God's revelation is present to every man, must be carefully distinguished from the reaction that sinful men make to this revelation. The revelation of God, not of *a* god, is so immediately present to every man, that, as Warfield, following Calvin, says: "The conviction of the existence of God bears the marks of an intuitive truth in so far as it is the universal and unavoidable belief of men, and is given in the very same act with the idea of self, which is known at once as dependent and responsible and thus implies one on whom it depends and to whom it is responsible."[28] It is to this sense of deity, even this knowledge of God, which, Paul tells us (Romans 1:19-20) every man has, but which, as Paul also tells us, every sinner seeks to suppress, that the Christian apologetic must appeal.

[27] Kampen, 1914, p. 165.
[28] *Studies in Theology*, p. 110.

What has been said up to this point may seem to be discouraging in the extreme. It would seem that the argument up to this point has driven us to a denial of *any* point of contact whatsoever with the unbeliever. Is it not true that men must have some contact with the truth if they are to receive further knowledge of it? If men are totally ignorant of the truth how can they even become interested in it? If men are totally blind why display before them the colors of the spectrum? If they are deaf why take them to the academy of music?

Moreover, is not reason itself a gift of God? And does not the scientist, though not a Christian, know much about the universe? Does one need to be a Christian to know that two times two are four? And besides all this, does Christianity, while telling us of much that is *above* reason, require of us to accept anything that is *against* reason?

Our answer to this type of query is that it is precisely in the Reformed conception of the point of contact, and in it alone, that the historically so famous dilemma about the wholly ignorant, or the wholly omniscient, can be avoided. But before showing this positively it is necessary to indicate that in the Roman Catholic view this dilemma is insoluble.

If a man is wholly ignorant of the truth he cannot be interested in the truth. On the other hand if he is really interested in the truth it must be that he already possesses the main elements of the truth. It is in the interest of escaping the horns of this dilemma that Rome and evangelical Protestantism seek a point of contact in some area of "common knowledge" between believers and unbelievers. Their argument is that in teaching the total depravity of man in the way he does the Calvinist is in the unfortunate position of having to speak to deaf men when he preaches the gospel. We believe, on the contrary, that it is only the Calvinist who is not in this position.

Plato's famous allegory of the cave may illustrate the Roman Catholic position. The dwellers of this cave had chains about their necks and on their legs. They saw nothing but shadows and attributed echoes to these shadows. Yet they supposed that "they were naming what was actually before them." If one of them should be released, says Plato, he would need to get accustomed to the light of the sun. But he would pity those who were still in the cave. And "if he had to compete in measuring the shadows with the prisoners who have never moved out of the den . . . would he not be ridiculous" in their view? "Men would say of him that up he went and down he comes without his eyes; and that there is no use in even thinking of ascending; and if anyone tried to loose another and lead him up to the light, let them only catch the offender in the act, and they would put him to death."

Plato himself interprets this allegory in relation to man's capacity for and knowledge of the truth. The prisoners have eyes with which to see the truth; all they need is to have their heads turned about so they may face the truth.

It is in some such fashion that Rome thinks of the natural man. Following Aristotle's general method of reasoning Thomas Aquinas argues that the natural man can, by the ordinary use of his reason, do justice to the natural revelation that surrounds him. He merely needs some assistance in order that he may also see and react properly to the supernatural revelation that is found in Christianity.

According to the Roman view then, the natural man is already in possession of the truth in terms of a true interpretation of natural revelation. And he interprets natural revelation aright because he participates in the being of God. To be sure, he is said to be in possession of the truth only with respect to natural revelation. But if the natural man can and does interpret natural revelation in a way that is essentially correct there is no reason why he should need supernatural aid in order to interpret Christianity truly. At most he would need the information that Christ and his Spirit have come into the world. Hearing this news he would not fail, as a rational being, to make the proper reaction to it. If the natural man's eyes (reason) enable him to see correctly in one dimension, there is no good reason to think that these same eyes will not enable him, without further assistance from without, to see correctly in all dimensions. There would be no reason why all of the prisoners of the cave could not break their chains and walk in the light of day. In fact, Plato gives no reason why those who did not escape could not have escaped as well as the one who did.

On the other hand, it may be said that according to the Roman Catholic view the natural man does not give a fully correct interpretation of natural revelation. Does not Thomas Aquinas correct the interpretations that "the philosopher" has given of the things of nature? And does not the Roman Catholic view of the image of God in man itself imply that even originally, before the fall, man was unable, without the *donum superadditum* to know anything in a perfect way?

We reply that though Aquinas does correct some of the conclusions of Aristotle, he accepts the method of Aristotle as essentially sound. But, ignoring this, and granting for the sake of the argument that according to Rome the natural man's view of natural revelation is not fully correct, it should be noted that the only reason Rome can adduce for this fact is a defect in revelation itself. The prisoners of Plato's cave are not to be blamed for the fact that they see shadows only. They are doing full justice by the position in which they find themselves. If their heads are bound so that they see shadows only, this is due to no fault of theirs. It is due to the constitution and course of nature. According to this view the human mind is not originally and naturally in contact with the truth. The idea of freedom, as entertained by Roman theology, is based upon man's being metaphysically distinct from "god." And this is tantamount to saying that man is free to the extent that he has no "being." There is on this basis no genuine point of contact with the mind of the natural man at all. The ideas that man is out of contact with God and that he participates in the being of God are correlative to one another.

We do not object to the idea that the mind of man is said to be always in need of supernatural revelation. On the contrary we would stress the fact that even in paradise the mind of man needed and enjoyed a supernatural revelation. What we object to is the reason given for the need that man had of supernatural revelation even in paradise. The reason for this need, according to the Roman Catholic view, is virtually a defect in the original constitution of man. This implies that man is naturally, according to his original constitution, prone to error as well as to truth. The reason for this is that the god of Roman Catholicism does not control "whatsoever comes to pass." Man is, accordingly, not exclusively confronted with that which reveals God. Man is also confronted with the ultimately non-rational. On such a conception of reality in general it is natural that man's constitution should be thought of, on the one hand, as of itself possessing the truth and, on the other hand, as never able, by its natural action, to come into possession of the truth.

On such a basis too, the addition of supernatural to natural revelation would not remedy matters. It would be as true of supernatural as of natural revelation that either it would not reach man or else if it did reach man he would not be in need of it.

If natural revelation does not so envelop man as to make it impossible for him to look at anything that does not speak of God, then supernatural revelation will not do this either. If natural revelation does not speak of such a God as by his counsel surrounds man completely, then neither can supernatural revelation speak of such a God. But if it did, *per impossible,* speak of such a God, it could mean nothing to the mind of man as Rome conceives of it. *The revelation of a self-sufficient God can have no meaning for a mind that thinks of itself as ultimately autonomous.* The possibility for a point of contact has disappeared. The whole idea of the revelation of the self-sufficient God of Scripture drops to the ground if man himself is autonomous or self-sufficient. If man is not himself revelational in the internal structure of his being, he can receive no revelation that comes to him from without.

On the other hand, if man is in any sense autonomous he is not in need of revelation. If he is then said to possess the truth he possesses it as the product of the ultimately legislative powers of his intellect. It is only if he can virtually control by means of the application of the law of non-contradiction all the facts of reality that surround him, that he can know any truth at all. And thus, if he knows any truth in this way, he, in effect, knows all truth.

On the Roman Catholic position, then, man is, with the cave dwellers of Plato, by virtue of his own constitution, adapted to semi-darkness. Revelation would not do him any good, even though we might think of him as in need of it. If revelation is to come to him, it must come to him as the truth came to one of

Plato's cave-dwellers, in an accidental fashion. Or else man is, with the accidentally liberated cave-dweller of Plato, not in need of supernatural revelation; potentially he has all truth within his reach.

IV

The Reformed Position

The fully Biblical conception of the point of contact, it ought now to be clear, is the only one that can escape the dilemma of absolute ignorance or absolute omniscience.

The one great defect of the Roman Catholic and the Arminian view is, as noted, that it ascribes ultimacy or self-sufficiency to the mind of man. Romanism and Arminianism do this in their views of man as stated in their works on systematic theology. It is consistent for them, therefore, not to challenge the assumption of ultimacy as this is made by the non-believer. But Reformed theology, as worked out by Calvin and his recent exponents such as Hodge, Warfield, Kuyper and Bavinck, holds that man's mind is derivative. As such it is naturally in contact with God's revelation. It is surrounded by nothing but revelation. It is itself inherently revelational. It cannot naturally be conscious of itself without being conscious of its creatureliness. For man self-consciousness presupposes God-consciousness. Calvin speaks of this as man's inescapable sense of deity.

For Adam in paradise God-consciousness could not come in at the end of a syllogistic process of reasoning. God-consciousness was for him the presupposition of the significance of his reasoning on anything.

To the doctrine of creation must be added the conception of the covenant. Man was created as a historical being. God placed upon him from the outset of history the responsibility and task of reinterpreting the counsel of God as expressed in creation to himself individually and collectively. Man's creature-consciousness may therefore be more particularly signalized as covenant-consciousness. But the revelation of the covenant to man in paradise was supernaturally mediated. This was naturally the case inasmuch as it pertained to man's historical task. Thus, the sense of obedience or disobedience was immediately involved in Adam's consciousness of himself. Covenant consciousness envelops creature-consciousness. In paradise Adam knew that as a creature of God it was natural and proper that he should keep the covenant that God had made with him. In this way it appears that man's proper self-consciousness depended, even in paradise, upon his being in contact with both supernatural and natural revelation. God's natural revelation was within man as well as about him. Man's very constitution as a rational and moral being is itself revelational to man as the ethically responsible reactor to revelation. And natural revelation is itself incomplete. It needed from the outset to be supplemented with supernatural revelation about man's future. Thus the very idea of supernatural revelation is correlatively embodied in the idea of man's proper self-consciousness.

It is in this way that man may be said to be by his original constitution in contact with the truth while yet not in possession of all the truth. Man is not in Plato's cave. He is not in the anomalous position of having eyes with which to see while yet he dwells in darkness. He has not, as was the case with the cave-dwellers of Plato, some mere capacity for the truth that might never come to fruition. Man had originally not merely a capacity for receiving the truth; he was in actual possession of the truth. The world of truth was not found in some realm far distant from him; it was right before him. That which spoke to his senses no less than that which spoke to his intellect was the voice of God. Even when he closed his eyes upon the external world his internal sense would manifest God to him in his own constitution. The *matter* of his experience was in no sense in need of a mere *form* with which he might organize the raw material. On the contrary the *matter* of his experience was lit up through and through. Yet it was lit up for him by the voluntary activity of God whose counsel made things to be what they are. Man could not be aware of himself without also being aware of objects about him and without also being aware of his responsibility to manage himself and all things for the glory of God. Man's consciousness of objects and of self was not static. It was consciousness in *time*. Moreover, consciousness of objects and of self in time meant consciousness of *history* in relationship to the plan of God back of history. Man's first sense of self-awareness implied the awareness of the presence of God as the one for whom he had a great task to accomplish

It is only when we begin our approach to the question of the point of contact by thus analyzing the situation as it obtained in paradise before the fall of man that we can attain to a true conception of the natural man and his capacities with respect to the truth. The apostle Paul speaks of the natural man as actually possessing the knowledge of God (Rom. 1:19-21). The greatness of his sin lies precisely in the fact that "when they knew God, they glorified him not as God." No man can escape knowing God. It is indelibly involved in his awareness of anything whatsoever. Man *ought*, therefore, as Calvin puts it, to recognize God. There is no excuse for him if he does not. The reason for his failure to recognize God lies exclusively in him. It is due to his willful transgression of the very law of his being.

Neither Romanism nor Protestant evangelicalism can do full justice to this teaching of Paul. In effect both of them fail to surround man exclusively with God's revelation. Not holding to the counsel of God as all-controlling they cannot teach that man's self-awareness always pre-supposes awareness of God. According to both Rome and evangelicalism man may have some measure of awareness of objects about him and of himself in relation to them without being aware at the same time of his responsibility to manipulate both of them in relation to God. Thus man's consciousness of objects, of self, of time and of history are not from the outset brought into an exclusive relationship of dependence upon God. *Hinc illae lacrimae!*

Of course, when we thus stress Paul's teaching that all men do not have a mere capacity for but are in actual possession of the knowledge of God, we have at once to add Paul's further instruction to the effect that all men, due to the sin within them, always and in all relationships seek to "suppress" this knowledge of God (Rom. 1:18, *American Standard Version*). The natural man is such a one as constantly throws water on a fire he cannot quench. He has yielded to the temptation of Satan, and has become his bondservant. When Satan tempted Adam and Eve in paradise he sought to make them believe that man's self-consciousness was ultimate rather than derivative and God-dependent. He argued, as it were, that it was of the nature of self-consciousness to make itself the final reference point of all predication. He argued, as it were, that God had no control over all that might come forth in the process of time. That is to say, he argued, in effect, that as any form of self-consciousness must assume its own ultimacy, so it must also admit its own limitation in the fact that much that happens is under no control at all. Thus Satan argued, as it were, that man's consciousness of time and of time's products in history, is, if intelligible at all, intelligible in some measure independently of God.

Romanism and Evangelicalism, however, do not attribute this assumption of autonomy or ultimacy on the part of man as due to sin. They hold that man should quite properly think of himself and of his relation to objects in time in this way. Hence they do injustice to Paul's teaching with respect to the effect of sin on the interpretative activity of man. As they virtually deny that originally man not merely had a capacity for the truth but was in actual possession of the truth, so also they virtually deny that the natural man suppresses the truth.

It is not to be wondered at that neither Romanism nor Evangelicalism are little interested in challenging the "philosophers" when these, as Calvin says, interpret man's consciousness without being aware of the tremendous difference in man's attitude toward the truth before and after the fall. Accordingly they do not distinguish carefully between the natural man's own conception of himself and the Biblical conception of him. Yet for the question of the point of contact this is all-important. If we make our appeal to the natural man without being aware of this distinction we virtually admit that the natural man's estimate of himself is correct. We may, to be sure, even then, maintain that he is in need of information. We may even admit that he is morally corrupt. But the one thing which, on this basis, we cannot admit, is that his claim to be able to interpret at least some area of experience in a way that is essentially correct, is mistaken. We cannot then challenge his most basic epistemological assumption to the effect that his self-consciousness and time-consciousness are self-explanatory. We cannot challenge his right to interpret all his experience in exclusively immanentistic categories. And on this everything hinges. For if we first allow the legitimacy of the natural man's assumption of himself as the ultimate reference point in interpretation in any dimension we cannot deny his right to interpret Christianity itself in naturalistic terms.

The point of contact for the gospel, then, must be sought within the natural man. Deep down in his mind every man knows that he is the creature of God and responsible to God. Every man, at bottom, knows that he is a covenant-breaker. But every man acts and talks as though this were not so. It is the one point that cannot bear mentioning in his presence. A man may have internal cancer. Yet it may be the one point he will not have one speak of in his presence. He will grant that he is not feeling well. He will accept any sort of medication so long as it does not pretend to be given in answer to a cancer diagnosis. Will a good doctor cater to him on this matter? Certainly not. He will tell his patient that he has promise of life, but promise of life on one condition, that is, of an immediate internal operation. So it is with the sinner. He is alive but alive as a covenant-breaker. But his own interpretative activity with respect to all things proceeds on the assumption that such is not the case. Romanism and evangelicalism, by failing to appeal exclusively to that which is within man but is also suppressed by every man, virtually allow the legitimacy of the natural man's view of himself. They do not seek to explode the last stronghold to which the natural man always flees and where he always makes his final stand. They cut off the weeds at the surface but do not dig up the roots of these weeds, for fear that crops will not grow.

The truly Biblical view, on the other hand, applies atomic power and flame-throwers to the very presupposition of the natural man's ideas with respect to himself. It does not fear to lose a point of contact by uprooting the weeds rather than by cutting them off at the very surface. It is assured of a point of contact in the fact that every man is made in the image of God and has impressed upon him the law of God. In that fact alone he may rest secure with respect to the point of contact problem.[29] For that fact makes men always accessible to God. That fact assures us that every man, to be a man at all, must already be in contact with the truth. He is so much in contact with the truth that

[29] Here, as throughout this chapter, the argument is not that we should start our analysis of the knowledge of the natural man from the notion of an "absolute ethical antithesis" but from the sense of deity in the way that Calvin does.

much of his energy is spent in the vain effort to hide this fact from himself. His efforts to hide this fact from himself are bound to be self-frustrative.

Only by thus finding the point of contact in man's sense of deity that lies underneath his own conception of self-consciousness as ultimate can we be both true to Scripture and effective in reasoning with the natural man. Man, knowing God, refuses to keep God in remembrance (Rom. 1:28).

Chapter VI

CHRISTIAN APOLOGETICS (THE PROBLEM OF METHOD)

A discussion of the problem of methodology naturally follows upon that of the problem of the point of contact. If we have discovered what we shall think of the person to whom we are to make our address in the interest of winning him to an acceptance of Christianity, we must next inquire as to the way by which we shall lead him to a knowledge of the truth.

The Christian view of man and the Christian view of method are alike aspects of the Christian position as a whole. So also the non-Christian view of man and the non-Christian view of method are alike aspects of the non-Christian position as a whole. That such is indeed the case will appear as we proceed. For the moment the point is dogmatically asserted in order to indicate the plan of procedure for this chapter.

Our concern throughout is to indicate the nature of a truly Protestant, that is a Reformed, apologetic. A Reformed method of apologetics must seek to vindicate the Reformed life and world view as Christianity come to its own. It has already become plain that this implies a refusal to grant that any area or aspect of reality, any fact or any law of nature or of history can be correctly interpreted except it be seen in the light of the main doctrines of Christianity. But if this be true, it becomes quite impossible for the apologist to do what Roman Catholics and Arminians must do on the basis of their view of Christianity, namely, agree with the non-Christian in his principles of methodology to see whether or not Christian theism be true. From the Roman Catholic and the Arminian point of view the question of methodology, like that of starting-point, is a neutral matter. According to these positions the Christian apologist can legitimately join the non-Christian scientist or philosopher as he, by his recognized methods, investigates certain dimensions of reality. Neither the follower of Thomas Aquinas nor the follower of the "judicious Butler" would *need*, on his principles, to object when, for instance, A. E. Taylor says: "Natural science, let me say again, is exclusively concerned with the detection of 'laws of nature,' uniformities of sequence in the course of events. The typical form of such a law is the statement that whenever certain definitely measurable events occur some other measurable event will also be found to occur. Any enquiry thus delimited obviously can throw no light on the question . . . whether God exists or not, the question whether the whole course of events among which the man of science discovers these uniformities of sequence is or is not guided by a supreme intelligence to the production of an intrinsically good result."[1] The Reformed apologist, on the other hand, would compromise what he holds to be of the essence of Christianity if he agreed with Taylor. For him the whole of created reality, including therefore the fields of research with which the various sciences deal, reveals the same God of which Scripture speaks. The very essence of created reality is its revelational character. Scientists deal with that which has the imprint of God's face upon it. Created reality may be compared to a great estate. The owner has his name plainly and indelibly written at unavoidable places. How then would it be possible for some stranger to enter this estate, make researches in it, and then fairly say that in these researches he need not and cannot be confronted with the question of ownership? To change the figure, compare the facts of nature and history, the facts with which the sciences are concerned, to a linoleum that has its figure indelibly imprinted in it. The pattern of such a linoleum cannot be effaced till the linoleum itself is worn away. Thus inescapably does the scientist meet the pattern of Christian theism in each fact with which he deals. The apostle Paul lays great stress upon the fact that man is without excuse if he does not discover God

[1] *Does God Exist?* London, 1947, pp. 13, 14.

in nature. Following Paul's example Calvin argues that men *ought* to see God, not *a* god, not some supernatural power, but the only God, in nature. They have not done justice by the facts they see displayed before and within them if they say that *a* god exists or that God *probably* exists. The Calvinist holds to the essential perspicuity of natural as well as Biblical revelation. This does not imply that a non-Christian and non-theistic interpretation of reality cannot be made to appear plausible. But it does mean that no non-Christian position can be made to appear *more* than merely plausible.

Roman Catholic apologists can, therefore, to the extent that their own theology does not teach the perspicuity of natural revelation, with consistency use the method of the natural man. Just as Rome, having a semi-pagan conception of the nature of man, can agree with the natural man's conception of the starting-point in knowledge, so also, having a semi-pagan concept of the nature of the objects man must know, can, to a large extent, agree with the natural man's conception of the method of knowledge.

Arminian apologists also, to the extent that their theology is faulty, can consistently agree with the non-believer on the question of methodology. Believing to some extent in the autonomy and ultimacy of human personality Arminianism can, in a measure, agree on the question of starting-point with those who make men the final reference point in all human predication. So also, believing to some extent in the existence of facts that are not wholly under the control and direction of the counsel of God, Arminianism can agree on the question of method with those for whom the object of knowledge has nothing at all to do with the plan of God.

In contradistinction from both Roman Catholics and Arminians, however, the Reformed apologist cannot agree at all with the methodology of the natural man. Disagreeing with the natural man's interpretation of himself as the ultimate reference-point, the Reformed apologist must seek his point of contact with the natural man in that which is beneath the threshold of his working consciousness, in the sense of deity which he seeks to suppress. And to do this the Reformed apologist must also seek a point of contact with the systems constructed by the natural man. But this point of contact must be in the nature of a head-on collision. *If there is no head-on collision with the systems of the natural man there will be no point of contact with the sense of deity in the natural man.* So also, disagreeing with the natural man on the nature of the object of knowledge, the Reformed apologist must disagree with him on the method to be employed in acquiring knowledge. According to the doctrine of the Reformed faith all the facts of nature and of history are what they are, do what they do and undergo what they undergo, in accord with the one comprehensive counsel of God. All that may be known by man is already known by God. And it is already known by God because it is controlled by God.

The significance of this for the question of method will be pointed out soon. For the moment this simple fact must be signalized as the reason which precludes the possibility of agreement on methodology between the Reformed theologian and the non-Christian philosopher or scientist. We may mention one point that brings out the difference in methodology between the two positions. It is the point with reference to the relevancy of hypotheses. For the non-Christian any sort of hypothesis may, at the outset of an investigation, be as relevant as any other. This is so because on a non-Christian basis facts are not what they are because of the systematic relation they sustain to God. On a non-Christian basis facts are "rationalized" for the first time when interpreted by man. But for one who holds that the facts are already part of an ultimately rational system by virtue of the plan of God it is clear that such hypotheses as presuppose the non-existence of such a plan must, even from the outset of his investigation, be considered irrelevant.

I

Reasoning by Presupposition

These things being as they are it will be our first task in this chapter to show that a consistently Christian method of apologetic argument, in agreement with its own basic conception of the starting point, must be by presupposition. To argue by presupposition is to indicate what are the epistemological and metaphysical principles that underlie and control one's method. The

Reformed apologist will frankly admit that his own methodology presupposes the truth of Christian theism. Basic to all the doctrines of Christian theism is that of the self-contained God, or, if we wish, that of the ontological trinity. It is this notion of the ontological trinity that ultimately controls a truly Christian methodolgy. Based upon this notion of the ontological trinity and consistent with it, is the concept of the counsel of God according to which all things in the created world are regulated.

Christian methodology is therefore based upon presuppositions that are quite the opposite of those of the non-Christian. It is claimed to be of the very essence of any non-Christian form of methodology that it cannot be determined in advance to what conclusions it must lead. To assert, as the Christian apologist is bound to do if he is not to deny the very thing he is seeking to establish, that the conclusion of a true method is the truth of Christian theism is, from the point of view of the non-Christian, the clearest evidence of authoritarianism. In spite of this claim to neutrality on the part of the non-Christian the Reformed apologist must point out that *every* method, the supposedly neutral one no less than any other, presupposes either the truth or the falsity of Christian theism.

The method of reasoning by presupposition may be said to be indirect rather than direct. The issue between believers and non-believers in Christian theism cannot be settled by a direct appeal to "facts" or "laws" whose nature and significance is already agreed upon by both parties to the debate. The question is rather as to what is the final reference-point required to make the "facts" and "laws" intelligible. The question is as to what the "facts" and "laws" really are. Are they what the non-Christian methodology assumes that they are? Are they what the Christian theistic methodology presupposes they are?

The answer to this question cannot be finally settled by any direct discussion of "facts." It must, in the last analysis, be settled indirectly. The Christian apologist must place himself upon the position of his opponent, assuming the correctness of his method merely for argument's sake, in order to show him that on such a position the "facts" are not facts and the "laws" are not laws. He must also ask the non-Christian to place himself upon the Christian position for argument's sake in order that he may be shown that only upon such a basis do "facts" and "laws" appear intelligible.

To admit one's own presuppositions and to point out the presuppositions of others is therefore to maintain that all reasoning is, in the nature of the case, *circular reasoning*. The starting-point, the method, and the conclusion are always involved in one another.

Let us say that the Christian apologist has placed the position of Christian theism before his opponent. Let us say further that he has pointed out that his own method of investigation of reality presupposes the truth of his position. This will appear to his friend whom he is seeking to win to an acceptance of the Christian position as highly authoritarian and out of accord with the proper use of human reason. What will the apologist do next? If he is a Roman Catholic or an Arminian he will tone down the nature of Christianity to some extent in order to make it appear that the consistent application of his friend's neutral method will lead to an acceptance of Christian theism after all. But if he is a Calvinist this way is not open to him. He will point out that the more consistently his friend applies his supposedly neutral method the more certainly he will come to the conclusion that Christian theism is not true. Roman Catholics and Arminians, appealing to the "reason" of the natural man as the natural man himself interprets his reason, namely as autonomous, are bound to use the direct method of approach to the natural man, the method that assumes the essential correctness of a non-Christian and non-theistic conception of reality. The Reformed apologist, on the other hand, appealing to that knowledge of the true God in the natural man which the natural man suppresses by means of his assumption of ultimacy, will also appeal to the knowledge of the true method which the natural man knows *but suppresses*. The natural man at bottom knows that he is the creature of God. He knows also that he is responsible to God. He knows that he should live to the glory of God. He knows that in all that he does he should stress that the field of reality which he investigates has the stamp of God's ownership upon it. But he suppresses his knowledge of himself as he truly is. He is the man with the iron mask. A true method of apologetics must seek to tear off that iron mask. The Roman Catholic and the Arminian make no attempt to do so. They even flatter its wearer about his fine appearance. In the introductions of their books on apologetics Arminian as well as Roman Catholic apologists frequently seek to set their "opponents" at ease by assuring them that their method, in its field, is all that any Christian could desire. In contradistinction from this, the Reformed apologist will point out again and again that the only method that will lead to the truth in any field is that method which recognizes the fact that man is a creature of God, that he must therefore seek to think God's thoughts after him.

It is not as though the Reformed apologist should not interest himself in the nature of the non-Christian's method. On the contrary he should make a critical analysis of it. He should, as it were, join his "friend" in the use of it. But he should do so self-consciously with the purpose of showing that its most consistent application not merely leads away from Christian theism but in leading away from Christian theism leads to destruction of reason and science as well.

An illustration may indicate more clearly what is meant. Suppose we think of a man made of water in an infinitely extended and bottomless ocean of water. Desiring to get out of water, he makes a ladder of water. He sets this ladder upon the water and against the water and then attempts to climb out of the water. So hopeless and senseless a picture must be drawn of the natural man's methodology based as it is upon the assumption that time or chance is ultimate. On his assumption his own rationality is a product of chance. On his assumption even the laws of logic which he employs are products of chance. The rationality and purpose that he may be searching for are still bound to be products of chance. So then the Christian apologist, whose position requires him to hold that Christian theism is really true and as such must be taken as the presupposition which alone makes the acquisition of knowledge in any field intelligible, must join his "friend" in his hopeless gyrations so as to point out to him that his efforts are always in vain.

It will then appear that Christian theism, which was first rejected because of its supposed authoritarian character, is the only position which gives human reason a field for successful operation and a method of true progress in knowledge.

Two remarks may here be made by way of meeting the most obvious objections that will be raised to this method of the Reformed apologist. The first objection that suggests itself may be expressed in the rhetorical question "Do you mean to assert that non-Christians do not discover truth by the methods they employ?" The reply is that we mean nothing so absurd as that. The implication of the method here advocated is simply that non-Christians are never able and therefore never do employ their own methods consistently. Says A. E. Taylor in discussing the question of the uniformity of nature, "The fundamental thought of modern science, at any rate until yesterday, was that there is a 'universal reign of law' throughout nature. Nature is rational in the sense that it has everywhere a coherent pattern which we can progressively detect by the steady application of our own intelligence to the scrutiny of natural processes. Science has been built up all along on the basis of this principle of the 'uniformity of nature,' and the principle is one which science itself has no means of demonstrating. No one could possibly prove its truth to an opponent who seriously disputed it. For all attempts to produce 'evidence' for the 'uniformity of nature' themselves presuppose the very principle they are intended to prove."[2] Our argument as over against this would be that the existence of the God of Christian theism and the conception of his counsel as controlling all things in the universe is the only presupposition which can account for the uniformity of nature which the scientist needs. But the best and only possible proof for the existence of such a God is that his existence is required for the uniformity of nature and for the coherence of all things in the world. We cannot *prove* the existence of beams underneath a floor if by proof we mean that they must be ascertainable in the way that we can see the chairs and tables of the room. But the very idea of a floor as the support of tables and chairs requires the idea of beams that are underneath. But there would be no floor if no beams were underneath. Thus there is absolutely certain proof for the existence of God and the truth of Christian theism. Even non-Christians presuppose its truth while they verbally reject it. They need to presuppose the truth of Christian theism in order to account for their own accomplishments.

[2] *Idem,* p. 2.

The second objection may be voiced in the following words: "While a Christian can prove that his Christian position is fully as reasonable as the opponent's view, there is no such thing as an absolutely compelling proof that God exists, or that the Bible is the word of God, just as little as anyone can prove its opposite." In this way of putting the matter there is a confusion between what is objectively valid and what is subjectively acceptable to the natural man. It is true that no method of argument for Christianity will be acceptable to the natural man. Moreover, it is true that the more consistently Christian our methodology, the less acceptable it will be to the natural man. We find something similar in the field of theology. It is precisely the Reformed faith which, among other things, teaches the total depravity of the natural man, which is most loathsome to that natural man. But this does not prove that the Reformed faith is not true. A patient may like a doctor who tells him that his disease can be cured by means of external applications and dislike the doctor who tells him that he needs a major internal operation. Yet the latter doctor may be right in his diagnosis. It is the weakness of the Roman Catholic and the Arminian methods that they virtually identify objective validity with subjective acceptability to the natural man. Distinguishing carefully between these two, the Reformed apologist maintains that there is an absolutely valid argument for the existence of God and for the truth of Christian theism. He cannot do less without virtually admitting that God's revelation to man is not clear. It is fatal for the Reformed apologist to admit that man has done justice to the objective evidence if he comes to any other conclusion than that of the truth of Christian theism.

As for the question whether the natural man will accept the truth of such an argument, we answer that he will if God pleases by his Spirit to take the scales from his eyes and the mask from his face. It is upon the power of the Holy Spirit that the Reformed preacher relies when he tells men that they are lost in sin and in need of a Savior. The Reformed preacher does not tone down his message in order that it may find acceptance with the natural man. He does not say that his message is less certainly true because of its non-acceptance by the natural man. The natural man is, by virtue of his creation in the image of God, always accessible to the truth; accessible to the penetration of the truth by the Spirit of God. Apologetics, like systematics, is valuable to the precise extent that it presses the truth upon the attention of the natural man. The natural man must be blasted out of his hideouts, his caves, his last lurking places. Neither Roman Catholic nor Arminian methodologies have the flame-throwers with which to reach him. In the all-out war between the Christian and the natural man as he appears in modern garb it is only the atomic energy of a truly Reformed methodology that will explode the last *Festung* to which the Roman Catholic and the Arminian always permit him to retreat and to dwell in safety.[3]

II

Scripture

It has been pointed out that the difference between a Roman Catholic-Arminian and a Reformed type of argument lies in the fact that the former is direct and the latter is indirect. The former grants the essential truthfulness of the non-Christian theory of man and of method, while the latter challenges both. This difference will appear again and appear in its fundamental importance still more strikingly if the question of the place of Scripture in apologetics is brought up for consideration. A few remarks on this subject must suffice.

For better or for worse the Protestant apologist is committed to the doctrine of Scripture as the infallibly inspired final revelation of God to man. This being the case, he is committed to the defense of Christian theism as a unit. For him theism is not really theism unless it is Christian theism. The Protestant apologist cannot be concerned to prove the existence of any other God than the one who has spoken to man authoritatively and finally through Scripture.

The entire debate about theism will be purely formal unless theism be taken as the foundation of Christianity. But if it is so

[3] The use of such martial terminology is not inconsistent with the Christian principle of love. He who loves men most will tell them the truth about themselves in their own interest.

[4] Readers especially interested in the relation of one's doctrine of inspiration to questions of apologetics should consult this writer's syllabus *The Protestant Doctrine of Scripture*. Several chapters found in the present writer's syllabi *Introduction to Systematic Theology* and *Christian Theory of Knowledge* also deal with the question of inspiration and authority directly, while his "Introduction" to B. B. Warfield's *The Inspiration and Authority of Scripture* (Presbyterian and Reformed Publishing Co.) outlines what he believes to be a biblical method of presenting and defending the doctrine of inspiration in the context of modern theology.

taken it is no longer theism as such but Christian theism that is in debate. Pantheist, deists and theists, that is bare theists, may formally agree that God exists. Socrates, in arguing about the nature of piety within Euthyphro says that men "join issue about particulars." So if the whole debate in apologetics is to be more than a meaningless discussion about the *that* of God's existence and is to consider *what kind* of God exists, then the question of God's revelation to man must be brought into the picture. Even before the entrance of sin, as already noted, man required supernatural positive revelation as a supplement to revelation in the created universe around and within him. To understand God's general revelation in the universe aright it was imperative for man that he see this revelation in relationship to a higher revelation with respect to the final destiny of man and the universe. If then even man in paradise could read nature aright only in connection with and in the light of supernatural positive revelation, how much the more is this true of man after the fall. In paradise the supernatural revelation of God to man told him that if he would eat of the forbidden tree he would surely die. Having eaten of this fruit he could therefore expect nothing but eternal separation from God as his final destiny. Of God's intention to save a people for his own precious possession he could learn nothing from nature. Nor was this involved in the preredemptive supernatural revelation that had been vouchsafed to him in paradise. It had to come by way of post-lapsarian supernatural revelation. Covenant-breakers could expect nothing but covenant wrath. That God meant to bring covenant-breakers back into covenant communion with himself through the covenant of grace could in no wise be discovered other than by supernatural redemptive revelation. B. B. Warfield brings out this point when he says that in addition to believing the supernatural fact, that is, God as a transcendent, self-existent being and in the supernatural act exemplified in creation and providence, the Christian must also believe in supernatural redemption. "As certainly as the recognition of the great fact of sin is an element in the Christian's world-conception, the need and therefore the actuality of the direct corrective act of God—of miracle, in a word—enters ineradicably into his belief."[5]

[5] *Studies in Theology*, p. 38.

But supernatural redemption in itself would not be of any avail. "For how should we be advantaged by a supernatural redemption of which we know nothing? Who is competent to uncover to us the meaning of this great series of redemptive acts but God himself? . . . Two thousand years ago a child was born in Bethlehem, who throve and grew up nobly, lived a life of poverty and beneficence, was cruelly slain and rose from the dead. What is that to us? After a little, as his followers sat waiting in Jerusalem, there was a rush as of a mighty wind, and an appearance of tongues of fire descending upon their heads. Strange: but what concern have we in it all? We require the revealing Word to tell us who and what this goodly child was, why he lived and what he wrought by his death, what it meant that he could not be holden of the grave and what those cloven tongues of fire signified—before they can avail as redemptive facts to us."[6] Going a bit beyond this it may be asserted that sinful man would naturally want to destroy a supernatural revelation that portrays his sin and shame and tells him that he is helpless and undone. This is out of accord with the pride that is a prime mark of the sinner. Hence the necessity for the inscripturization of the God-given post-lapsarian supernatural revelation of God to man.

Thus the Bible, as the infallibly inspired revelation of God to sinful man, stands before us as that light in terms of which all the facts of the created universe must be interpreted. All of finite existence, natural and redemptive, functions in relation to one all-inclusive plan that is in the mind of God. Whatever insight man is to have into this pattern of the activity of God he must attain by looking at all his objects of research in the light of Scripture. "If true religion is to beam upon us, our principle must be, that it is necessary to begin with heavenly teaching, and that it is impossible for any man to obtain even the minutest portion of right and sound doctrine without being a disciple of Scripture."[7]

What has been said so far on the subject of Scripture has dealt primarily with its place in Protestant doctrine. What bearing does this fact have upon the place of Scripture in Christian apolo-

[6] *Idem*, p. 42.
[7] *Institutes*, Bk. I, Chap. VI, Sec. 2.

getics? And what bearing does it have upon the method of apologetics in general?

In the first place it must be affirmed that a Protestant accepts Scripture to be that which Scripture itself says it is on its own authority. Scripture presents itself as being the only light in terms of which the truth about facts and their relations can be discovered. Perhaps the relationship of the sun to our earth and the objects that constitute it, may make this clear. We do not use candles, or electric lights in order to discover whether the light and the energy of the sun exist. The reverse is the case. We have light in candles and electric light bulbs because of the light and energy of the sun. So we cannot subject the authoritative pronouncements of Scripture about reality to the scrutiny of reason because it is reason itself that learns of its proper function from Scripture.

There are, no doubt, objections that occur to one at once when he hears the matter presented so baldly. We cannot deal with these fully here. For the moment it is of the greatest importance that this simple but basic point be considered apart from all subsidiary matters. All the objections that are brought against such a position spring, in the last analysis, from the assumption that the human person is ultimate and as such should properly act as judge of all claims to authority that are made by any one. But if man is not autonomous, if he is rather what Scripture says he is, namely, a creature of God and a sinner before his face, then man should subordinate his reason to the Scriptures and seek in the light of it to interpret his experience.

The proper attitude of reason to the authority of Scripture, then, is but typical of the proper attitude of reason to the whole of the revelation of God. The objects man must seek to know are always of such a nature as God asserts they are. God's revelation is always authoritarian. This is true of his revelation in nature no less than of his revelation in Scripture. The truly scientific method, the method which alone can expect to make true progress in learning, is therefore such a method as seeks simply to think God's thoughts after him.

When these matters are kept in mind, it will be seen clearly that the true method for any Protestant with respect to the Scripture (Christianity) and with respect to the existence of God (theism) must be the indirect method of reasoning by presupposition. In fact it then appears that the argument for the Scripture as the infallible revelation of God is, to all intents and purposes, the same as the argument for the existence of God. Protestants are required by the most basic principles of their system to vindicate the existence of no other God than the one who has spoken in Scripture. But this God cannot be proved to exist by any other method than the indirect one of presupposition. No proof for this God and for the truth of his revelation in Scripture can be offered by an appeal to anything in human experience that has not itself received its light from the God whose existence and whose revelation it is supposed to prove. One cannot prove the usefulness of the light of the sun for the purposes of seeing by turning to the darkness of a cave. The darkness of the cave must itself be lit up by the shining of the sun. When the cave is thus lit up each of the objects that are in it "proves" the existence and character of the sun by receiving their light and intelligibility from it.

Now the Roman Catholic is not committeed to any such doctrine of Scripture as has been expressed above. He can therefore build up his apologetics by the direct method. He can, as has already been shown, to a large extent agree with the natural man in his conception of both the starting point and the method of human knowledge. He can therefore join the non-Christian in his search for the existence or non-existence of God by the use of reason without any reference to Scripture. That is, he and the natural man can seek to build up theism quite independently of Christianity. Then when the Romanist has, together with his friend the natural man, built the first story of the house to the satisfaction of both, he will ask his friend to help in building the second story, the story of Christianity. He will assure his friend that he will use the same principles of construction for the second story that they have together employed in their common construction of the first story. The second story is, according to Rome, to be sure, the realm of faith and of authority. But then this authority is but that of the expert. Rome knows of no absolute authority such as Protestantism has in its doctrine of Scripture. Rome's authority is the authority of those who are experts in what they say are reported to be the oracles of God. These oracles receive their authoritative illumination from the expert interpreters of them, from the Pope first of all. But such a concept of authority resembles that which Socrates referred to in *The Symposium* when he spoke of Diotima the inspired. When the effort at rational interpretation failed him, Socrates took refuge in mythology as a second best. The "hunch" of the wise is the best that is available to man with respect to that which he cannot reach by the methods of autonomous reason. No "wise man" ought to object to such a conception of the "supernatural." It merely involves the recognition that he has not yet discovered the truth about all of reality by means of reason. So then the natural man need not really object, even from his own point of view, to the presentation of supernatural revelation as it is offered to him by the Roman Catholic apologist.

If the Roman Catholic method of apologetic for Christianity is followed then Christianity itself must be so reduced as to make it acceptable to the natural man. Since Rome is more than willing to grant the essential correctness of the starting point and method of the natural man in the "realm of nature" he cannot logically object to the conclusion of the natural man with respect to supernatural reality. The natural man need only to reason consistently along the lines of his starting point and method in order to reduce each of the Christian doctrines that are presented to him to naturalistic proportions.

As for the Arminian way of reasoning, it is, as already noted, essentially the same as that of Rome. The method followed by Bishop Butler follows closely that of Thomas Aquinas. According to Butler some of those who have no belief in or knowledge of Christianity at all have, none the less, quite rightly interpreted the "course and constitution of nature." The cave has already been lit up by means of light that was not derived from the sun. By the use of the empirical method those who make no pretense of listening to Scripture are said or assumed to have interpreted nature for what it really is. It is no wonder then that the contents of Scripture too must be adjusted to the likes of the natural man. He will not accept them otherwise. And Butler is anxious to win him. So he says to him: "Reason can, and it ought to judge, not only of the meaning, but also of the morality and the evidence, of revelation. First, it is the province of reason to judge of the morality of Scripture; i.e., not whether it contains things different from what we should have expected from a wise, just, and good Being; for objections from hence have now been obviated; but whether it contains things plainly contradictory to wisdom, justice, or goodness—to what the light of nature teaches us of God."[8] Since even in the interpretation of "nature" the natural man must and does himself admit that he cannot know everything, he can certainly, without compromising himself in the least, allow that what Scripture claims about "supernatural" things may *probably* be true. Already accustomed to allowing for a measure of discontinuity even in his interpretation of the "course and constitution of nature" why should he not allow for a little more of this same sort of discontinuity in realms about which he admits that he still may learn? Such a concession will not break the principle of continuity that he has employed in all his interpretations of things that he knows; his principle of continuity needs merely to be stretched. The natural man does not object to stretching his principle of continuity if he is compelled to do so by virtue of the irrationality of reality; the only thing to which he strenuously objects is the submission of his own principles of continuity and of discontinuity to the counsel of God.

It appears then that as Arminianism together with Roman Catholicism is willing to join the natural man in his supposedly neutral starting point and method, so also Arminianism is forced to pay for these concessions by having the natural man to some extent dictate to him what sort of Christianity he may or may not believe. If the natural man is given permission to draw the floorplan for a house and is allowed to build the first story of the house in accordance with his own blueprint, the Christian cannot escape being controlled in a large measure by the same blueprint when he wants to take over the building of the second story of the house. Arminianism begins by offering to the natural man a Christian theology that has foreign elements in it. As over against the Reformed faith the Arminian has fought for the idea of man's ultimate ability to accept or reject salvation. His argument on this score amounts to saying that God's presentation of his claims upon mankind cannot reach down to the individual

[8] *The Works of Bishop Butler,* edited by W. E. Gladstone, New York, 1896, Vol. I, p. 238.

man; it can only reach to the *infima species.* God has to await the election returns to see whether he is chosen as God or is set aside. God's knowledge therefore stands over against and depends to some extent upon a temporal reality which he does not wholly control. When the Arminian has thus, as he thinks, established and defended human responsibility against the Calvinist he turns about to defend the Christian position against the natural man. But then he soon finds himself at the mercy of the natural man. The natural man is mercilessly consistent. He simply tells the Arminian that a little autonomy involves absolute autonomy, and a little reality set free from the plan of God involves all reality set free from the plan of God. After that the reduction process is simply a matter of time. Each time the Arminian presents to the natural man one of the doctrines of Christianity, the natural man gladly accepts it and then "naturalizes" it.

It is no valid objection against this contention to say that certainly many Arminians do not hold to any naturalistic conception of Christianity. For the question is not so much now what individual Arminians believe. Their belief at best involves a compromise with naturalism. But the point we are making now is about the method of apologetics that fits in with Arminian theology. And on that score we must, in simple honesty, assert that this method is essentially the same as the method of Roman Catholicism and is essentially reductionistic and therefore self-frustrative. It appears then that the first enemy of Arminianism, namely Calvinism, is its best friend. Only in the Reformed Faith is there an uncompromising statement of the main tenets of Christianity. All other statements are deformations. It is but to be expected that only in the Reformed Faith will we find an uncompromising method of apologetics. Calvinism makes no compromise with the natural man either on his views of the autonomy of the human mind or on his views of the nature of existence as not controlled by the plan of God. Therefore Calvinism cannot find a direct point of contact in any of the accepted concepts of the natural man. He disagrees with every individual doctrine of the natural man because he disagrees with the outlook of the natural man as a whole. He disagrees with the basic immanentistic assumption of the natural man. For it is this basic assumption that colors all his statements about individual teachings. It is therefore this basic assumption of the natural man that meets its first major challenge when it is confronted by the statement of a full-fledged Christianity.

The Reformed apologist throws down the gauntlet and challenges his opponent to a duel of life and death from the start. He does not first travel in the same direction and in the same automobile with the natural man for some distance in order then mildly to suggest to the driver that they ought perhaps to change their course somewhat and follow a road that goes at a different slant from the one they are on. The Reformed apologist knows that there is but one way to the truth and that the natural man is travelling it, but in the wrong direction. The service stations along the highway will service cars going in either direction. And as there are seemingly more cars going in the wrong direction than there are going in the right direction, the upkeep of the road will be supplied largely by those going in the wrong direction. Speaking together at one of these service stations, two travellers going in opposite directions may be in perfect agreement when they eulogize the turnpike on which they are travelling and the preumim quality of gasoline which they are getting. But like Bunyan's Christian the Reformed apologist will tell his friend that the way he is going leads to the precipice. He points to the signs made by the builder of the road which all point the opposite way from that which his friend, the natural man, is going. And when the reply is made by the natural man that he has been very successful in his trip so far, and that he too has been following signs, signs which point in the direction in which he is moving, the Reformed apologist will wipe out such of these signs as are near at hand and will challenge his friend to wipe out any of the signs he has ignored.

The Roman Catholic and the Arminian apologist would not be in a position to wipe out any of the signs that point in the wrong direction. An Arminian apologist meeting the natural man as both stop at one of the service stations is in a strange predicament. Since he is a Christian he should really speak to the natural man about the fact that he is following the wrong signs. His belief in creation demands of him that he warn his new acquaintance against following the wrong signs. But since he himself holds to a measure of autonomy for man and since this undermines his own belief in creation, he can at best say to his friend that it is *doubtful* which signs are right. Then as far as his "neutral" apologetic method is concerned, the Arminian, in the interest of getting his friend to go in the right direction, admits that the signs that point in the wrong direction are right. He himself goes in the wrong direction for some distance too with the natural man. He fully agrees with the natural man when together they start on their wrong course and he still fully agrees on the way to the city of destruction. Then suddenly he puts on the brakes and turns around, expecting that his friend will do the same. Thus in the whole business he has dishonored his God (a) by practically admitting that his revelation is not plain and (b) by himself running away from God in his interpretation of natural revelation and in his subjection of supernatural revelation to the illegitimate requirements of the natural man. Meanwhile he has failed in his purpose of persuading the natural man to go in the right direction. The Roman Catholic and Arminian views of theology are compromising; in consequence the Roman Catholic and the Arminian method of apologetics is both compromising and self-frustrative.

III

Block-house Methodology

A final point must be made before concluding this chapter. We have seen that the proper method for Protestant apologetics is that of presupposition instead of the direct approach. But the theology of Rome and the theology of Arminianism does not permit of such an argument. Roman Catholics and Arminians must of necessity argue by way of direct approach. As deformations of Christian theism they contain no clear challenge to the position of the natural man till it is too late.

We have also seen that the method of presupposition requires the presentation of Christian theism as a unit. But the theology of Roman Catholics compels them to deal with theism first and with Christianity afterwards. Assigning to reason the task of interpreting nature without dependence upon Scripture, this theology is bound to prove the truth of theism first. The theism that is proved in this way cannot be the only theism that any Christian should want to prove, namely, Christian theism. Yet having proved some sort of theism by "reason," the Roman Catholic is bound by virtue of his theology to prove a type of Christianity that will fit on to the deformation of theism it has "established." And what holds true of Roman Catholicism holds true fundamentally also of Arminianism.

It remains now to indicate more fully than has been done that the Roman Catholic and Arminian method of reasoning is bound, not merely to cut the unity of Christian theism in two, but is bound even to prove its theism piece by piece. Romanism and Arminianism lead not merely to dualism but to atomism in methodology.

A truly Protestant method of reasoning involves a stress upon the fact that the meaning of every aspect or part of Christian theism depends upon Christian theism as a unit. When Protestants speak of the resurrection of Christ they speak of the resurrection of him who is the Son of God, the eternal Word through whom the world was made. The truth of theism is involved in this claim that Christians make with respect to the domain of history. And what is true of the resurrection of Christ is true with respect to all the propositions about historical fact that are made in Scripture. No proposition about historical fact is presented for what it really is till it is presented as a part of the system of Christian theism that is contained in Scripture. To say this is involved in the consideration that all facts of the created universe are what they are by virtue of the plan of God with respect to them. Any fact in any realm confronted by man is what it is as revelational through and through of the God and of the Christ of Christian theism.

But if this is true—and it would seem to be of the very essence of the Biblical point of view to say that it is true—then it follows that the whole claim of Christian theism is in question in any debate about any fact. Christian theism must be presented as that light in terms of which any proposition about any fact receives meaning. Without the presupposition of the truth of Christian theism no fact can be distinguished from any other fact. To say this is but to apply the method of idealist logicians in a way that these idealist logicians, because of their own anti-

Christian theistic assumptions, cannot apply it. The point made by these logicians is that even the mere counting of particular things presupposes a system of truth of which these particulars form a part. Without such a system of truth there would be no distinguishable difference between one particular and another. They would be as impossible to distinguish from one another as the millions of drops of water in the ocean would be indistinguishable from one another by the naked eye. "The main point is this, that all counting presupposes and depends upon a qualitative Whole, and that the Collective Judgment asserts a generic connection within its group. Hence no mere particulars can be counted."[9]

It may be objected that one fact differs from other facts precisely because none of them are rationally controlled. Is it not the insertion of individual facts into a logically concatenated system that makes these facts lose their individuality? Has not Kant taught us that, if we are to have logical concatenation between the individual facts of our experience at all, we can have it just to the extent that we give up the impossible ideal of knowing individual things in themselves?

In reply we need only to observe that this way of escape is not open to the Reformed apologist. The Reformed apologist must, if he is at the same time a Reformed theologian, hold to what the average scientist and philosopher today will look upon as the most hopeless form of rationalism he has ever met. The historical forms of rationalism have done either of two things. If they were reasonably consistent then they were ready to deny the existence and meaning of individuality in history altogether. Parmenides claimed that the "great question, *Is it or is it not?*" was to be determined by what man can consistently say about it.[10] This was consistent raltionalism. Parmenides was therefore ready to assert the non-existence and meaninglessness of individual historical factuality. On the other hand, if rationalists were consistent they held to the same ideal of individuation by means of complete logical description on the part of man but they realized that such a description cannot be accomplished. Leibniz

[9] F. H. Bradley: *The Principles of Logic*, Vol. I, p. 369.

[10] Burnet: *Greek Philosophy, Part I, Thales to Plato*, London, 1920, p. 67.

was not less a rationalist in his hopes and ambitions than was Parmenides. He does not hesitate to make the "possibility of knowledge depend upon a knowledge of possibility." Yet, Leibniz questions whether man can ever attain to the perfect analysis, which would carry him back, without finding any contradiction, to the absolute attributes of God.[11] Thus, in spite of himself, Leibniz has to allow for the actual existence of individual, ultimately changing things. But then to do so he has to sacrifice his system of logic. He recognizes temporal individuality but can do so only at the expense of logical system. Thus the rationalist agrees with the irrationalist that individuality in fact can exist only at the expense of logical system. And the idealist logicians, such as F. H. Bradley and Bernard Bosanquet, are no exceptions to this rule. But in contradistinction from the rationalist and the irrationalist, and in contradistinction from the forms of thought that seek some sort of combination between these two, the Reformed apologist must hold both to the idea of absolute system and to that of genuine historic fact and individuality. He does not hold to "truths of fact" at the expense of "truths of reason." He holds to truths of fact only because to him they are truths of reason. But then it is obvious that he is not himself, as a human being, able to show the exhaustive logical relationships between the facts of history and nature which are in debate as between believers and disbelievers in Christian theism. In consequence he must maintain that the truths of fact presented in Scripture must be what Scripture says they are or else they are irrational and meaningless altogether. The true Christian apologist has his principle of discontinuity; it is expressed in his appeal to the mind of God as all-comprehensive in knowledge because all-controlling in power. He holds his principle of discontinuity then, not at the expense of all logical relationship between facts, but because of the recognition of his creaturehood. His principle of discontinuity is therefore the opposite of that of irrationalism without being that of rationalism. The Christian also has his principle of continuity. It is that of the self-contained God and his plan for history. His principle of continuity is therefore the opposite of that of rationalism without being that of irrationalism.

[11] Martin, Clark, Clarke, Ruddick: *A History of Philosophy*, New York, 1941, p. 396.

Conjoining the Christian principle of continuity and the Christian principle of discontinuity we obtain the Christian principle of reasoning by presupposition. It is the actual existence of the God of Christian theism and the infallible authority of the Scripture which speaks to sinners of this God that must be taken as the presupposition of the intelligibility of any fact in the world.

This does not imply that it will be possible to bring the whole debate about Christian theism to full expression in every discussion of individual historical fact. Nor does it imply that the debate about historical detail is unimportant. It means that no Christian apologist can afford to forget the claim of his system with respect to any particular fact. He must always maintain that the "fact" under discussion with his opponent must be what Scripture says it is, if it is to be intelligible as a fact at all. He must maintain that there can be no facts in any realm but such as actually do exhibit the truth of the system of which they are a part. If facts are what they are as parts of the Christian theistic system of truth then what else can facts do but reveal that system to the limit of their ability as parts of that system? It is only as manifestations of that system that they are what they are. If the apologist does not present them as such he does not present them for what they are.

Over against this Christian theistic position, any non-Christian philosophy virtually denies the unity of truth. It may speak much of it and even seem to contend for it, as idealistic philosophers do, but in the last analysis non-Christian philosophy is atomistic. This follows from the absolute separation between truth and reality that was introduced when Adam and Eve fell away from God. When Satan tempted Eve to eat of the forbidden fruit he tried to persuade her that God's announcement of the consequences of such an act would not come true. That was tantamount to saying that no assertion in terms of a rational scheme could predict the course of movement of time-controlled reality. Reality, Satan practically urged upon man, was to be conceived of as something that is not under rational control. Every non-Christian philosophy makes the assumption made by Adam and Eve and is therefore irrationalistic. This irrationalism comes to most consistent expression in various forms of empiricism and pragmatism. In them predication is frankly conceived of in atomistic fashion.

On the other hand when Satan tempted Eve he virtually asked her to become a rationalist. He asked her to take the position that she needed not to obtain any information about the course of factual eventuation from any source but her own mind. Prior to any tendency that had developed in the course of historical events she, following Satan's advice, made what was tantamount to a universal negative judgment about temporal reality. She took for granted that punishment could not come as a consequence of her eating of the forbidden fruit. This rationalism appears most consistently in such men as Parmenides. But even the inconsistent rationalists are really *a priorists*; they make concessions only because they cannot realize their ideal.

In modern times Kant has combined the principles of rationalism and empiricism. "He described the contribution of reason to knowledge as exactly so and so and the contribution of sense as exactly such and such."[12] This position of Kant is the dominating position that confronts us today. It is usually spoken of as phenomenalistic. It is characterized by an attempt to bridge the gulf between fact and mind that was brought into the world as the consequence of the sin of Adam. But it cannot be a remedy for this dualism. Phenomenalism is still basically atomistic inasmuch as it still maintains that factuality in itself is non-rational in character. At the same time phenomenalism is still rationalistic in that whatever of unity it thinks it finds in this atomistically conceived reality virtually proceeds from the human mind. At least this rationality is not taken as proceeding from the mind of God. The rationalizing effort that is inherent in phenomenalism would, if successful, destroy all individuality. Its rationalizing effort is admittedly a step-by-step affair. *That this is so is evident from the fact that its rationalizations are rationalizations of admittedly non-rational material.* Phenomenalism builds up its island of rationality by taking dirt from its center and patching it on to its side, much as the Chicago lake front was built up gradually with dirt hauled into the water from the land. The difference is that the phenomenalists have no right to think of a bottom underneath the water into which they throw their dirt.

The dilemma that confronts the non-Christian methodology in general, and that of modern phenomenalism in particular, is

[12] Gordon H. Clark in *Christian Opinion*, January, 1945.

therefore that one must either know everything or one cannot know anything. One assumption is that unless one knows the terms or objects of propositions in the fulness of their relationships one does not know them at all. A second assumption is that the terms of propositions are not merely unknown but ultimately unknowable in all their relationships. And what is called scientific knowledge is a cross between knowing everything about nothing and knowing nothing about everything. "A completed rational system having nothing outside of it nor any possible alternative to it, is both presupposed and beyond the actual attainment of any one moment."[13]

The point we are now concerned to stress is the atomistic character of the non-Christian methodology. The idea of system is for it merely a limiting notion. It is merely an ideal. What is more, it must forever remain but an ideal. To become a reality this ideal would have to destroy science itself. It would have to demolish the individuality of each fact as it became known. Thus there would no longer be knowledge of a fact that is different from any other fact. The method of non-Christian science then requires that to be known facts must be known as part of a system. And since the Christian idea of system as due to the counsel of God is by definition excluded, it is man himself that must know this system. But to know the system he must know it intuitively. He cannot know it discursively because discursive thought, if it is to be in contact with reality at all, must partake of the piecemeal character of non-rational being. Each individual concept that pretends to be a concept with respect to things that have their existence in the world of time must partake of the *de facto* character of these facts themselves. In consequence each judgment or each proposition that is made by discursive thought about temporal existence is also characterized by the *de facto* character of temporal existence itself. Each proposition then, as far as all practical purposes are concerned, would have to be thought of as standing essentially by itself and as intelligible by itself. There could be no logically necessary connection between the various judgments of discursive thought; there could only be an intuition that, as F. H. Bradley puts it, *somehow* Reality contains the harmony that is not found in appearance.

[13] Cohen: *Reason and Nature,* New York, 1931, p. 158.

If at this point the idea of God is introduced and it is said that while man of necessity cannot know otherwise than discursively and therefore cannot know all things but that God knows intuitively and therefore does know all things, the reply would be that such a God must then stand in a non-rational relation to the universe and to the knowledge which man possesses. Always bound to think atomistically man could know nothing of a God who knows intuitively and yet knows individuality and concrete historical factuality. Aristotle's God is just such a God. To the extent that he knows intuitively he knows nothing of individual existence. He knows himself and men only to the extent that they are exhaustively classified and when they are so classified and he therefore knows them, he does not know *them*. And Aristotle's man knows nothing of Aristotle's God as Aristotle's God knows nothing of Aristotle's man.

It is not difficult to see that the Christian position requires the apologist to challenge this whole approach in the interest of the knowledge of the truth. If man's necessarily discursive thought is not to fall into the ultimate irrationalism and scepticism that is involved in modern methodology we must presuppose the conception of the God that is found in Scripture. Scripture alone presents the sort of God whose intuition of system is not bought at the price of his knowledge of individuality, and whose knowledge of individuality is not bought at the expense of intuitional knowledge of system. But such a God must really be presupposed. He must be taken as the prerequisite of the possibility and actuality of relationship between man's various concepts and propositions of knowledge. Man's system of knowledge must therefore be an analogical replica of the system of knowledge which belongs to God.

We need not now pursue this matter further. It must rather be pointed out in this connection that since Roman Catholicism and Arminianism are committed to a neutral starting point and methodology they are bound also to fall into the atomism of non-Christian thought. Since they will not look at all the facts as facts of the Christian theistic system, and flatly refuse to maintain that anything but a Christian theistic fact can exist at all, and with this claim challenge the non-Christian methodology from the outset of the argument, they are bound to be carried away to a non-Christian conclusion. It is of the essence of both the Romanist and the Arminian method of argumentation to agree with the non-Christian that individual propositions about many dimensions of reality are true whether Christianity is true or not. Neither Roman Catholics nor Arminian apologists are in a position to challenge the natural man's atomistic procedure. Their own theologies are atomistic. They are not built along consistently Christian lines. Their individual doctrines are therefore not presented as being what they are exclusively by virtue of their relation to the main principles of the Christian position. Their contention that the Reformed faith is wrong in thinking of all things in the world as being what they are ultimately in virtue of God's plan with respect to them compels the Roman Catholic and the Arminian apologist to admit the essential correctness of non-Christian atomism. And herewith they have at the same time lost all power to challenge the non-Christian methodology at the outset of its career. Instead they themselves become the victims of this method. Since the principles of their theology will not permit them to argue by way of presupposition, their own piece-meal presentation of Christian theism constantly comes to a sorry end. It is as though an army were sending out a few individual soldiers in order to wrest some atoll from a powerful concentration of an enemy's forces. There can be no joining of issues at the central point of difference, the interpretation by exclusively immanentistic categories or the interpretation in terms of the self-sufficient God, unless it be done by way of presupposition. And the Reformed apologist has a theology that both permits and requires him to do this.

Chapter VII

CHRISTIAN APOLOGETICS (AUTHORITY AND REASON)

The general principles of methodology that have been discussed in the preceding chapter must now be applied more fully to the problem of authority. Here, if anywhere, the difference between the Protestant and the Roman Catholic methodology becomes clearly apparent. For Rome the authority of the church, in particular that of the Pope, speaking *ex cathedra* is ultimate; for Protestantism the Scripture stands above every statement of the church and its teachers.

The question that now requires fuller discussion is as to how the Roman Catholic and how the Protestant approaches the non-believer on the question of authority.

I

Non-Christian Views

To answer this question it is well that we begin by asking what place the non-believer himself attributes to authority. And in order to discover the place allowed to authority by the natural man it is imperative to note what he means by authority.

There are those, of course, who deny that they need any form of authority. They are the popular atheists and agnostics. Such men say that they must be shown by "reason" whatever they are to accept as true. But the great thinkers among non-Christian men have taken no such position. They know that they cannot cover the whole area of reality with their knowledge. They are therefore willing to admit that there may be others who have information that they themselves do not possess. In everyday life this sort of thing is illustrated in the idea of the expert. A medical doctor knows much about the human body that the rest of us do not know. Then among medical men there are those who, because of natural ability, industry and opportunity, make such discoveries as their fellows do not make. So everywhere and in all respects the lesser minds are bound to submit to the authority of greater minds.

In putting the matter in this way the nature of the authority that can be allowed by the natural man is already indicated. The natural man will gladly allow for the idea of authority if only it be the authority of the expert in the use of reason. Such a conception of authority is quite consistent with the assumption of the sinner's autonomy.

On the other hand the conception of authority as something that stands "above reason" is unacceptable to the natural man. But it is not easy to distinguish in every instance when authority is considered to be "above reason." There are some forms of authority that might seem, at first sight, to be "above reason" while in reality they are not. Some discussion of this matter must therefore precede our analysis of the difference between the Roman Catholic and the Protestant methods of presenting the authority of Christianity to the natural man.

Let us note then some of the forms of authority that are quite acceptable to the natural man because, to his mind, they do not violate the principle of autonomy.

First there is the need for authority that grows out of the existence of the endless multiplicity of factual material. Time rolls its ceaseless course. It pours out upon us an endless stream of facts. And the stream is really endless on the non-Christian basis. For those who do not believe that all that happens in time happens because of the plan of God, the activity of time is like to that, or rather is identical with that, of Chance. Thus the ocean of facts has no bottom and no shore. It is this conception of the ultimacy of time and of pure factuality on which modern philosophy, particularly since the days of Kant, has laid such great stress. And it is because of the general recognition of the ultimacy of chance that rationalism of the sort that Descartes, Spinoza and Leibniz represented, is out of date. It has become customary to speak of post-Kantian philosophy as irrationalistic. It has been said that Kant limited reason so as to make room for faith. Hence there are those who are willing to grant that man's emotions or his will can get in touch with such aspects of reality as are not accessible to the intellect. The intellect, it is said, is not the only, and in religious matters not even the primary, instrument with which men come into contact with what is ultimate in human experience. There is the world of the moral imperative, of aesthetic appreciation, of the religious *a priori* as well as the world of science. There is in short the world of "mystery" into which the prophet or genius of feeling or of will may lead us.

It is of the greatest import to note that the natural man need not in the least object to the kind of authority that is involved in the idea of irrationalism. And that chiefly for two reasons. In the first place the irrationalism of our day is the direct lineal descendent of the rationalism of previous days. The idea of pure chance has been inherent in every form of non-Christian thought in the past. It is the only logical alternative to the position of Christianity according to which the plan of God is back of all. Both Plato and Aristotle were compelled to make room for it in their maturest thought. The pure "non-being" of the earliest rationalism of Greece was but the suppressed "otherness" of the final philosophy of Plato. So too the idea of pure factuality or pure chance as ultimate is but the idea of "otherness" made explicit. Given the non-Christian assumption with respect to man's autonomy the idea of chance has equal rights with the idea of logic.

In the second place modern irrationalism has not in the least encroached upon the domain of the intellect as the natural man thinks of it. Irrationalism has merely taken possession of that which the intellect, by its own admission, cannot in any case control. Irrationalism has a secret treaty with rationalism by which the former cedes to the latter so much of its territory as the latter can at any given time find the forces to control. Kant's realm of the noumenal has, as it were, agreed to yield so much of its area to the phenomenal, as the intellect by its newest weapons can manage to keep in control. Moreover, by the same treaty irrationalism has promised to keep out of its own territory any form of authority that might be objectionable to the autonomous intellect. The very idea of pure factuality or chance is the best guarantee that no true authority, such as that of God as the Creator and Judge of men, will ever confront man. If we compare the realm of the phenomenal as it has been ordered by the autonomous intellect to a clearing in a large forest we may compare the realm of the noumenal to that part of the same forest which has not yet been laid under cultivation by the intellect. The realm of mystery is on this basis simply the realm of that which is not yet known. And the service of irrationalism to rationalism may be compared to that of some bold huntsman in the woods who keeps all lions and tigers away from the clearing. This bold huntsman covers the whole of the infinitely extended forest, ever keeping away all danger from the clearing. This irrationalistic Robin Hood is so much of a rationalist that he virtually makes a universal negative statement about what *can* happen in all future time. In the secret treaty spoken of he has assured the intellect of the autonomous man that the God of Christianity cannot possibly exist and that no man therefore need to fear the coming of a judgment. If the whole course of history is, at least in part, controlled by chance, then there is no danger that the autonomous man will ever meet with the claims of authority as the Protestant believes in it. For the notion of authority is but the expression of the idea that God by his counsel controls all things that happen in the course of history.

There is a second kind of authority that the natural man is quite ready to accept. It does not spring, as did the first, from the fact that the intellect can by definition not control the whole realm of chance. It springs from the fact that even that which the intellect does assert about the objects of knowledge is, of necessity, involved in contradiction. F. H. Bradley's great book, *Appearance and Reality,* has brought out this point with the greatest possible detail. The point is not that the many philosophers who have speculated on the nature of reality have actually contradicted each other and themselves. The point is rather that in the nature of the case all logical assertion with respect to the world of temporal existence must needs be, it is said, self-contradictory in character.

On the assumptions of the natural man logic is a timeless

impersonal principle, and facts are controlled by chance. It is by means of universal timeless principles of logic that the natural man must, on his assumptions, seek to make intelligible assertions about the world of reality or chance. But this cannot be done without falling into self-contradiction. About chance no manner of assertion can be made. In its very idea it is the irrational. And how are rational assertions to be made about the irrational? If they are to be made then it must be because the irrational is itself wholly reduced to the rational. That is to say if the natural man is to make any intelligible assertions about the world of "reality" or "fact" which, according to him is what it is for no rational reason at all, then he must make the virtual claim of rationalizing the irrational. To be able to distinguish one fact from another fact he must reduce all time existence, all factuality to immovable timeless being. But when he has done so he has killed all individuality and factuality as conceived of on his basis. Thus the natural man must on the one hand assert that all reality is non-structural in nature and on the other hand that all reality is structural in nature. He must even assert on the one hand that all reality is non-structurable in nature and on the other hand that he himself has virtually structured all of it. Thus all his predication is in the nature of the case self-contradictory.

Realizing this dilemma, many modern philosophers have argued that any intellectual system of interpretation is therefore no more than a perspective. No system, these men assert, should pretend to be more than a system "for us." We have to deal with reality *as if* it will always behave as we have found it behaving in the past. The world of appearance formed by means of the exercise of the intellect must be taken as "somehow" similar to the world of Reality. And thus we seem to have come again upon the idea of mystery, the world of "faith" and of "authority" where prophets and seers may suggest to us the visions they have seen in the night.

Such then seems to be the present situation. Modern philosophy in practically all of its schools admits that all its speculations end in mystery. Speaking generally, modern philosophy (and science) is phenomenalistic. It admits that ultimate reality is unknowable to man. All systems of interpretation are said to be necessarily relative to the mind of man. And so it seems at first sight that modern philosophy ought, on its own principles, to admit that there is a dimension of reality that is beyond its reach and about which it ought therefore to be ready to listen by the avenue of authority. Modern philosophy would seem to be ready therefore to listen to the voice of "religion." So for instance Dorothy Emmet views the matter. "The heart of religion, as far as I can see it, seems to be an intuitive response to something which evokes our worship. Let me first explain what I here understand by 'intuitive.' I am using the word to mean a kind of apprehension which is reached by methods other than those of critical reflection. It is the kind of apprehension we use when we grasp the character of a person, or the demands of a situation, without being aware of the steps by which we have arrived at our judgment."[1] On such a view it might seem that one should be able to accept the authority of Jesus. And Miss Emmet can allow for the authority of Jesus. But it is still no more than the authority of the expert. For those who think as she does, Jesus is nothing more than the kind of person they would like to be and could be if only they lived up to their own ideals.

The natural man then assumes that he has the final criterion of truth within himself. Every form of authority that comes to him must justify itself by standards inherent in man and operative apart from the authority that speaks.

But what has been said has dealt only with modern philosophy. A word must be added about modern theology. Surely we shall find here a more ready recognition of the need of authority! More than that we shall expect to find here the advocates of authority! But in this we are disappointed. Modern theology is, to be sure, ready to defend the need and place of authority. But it will defend no authority that is not acceptable to modern philosophy and science. It too advocates the authority of the expert only.

II

Modern Theological Views

It needs no argument to prove this contention true with respect to Schleiermacher, the father of modern theology. His great work *The Christian Faith* is largely controlled in its epis-

[1] *Philosophy and Faith*, London, 1936, p. 84.

temology by the principles of Kant's *Critique of Pure Reason.* He speaks, to be sure, of the religious man and of his absolute dependence upon God. He seems to limit the claims of the human intellect. He says that by means of it we cannot reach God. It is by our feeling of dependence that we have contact with God. But in all this he is simply setting forth a religious phenomenalism. It is no virtue to decry the autonomous intellect if one sets up in its stead an autonomous feeling. And that is precisely what Schleiermacher does. In his theology it is still the human personality as such that has the final criterion of truth within itself.

For a contemporary discussion of the relation between authority and reason on the part of a great churchman and a great philosopher we may turn to the work of A. E. Taylor, *The Faith of a Moralist.* Taylor pleads for a place for authority in human thought. But no authority, he says, can be absolute. An absolute authority could not be transmitted through history and if it could be transmitted it could not be received. The mind of man contributes to all that it receives. Kant has taught us this once for all and we cannot depart from it. Hence no orthodox doctrine of authority can ever be accepted. Such is the burden of Taylor's argument and it is typical of what one hears in varying forms.[2]

The late archbishop William Temple also asks for no higher authority than that of the expert in his work, *Nature, Man and God,* London, 1925. The spiritual authority of revelation, he contends, "depends wholly upon the spiritual quality of what is revealed."[3] And whether what is revealed be spiritual, of that, argues Temple in effect, man himself must ever be the final judge.

But what of Karl Barth and Emil Brunner? Have they not bravely contended for the "absolutely other" God? Are not they the "theologians of the Word"? Look at the lashing Barth gives the "consciousness theologians," the followers of Schleiermacher and Ritschl, just because they have been virtual ventriloquists, speaking in the name of God that which in reality proceeds only from themselves (*Dogmatik,* 1927). Note too with what increasing consistency through the periods of his development Barth has set his theology over against that of "modern Protestantism." A true theology, argues Barth, has its chief canon in the first com-

[2] London, 1931, Vol. II, p. 200 ff.

[3] Page 347.

mandment, "Thou shalt have no other gods before me" instead of in the logic of Aristotle or Kant. A true theology must break with all systems of philosophy, with all the Promethean constructions of the human intellect and reach man in the depth of his being with the voice of God's authority speaking in its own name. Here then it would seem that among all the "types of modern theology" we have found one that stands up like a Daniel against modern philosophy and science with the voice of the living God.

Sad to say, however, the "absolutely other" God of Barth is absolutely other only in the way that a sky-rocket is "absolutely other" to the mind of the child. Barth's god has first been cast up into the heights by the projective activity of the would-be auton-escape it, still controlled by some form of modern critical philosophy. And this means that the mind of man is always thought of as contributing something ultimate to all the information it receives. Accordingly the "absolutely other" god of Barth remains absolute just so long as he is absolutely unknown. In that case he is identical with the realm of mystery which the autonomous man admits of as existing beyond the reach of his thought. It then has no more content and significance than the vaguest conception of something indeterminate. There is no more meaning in the idea of God as Barth holds it than there was in the idea of the *apeiron*, the indefinite, of Anaximander the Greek philosopher. On the other hand when the god of Barth does reveal himself he reveals himself wholly. For Barth God is exhaustively known if he is known at all. That is to say to the extent that this god is known he is nothing distinct from the principles that are operative in the universe. He is then wholly identical with man and his world. It appears then that when the god of Barth is wholly mysterious and as such should manifest himself by revelation only, he remains wholly mysterious and does not reveal himself. On the other hand when this god does reveal himself his revelation is identical with what man can know apart from such a revelation. Thus there is absolute authority which either says nothing or when it says something has lost its character as authority. And the fact that Barth thinks of revelation dialectically means in this connection only that his god is both absolutely hidden and absolutely revealed simultaneously. And this can be maintained only if the very idea of authority as orthodox Christianity conceives of it on the basis of the Creator-creature distinction has first been discarded. If this distinction is maintained there can be no such dialectical relationship between the hidden and the revealed character of God. In that case God cannot, to be sure, ever reveal himself exhaustively. The mind of man is finite and knows only by thinking God's thoughts after him. But what it knows it then knows truly. It has at its disposal the revelation of God. This revelation does not hide God while it reveals him; it reveals him truly, though not exhaustively.

What has been said about Barth holds, with minor changes, also for Emil Brunner and for such other theologians as Reinhold Niebuhr and John A. Mackay.[4] In their theology, as in that of Barth, it is the autonomous religious consciousness that divides itself into two sections after the style of Dr. Jekyll and Mr. Hyde. The higher aspect addresses itself to the lower aspect and insists upon obedience to its voice. Thus men tell themselves that they have listened to and obeyed the voice of Jesus or of God, while they have only obeyed themselves.

It appears then that, in Protestant circles at least, there seems in our day to be general agreement as to the nature of authority and the relation it is to sustain to reason. There is a quite general acceptance of authority but it is merely the authority of the expert. And this authority presupposes that, in the last analysis, man is dealing with an ultimately mysterious environment. It takes for granted that God, no less than man, is surrounded by mystery. It is no wonder that those who work on the principle of the autonomy of reason have no difficulty in accepting such a concept of authority. The followers of the autonomous reason have, in modern times, themselves asserted the need of the idea of the ultimately mysterious. *The Mysterious Universe*, the universe in which facts are what they are for no rational reason, is the presupposition both of modern science and of modern philosophy. And this position is not challenged by modern theology.

[4] For a discussion of Emil Brunner's views see the writer's *The New Modernism;* for those of Reinhold Niebuhr see *Christianity in Modern Theology;* for those of John A. Mackay see *The Confession of 1967: Its Theological Background and Ecumenical Significance* (Presbyterian and Reformed Publishing Co.).

III

THE ROMAN CATHOLIC VIEW

Is it then to the church of Rome that we must go in order to find a challenge to this modern concept of reason as autonomous, and of authority as merely that of those who have probed the realm of utter darkness a little more deeply than others? At first sight this might seem to be the case. A. E. Taylor relates a little story that might seem to point in that direction. "It relates," he says, "that a Roman Catholic theologian was in conversation with an outsider, who remarked that there seemed to be no real difference between the position of Rome and that of a well-known and highly respected 'Anglo-Catholic.' 'Pardon me,' replied the theologian, 'we are at the opposite pole from X. He holds every doctrine we hold, but holds them all for the entirely irrelevant reason that he thinks them true.' "[5] But this story in and by itself would not give an adequate notion of the Roman Catholic position either on the meaning of authority or on its relation to reason. A brief word must therefore be said on the subject.

To ascertain the Romish concept of reason, we may start from the fact that by Roman Catholic theologians Aristotle is taken to be the "philosopher *par excellence*, as St. Thomas is the theologian."[6] Now theology, says Maritain, presupposes certain truths of the "natural order." These truths are naturally known to all men and are worked out scientifically by the philosophers and particularly by Aristotle. "The premises of philosophy are self-supported and are not derived from those of theology."[7] Ettienne Gilson expresses the same thought when he says: "The heritage of Greek thought, even when cut to the minimum and judged most critically, is still worthy of admiration. So true is this that a number of the Fathers were convinced that the pagan thinkers had access to the Bible without admitting it. One first being, the supreme principle and cause of nature, source of all intelligibility, of all order, and of all beauty, who eternally leads a life of happiness, because, being thought itself, it is an eternal

[5] *The Faith of a Moralist,* II, 198.

[6] J. Maritain: *An Introduction to Philosophy,* London, 1937, p. 91.

[7] *Idem,* p. 126.

contemplation of its own thought, all that was taught by Aristotle; and if we compare his theology to the ancient mythologies we will see at a glance what immense progress human reason had made since the era of Chronos and Jupiter without the aid of Christian Revelation. Doubtless there were many lacunae, and numberless errors mingled with these truths. But they were still truths. Discovered by the natural reason of the Greeks, they owed nothing to faith; still discoverable today, with even greater ease, by the same natural reason, why should they owe more to faith in our own reason than in Aristotle's?"[8]

Besides this "natural order" which can be discovered by reason apart from faith, there is the order of faith. And as the assertions by reason in the natural order do not depend for their validity upon faith, so those in the order of faith do not depend for their validity upon the assertions of reason. "The affirmations of Catholic faith ultimately depend on no reasoning, fallible or otherwise, but on the Word of God. For indeed whatever reason is able to know about God with a perfect knowledge, precisely because it is thus knowable, cannot essentially belong in the order of faith."[9]

The order of nature as set forth by autonomous reason and the order of faith accepted exclusively on authority both deal with God and his relation to man. The question that at once appears is as to how it may be known that the God of reason and the God of faith are the same God. There is the more reason for asking this question inasmuch as it is admitted that the reason which discovers the truths of the natural order is "wounded." "The true Catholic position consists in maintaining that nature was created good, that it has been wounded, but that it can be at least partially healed by grace if God so wishes."[10] It might seem that grace must first restore the powers of reason at least to the extent of healing its wounds before reason can function normally. And Gilson does in fact speak of a Christian philosophy which is the product of a reason that is restored by grace. Such a philosophy, he argues, is the best philosophy. It is the best philosophy because in it reason best comes to its own. But

[8] *Christianity and Philosophy,* London, 1939, pp. 35, 36.
[9] *Idem,* p. 56.
[10] *Idem,* p. 21.

even so the problem remains the same. Here it is Aristotle who has by means of his wounded reason constructed the truths of the natural order as noted. Is then the God whom Aristotle discovers the same God of whom Christian theology speaks?

Gilson himself confronts us with the seriousness of the problem when he says in pointed fashion that reason or philosophy can deal only with *essences* and not with existence. Yet it is of the existence of God that it is supposed to speak.

"When, for instance, Aristotle was positing his first self-thinking Thought as the supreme being, he certainly conceived it as a pure Act and as an infinitely powerful energy; still, his god was but the pure Act of a Thought. This infinitely powerful actuality of a self-thinking principle most certainly deserves to be called a pure Act, but it was a pure Act in the order of knowing, not in that of existence. Now nothing can give what it has not. Because the supreme Thought of Aristotle was not 'He who is,' it could not give existence: hence the world of Aristotle was not a created world. Because the supreme Thought of Aristotle was not the pure Act of existing, its self-knowledge did not entail the knowledge of all being, both actual and possible: the god of Aristotle was not a providence; he did not even know a world which he did not make and which he could not possibly have made because he was the thought of a Thought, nor did he know the self-awareness of 'Him who is.'"[11]

Taking over this philosophy of Aristotle, St. Thomas was bound, in consequence, to "translate all the problems concerning being from the language of essences into that of existences." But could he do so without suppressing reason? Was it St. Thomas the theologian who, because of his faith, was able to make this transposition from the realm of abstract essences to that of existence? If it was, then no progress has been made in solving the problem of the relation of authority and reason. In fact the problem then seems to be more difficult than ever. For the god of Aristotle has then begun to appear to be quite different from the God of the Christian faith. Aristotle's god, it is admitted, has not created the world and does not know the world. If such a god is the natural outcome of the activity of reason when it is not enlightened by faith does it not seem as though faith will have to

[11] *God and Philosophy*, London, 1941, p. 66.

reverse the decision of reason with respect to God? A philosophy that deals with essences only would seem to resemble a merry-go-round hovering above reality but never touching it. Yet according to Rome, St. Thomas the Christian theologian need not at all ask St. Thomas the autonomous philosopher to reverse his decisions on the fundamental question about the existence of God.

It would appear then that St. Thomas the theologian might appear with the God of Moses, the "He who is," in order to present him for acceptance to St. Thomas the philosopher. If the God of Moses, the Creator and controller of the world, is the one to be accepted by St. Thomas the philosopher, he must first be reduced from an existent God to a pure essence, from the "He who is" to the "it that is not." St. Thomas the philosopher is bound, by the principles of his reason, to bring the information given him by St. Thomas the theologian into orderly relation with the body of his beliefs about reality in general. And this involves the rejection of the existence of a God whose existence and knowledge cannot be thus related. There would seem to be no escape from the conclusion that if we start with autonomous reason and contend that it deals with essences only, the being which comes to expression through these essences is a being whose very existence is that of correlativity to the human mind. Kant and his followers were not illogical when they drew this conclusion. We cannot start with Aristotle without eventually falling prey to Kant.

Gilson seeks desperately to escape this conclusion. Like all Roman Catholic apologists he must at some time or other face this question as to how the "He who is" of Moses and the "it that is not" of Aristotle are related. He does so by arguing as follows: "Beyond a world wherein 'to be' is everywhere at hand, and where every nature can account for what other natures are but not for their common existence, there must be some cause whose very essence it is 'to be.' To posit such a being whose essence is a pure Act of existing, that is, whose essence is not to be this and that, but 'to be,' is also to posit the Christian God as the supreme cause of the universe."[12] But this argument does not

[12] *Idem*, pp. 71, 72.

escape the dilemma just mentioned. The logical implication of the method of Aristotle is his "god," the "it that is not." That has been asserted by Gilson himself and it is clearly correct. That is the only god that is accessible to reason alone. Yet Gilson constantly speaks as though "the existence of one God, the sole Creator of the world" is also accessible to reason.[13] And this God is supposed to be accessible to reason in the way that is shown in the quotation just given. But how can a god who is not and a God who is the Creator of the world both be the logical implication of the one true method of philosophy?

Yet it might seem that we have reached a position which involves the idea of absolute authority for at least one dimension of life. The order of faith and all that it contains is to be accepted purely on authority. Here then we seem to have reached the idea of absolute rather than expert authority. Before we have finished with the Roman Catholic view of the relation of authority to reason, however, there are further matters to be considered.

In the first place it has been noted how valiantly Gilson seeks to defend the idea of the autonomy of reason. If then the dimensions of reason and of faith are finally to be brought together into union with one another there will have to be a compromise. If there is one thing on which Roman Catholics insist, it is that only on their position is it possible to do justice to the statement of St. Paul that every man naturally knows something of God, without compromising the uniqueness of the Christian faith. In other words they maintain that it is in their system as a whole that there is a true union of the natural and the supernatural. But it is not difficult to see that if the autonomy of reason is to be maintained and the absolute authority of faith as well, any union between them must be one of compromise.

In the second place we may discover the nature of the compromise if we go back to the Roman Catholic conception of the nature of man, and especially of man's freedom in relation to God. According to Roman Catholic theology man has a measure of autonomy over against the plan of God. God has to await man's decisions on many points. Thus God does not really control whatsoever comes to pass. And this means that man's ulti-

[13] *Christianity and Philosophy*, p. 60.

mate environment is only partly under God's direction. All of this implies, in effect, that on the basis of Roman Catholic theology there is mystery for God as well as for man. God himself is therefore on this basis surrounded by brute fact. Man's dealings are partly with God but also partly with brute fact. It is no wonder then that, holding this doctrine of the ultimacy of the mind and will of man in its theology, Romish theology should recognize the legitimacy of the idea of autonomy in the field of philosophy. Even when it speaks of Christian philosophy, as Gilson does, it must still base this philosophy upon the idea of autonomy. And even when it speaks of the original perfection of man when his reason was not "wounded" Rome still holds to the idea of autonomy for the mind and will of man to some extent. In all stages and in all respects of its thinking it is committed to this idea. In all stages and in all respects it is therefore also committed to the idea of brute fact as a part of man's ultimate environment.

Now it is this fact that Rome is always and everywhere committed to the idea of brute fact as such, to eventuation apart from the counsel of God, that is all-determinative on the question of its conception of the relation of reason to authority. Rome simply has not the materials with which to build a really Christian concept of authority. A truly Christian concept of authority presupposes that in all he does man is face to face with the requirement of God. But how could man be face to face with the requirement of God if God does not control all things? How could God face man with his requirements there where he has no power to rule? It is only on the idea of the comprehensiveness of the plan of God that a true concept of authority can be based. And this is to say, in effect, that only on the idea of the covenant as all comprehensive with respect to every phase of human life can the idea of authority find a footing.

Our conclusion then is that while the Roman Catholic notion of authority seems at first sight to be very absolute—in fact even more absolute than that of Protestantism—it is in reality not absolute at all. Its idea of autonomy wins out in every case. And so it comes to pass that the Roman Catholic doctrines of faith are in every instance adjusted to the idea of human autonomy. To be sure, the natural man is said to be fallen, but he has fallen but a little way; even in the state of rectitude he justly insisted on autonomy. Does the fallen character of man consist in his using this autonomy unwisely? To be sure, the Christian man is *healed* by grace; but even when he is healed he is still advised to exercise his autonomous will to some extent over against the plan of God. The concept of *covenant obedience* does not fit in anywhere in Roman Catholic theology or philosophy. Our conclusion must therefore be that even Rome offers nothing in the way of authority that is clearly different from the idea of the expert as this is willingly granted by the natural man.

The Roman Catholic concept of tradition only corroborates what has been said. In its "Decree concerning the canonical Scriptures" the Council of Trent speaks of "unwritten traditions" which are as it were transmitted from hand to hand. These unwritten traditions are accorded the same authority as Scripture. Christian truth, it is said, has come to us by way of two distinct streams, one of which is found in Scripture and the second of which is found in tradition. To be sure this tradition may, to some extent at least, be itself reduced to writing. Yet there is no body of writings which the church officially accepts as containing the written statement of what it accepts as tradition. It is the living voice of the Church speaking in its official ministers, and especially through the Pope, that is the final guardian of this tradition. Tradition is therefore finally that which the church propounds from time to time.

The bearing of this conception of tradition on the questions of authority and its relation to reason must now be drawn. The hierarchy of the church in general, and of the Pope in particular, is not to be thought of as itself subject to the final and comprehensive revelation of God. There is no place anywhere in the whole of Roman Catholic thought for the idea that any human being should be wholly subject to God. On the contrary, the position of Rome requires the rejection of the counsel of God as all-determinative. Hence the Pope himself, as he makes up his mind with respect to the infallible pronouncement that his office requires or permits him to make from time to time, must seek as an expert to interpret the meaning of brute fact, of being in general. What the Bible teaches him he will be required to relate to what his autonomous reason teaches him with respect to being in general. The result is that the voice of God as the controller and governor of man and the universe can never speak through the voice of the Pope. Those who listen to the voice of the Pope are listening to the voice of an expert who is supposed, for some wholly non-rational reason, to be able to peer more deeply into the realm of "Being" than other men.

It appears then, that so far from being the defender of the true Christian concept of authority and of reason, Rome offers a compromise on both ideas and therefore on the relation between them. Holding to a concept of reason that is not itself interpreted in terms of the doctrine of God as self-contained it can offer no concept of authority that really stands above reason. Its authority therefore is the galling authority of one man dealing with "being in general" and guessing about it, over another man also dealing with "being in general" and guessing about it. It is the authority that brings men into bondage.

The entire position of Rome then with respect to authority and its relations to reason illustrates the weakness of Roman Catholic apologetics in general. It has no clear-cut position that can be contrasted with that of the natural man. It cannot therefore challenge the position of the natural man with any effectiveness at any point. Assuming the correctness of the starting point and the method of the natural man in the natural sphere it cannot logically ask men to accept the authority of God even in the spiritual sphere.

IV

The Arminian View

It will appear to many as a very strange thing to say that Arminian theology is similar to that of Romanism on the question of authority. Yet this is really the case. Of course it is true that evangelical Arminians reject the ritualism and the hierarchy of Rome. It is also true that individual Arminians are much better in their practical attitude toward Scripture than their system of theology permits them to be. It is only of this system of theology that we speak. And of it—there is no escape from it—the assertion must be made that its conception of reason is similar to that of

Rome and therefore its conception of authority cannot be very different from that of Rome.

There is nothing on which Arminian theology is more insistent than that the Reformed doctrine of election does injustice to man's responsibility. Yet the Reformed doctrine of election is but the consistent expression in the field of man's relation to God of the general teaching of Scripture that all things in history happen by the plan of God. The Arminian doctrine of responsibility therefore presupposes the rejection of the idea of the plan of God as all-inclusive. And this means that the idea of brute fact is one of the basic ingredients of the Arminian position. Man is therefore once again partly related to God and partly to some form of "being in general." And this in turn means that God himself is confronted with that which determines his powers and actions. He is limited by the facts of Reality about him and his knowledge is accordingly surrounded by mystery.

Thus we are back at that arch foe of Christianity, namely, the idea of human ultimacy or autonomy. This idea of autonomy expresses itself in modern times by holding that in all that comes to man he gives as well as takes. Modern philosophy has, particularly since the day of Kant, boldly asserted that only that is real for man which he has, in part at least, constructed for himself.

Nor is this modern form of manifestation of the would-be autonomous man illogical. In every non-Christian concept of reality brute facts or chance plays a basic role. This is so because any one who does not hold to God's counsel as being man's ultimate environment, has no alternative but to assume or assert that chance is ultimate. Chance is simply the metaphysical correlative of the idea of the autonomous man. The autonomous man will not allow that reality is already structural in nature by virtue of the structural activity of God's eternal plan. But if reality is non-structural in nature then man is the one who for the first time, and therefore in an absolutely original fashion, is supposed to bring structure into reality. But such a structure can be only "for him." For, in the nature of the case, man cannot himself as a finite and therefore temporally conditioned being, control the whole of reality. But all this amounts only to saying that modern philosophy is quite consistent with its own principles when it contends that in all that man knows he gives as well as takes. It is merely the non-rational that is given to him; he himself rationalizes it for the first time. And so that which appears to him as rationally related reality is so related primarily because he himself has rationalized it.

The modern form of autonomy expresses itself then both in a negative and in a positive fashion. Negatively it assumes or asserts that that which is "out there," that is, that which has not yet come into contact with the human mind, is wholly non-structural or non-rational in character. We are not now concerned so much to point out that this assumption is itself not very reasonable to make for one who claims to limit his assertions to what human experience can control. Human experience can hardly establish the universal negative assertion about the whole of reality and therefore about all future eventuality that is implied in the assumption of the average modern philosopher or scientist. What it is our main concern, however, to point out now is that the Arminian theologian is not in a good position to challenge this modern man in his attitude toward the authority of Scripture.

What is the attitude toward the idea of Scripture that we would expect to find on the part of modern man? Will he readily accept the idea? Will he be open-minded with respect to the "evidence" for the Scriptural teaching with respect to such doctrines as creation, providence, and miracles? Will he be open-minded with respect to revelation given about future eventuation? That is to say, will he be ready to accept information about that which happens in a realm totally beyond human experience or what has happened, does happen and will happen by way of influence from that realm that is totally beyond human experience upon the realm of human experience? The answer is obvious. The entire idea of inscripturated supernatural revelation is not merely foreign to but would be destructive of the idea of autonomy on which the modern man builds his thought. If modern man is right in his assumption with respect to his own autonomy then he cannot even for a moment logically consider evidence for the fact of the supernatural in any form as appearing to man. The very idea of God as self-contained is meaningless on his principles. The idea of such a God, says the modern follower of Kant, is fine as a limiting notion. Taken as a limiting notion it is quite innocent and even useful. For then it stands merely for the ideal of exhaustive rationality. And science requires such an ideal. But the idea of such a God as taken by orthodox Christians, that is as a constitutive rather than as a limiting concept, is meaningless; it would kill the idea of pure facts as the correlative to pure rationality. And the idea of pure fact as a limiting concept is as necessary to modern science as is the idea of pure rationality.

It is therefore logically quite impossible for the natural man, holding as he does to the idea of autonomy, even to consider the "evidence" for the Scripture as the final and absolutely authoritative revelation of the God of Christianity. The God of Christianity is for him logically irrelevant to human experience. It would therefore be as sensible to talk about his revealing himself either in nature or in Scripture as it would be to ascribe to the man in the moon the perpetration of some murder in one's neighborhood.

This way of putting the matter may seem to some to be extreme. Yet we believe it to be strictly in accord with the facts. There are, to be sure, some among modern philosophers, particularly those of the theistic and personalist schools, who seem to be favorably disposed to what they call a positive religion. And among the positive religions they will pick out Christianity as the most acceptable. Mention may again be made of A. E. Taylor. In his recent book *Does God Exist?* Taylor argues for "the existence of God." But since he works on the assumption of the autonomy of man, the kind of god he believes in is, after all, a finite deity. When he deals with the tenets of historic Christianity Taylor makes perfectly clear that, on his principles, one could not accept them as being what they are presented as being in Scripture. Speaking of the resurrection of Jesus he says: "That St. Paul and the other Apostles believed this is as certain as any fact of past history can be; it is quite another question whether that belief was not a mistaken interpretation of their experiences. Since it is a familiar fact that men do sometimes misinterpret their experience, there is nothing in principle irrational in the suggestion that St. Paul and the other Apostles did this, and no man can *prove* 'beyond all shadow of doubt' that they did not."[14] Taylor simply assumes that every human mind, that

[14] London, 1947, p. 127.

of an apostle no less than that of any other man, contributes in an original sense to what it receives. The result is that even if he could believe in a self-contained God—which on his premises he cannot—Taylor cannot believe that any man could receive any revelation from such a God without to some extent, in the very act of reception, confusing it with his own experiences that operate independently of this God.

The whole attitude of the modern man with respect to the idea of authoritative revelation such as is given in Scripture may therefore be summed up in the following points. Such a God as Scripture speaks of simply does not exist. This idea of the non-existence of God is involved, as has been noted, in the assumption of brute factuality. In the second place, if such a God did exist he could not manifest himself in the world that we know. For that world is known to be something other than the revelation of God; it is known to be a combination of brute factuality and the rationalizing activity of autonomous man with respect to them. In the third place, even if such a God did reveal himself in such a world as is known to be something other than a manifestation of him, no man could receive such a revelation without falsifying it. In the fourth place, if in spite of these three points a revelation had been received in the past it could not be transmitted to men of the present time without their again falsifying it. In the fifth place, if in spite of everything such a revelation of such a God as the Bible speaks of came to man today he in turn could not receive it without falsifying it.

Now, Arminianism has no valid argument for the idea of Biblical authority with which to challenge the position of modern man. Its own concept of man, as acting independently of the plan of God to some extent, and therefore its own view of the human mind as being ultimate in some respects, paralyzes its apologetical efforts. Like the Roman Catholic, the Arminian apologist is bound to start with his opponent on a supposedly common basis. The Arminian must grant that his opponent has rightly interpreted much of human experience in terms of the autonomy of the human mind and the ultimacy of chance. But if the natural man who works with the idea of autonomy can correctly interpret the phenomenal world aright without God, why should he be ready to turn about suddenly and interpret spiritual things in terms of God? If he is consistent with himself he will not do so.

As has been noted earlier, the Arminian is bound to present the Christian position in atomistic fashion. He will therefore first speak to the non-believer about the *possibility* of supernatural revelation as though the word possibility meant the same thing for the natural man and for the believer. But it does not. For the natural man the idea of possibility is on the one hand identical with chance and on the other hand with that which the natural man himself can rationalize. For him only that is practically possible which man can himself order by his logical faculties. But the word possibility means for the Christian that which may happen in accord with the plan of God.

Secondly the Arminian may speak to the natural man of the *probability* of supernatural revelation as though the word probability meant the same thing for the believer and for the non-believer. But it does not. For the non-believer the meaning of the word probability is involved in his concept of the idea of possibility as just before discussed. Therefore, as Hume has effectively shown in his criticism of the empirical probability argument for Christianity, there can be no presumption at all for the eventuation of certain things rather than of others, once one allows the idea of chance in his system at all. There can be no probability that God will supernaturally reveal himself to man unless it is certain that without the presupposition of such a revelation man's experience, even of the realm of natural things, is meaningless.

In the third place the Arminian will speak to the natural man about the historical *fact* of revelation as recorded in Scripture. He will stress the fact that Christianity is a historical religion. To that he will add that therefore it is simply a matter of evidence whether or not, say, the resurrection of Christ, is a fact. On this question, he will insist, anybody who is able to use the canons of historical study is as good a judge as any other. The proof for the resurrection is then said to be just the sort of proof that men demand everywhere in questions of history.

But this argument about the facts of supernatural revelation again forgets that the natural man's entire attitude with respect to the facts that are presented to him will naturally be controlled by his notions of possibility and probability as already discussed. He may therefore grant that a man named Jesus of Nazareth arose from the dead. He need not hesitate, on his principles, to accept the *fact* of the resurrection at all. But for him that fact is a different sort of fact from what it is for the Christian. It is not the same fact at all. It is in vain to speak about the fact without speaking of the meaning of the fact. For the factness of the fact is to any mind that deals with it that which he takes it to mean. It is his meaning that is virtually the fact to him. And it is impossible even to present the fact for what it really is, namely, that which it is according to its interpretation as given in Scripture, to the natural man, if one does not challenge his notions of possibility and probability that underlie his views of the facts of history. To talk about presenting to him the fact of the resurrection without presenting its meaning is to talk about an abstraction. The resurrection either *is* what the Christian says it is, or it is not. If it *is*, then it is as such that it actually appears in history.

Yet the Arminian position is committed to the necessity of presenting the facts of Christianity as being something other than he himself as a Christian knows they are. He knows that it is the Son of God who died in his human nature and rose again from the dead. But the fact of the resurrection about which he speaks to unbelievers is some nondescript something or other about which believers and non-believers are supposed to be able to agree.

In the fourth place, then, the Arminian will speak to the unbeliever about the Bible as the inspired and infallible revelation of God. He will argue that it is the most wonderful book, that it is the best seller, that all other books lose their charm while the Bible does not. All of these things the unbeliever may readily grant without doing any violence to his own position and without feeling challenged to obey its voice. It means to him merely that some experts in religion have somehow brought to expression some of the deep fellow feeling with Reality that they have experienced. Their position allows for sacred books and even for a superior book. But the one thing it does not allow for is an absolutely authoritative book. Such a book presupposes the existence and knowability of the self-contained God of Christianity. But such a God, and the revelation of such a God in the universe and to man, are notions that, as has already been observed, the natural man must reject. So he will naturally also reject that which is simply the logical implicate, of the idea of such a God and of such a revelation. The very idea of sin, because of which the idea of an externally promulgated supernatural revelation of grace became imperative, is meaningless for him. For him sin or evil is a metaphysical action that is inherent in the concept of Chance.

V

The Reformed View

Enough has now been said to indicate that the Roman Catholic and the Arminian methods, proceeding as they do by way of accepting the starting point and the method of the natural man with respect to a supposedly known area of experience, are self-refuting on the most important question of the Bible and its authority. We repeat that many Arminians are much better than their position. We also stress the fact that many of the things that they say about points of detail are indeed excellent. In other words our aim is not to depreciate the work that has been done by believing scholars in the Arminian camp. Our aim is rather to make better use of their materials than they have done by placing underneath it an epistemology and metaphysic which make these materials truly fruitful in discussion with non-believers.

Such a foundation it is that is furnished in the Reformed position. But it is furnished by the Reformed position simply because this position seeks to be consistently Christian in its starting-point and methodology. And here it must be confessed that those of us who hold this position are all too often worse than our position. Those who hold the Reformed position have no reason for boasting. What they have received they have received by grace.

The Reformed position seeks to avoid the weaknesses of the Roman Catholic and the Arminian positions. Since these positions have now been discussed at length it will be immediately apparent what is meant. Since the natural man assumes the idea of brute fact in metaphysics and the idea of the autonomy of the human mind in epistemology, the Reformed apologist realizes that he should first challenge these notions. He must challenge these notions in everything that he says about anything. It is these notions that determine the construction that the natural man puts upon everything that is presented to him. They are the colored glasses through which he sees all the facts. Now Romanism and Arminianism also seek to present to the unbelievers the facts of Christianity. We have seen that in reality their own false interpretations of the facts of Christianity mean that they do not really present the facts fully for what they are. But to the extent that they do present the facts as they are, they still do not challenge the natural man to take off his colored glasses. And it is precisely this that the Reformed apologist seeks to do. He will first present the facts for what they really are and then he will challenge the natural man by arguing that unless they are accepted for what they are according to the Christian interpretation of them, no facts mean anything at all.

Here then are the facts, or some of the main facts that the Reformed apologist presents to the natural man. There is first the fact of God's self-contained existence. Second, the fact of creation in general and of man as made in God's image in particular. Third, there is the fact of the comprehensive plan and providence of God with respect to all that takes place in the universe. Then there is the fact of the fall of man and his subsequent sin. It is in relation to these facts and only in relation to these facts that the other facts pertaining to the redemptive work of Christ, are what they are. They would not be what they are unless the facts just mentioned are what they are. Thus there is one system of reality of which all that exists forms a part. And any individual fact of this system is what it is in this system. It is therefore a contradiction in terms to speak of presenting certain facts to men unless one presents them as parts of this system. The very factness of any individual fact of history is precisely what it is because God is what he is. It is God's counsel that is the principle of individuation for the Christian man. God makes the facts to be what they are.

To be sure, man's actions have their place in this system.

But they are not ultimately determinative; they are subordinately and derivatively important. Hence the idea of human autonomy can find no place in the truly Christian system any more than can the idea of chance. The human being is analogical rather than original in all the aspects of its activity. And as such its activity is truly significant.

It is natural that only the supernatural revelation of God can inform man about such a system as that. For this system is of a nature quite different from the systems of which the natural man speaks. For the latter a system is that which man, assumed to be ultimate, has ordered by his original structural activity. The natural man virtually attributes to himself that which a true Christian theology attributes to the self-contained God. The battle is therefore between the absolutely self-contained God of Christianity and the would-be wholly self-contained mind of the natural man. Between them there can be no compromise.

The idea of supernatural revelation is inherent in the very idea of this system of Christianity which we are seeking to present to the natural man. But if this is so then the idea of a supernatural, infallibly inscripturated revelation is also inherent in this system. Man as the creature of God needs supernatural revelation and man, become a sinner, needs supernatural redemptive revelation. He needs this revelation in infallibly inscripturated form lest he himself destroy it. As a hater of God he does not want to hear about God. The natural man seeks to suppress the pressure of God's revelation in nature that is about him. He seeks to suppress the pressure of conscience within him. So he also seeks to suppress the idea of the revelation of grace that speaks in Scripture. In every case it is God as his Creator and as his judge that asks of him to listen and be obedient. How can the autonomous man be obedient on his own assumptions? He cannot be obedient unless he reverses his entire position, and this he cannot do of himself. It takes the regenerating power of the Spirit to do that.

Having reached this point the Roman Catholic and the Arminian may argue that it was in the interest of avoiding this very impasse that they sought to make their point of contact with the natural man on a neutral basis. The reply of the Reformed apologist is as follows. Good preaching, he will say, will recognize the truth of Scripture that man has been blinded by sin, and that his will is perverted toward seeking self instead of God. But how can deaf ears hear, and blind eyes see? That is to say preaching is confronted with the same dilemma as is apologetical reasoning. In both cases the Roman Catholic and the Arminian tone down the facts of the gospel in order to gain acceptance for them on the part of the natural man. In neither case will the Reformed apologist do so. In both cases he will challenge the natural man at the outset. Both in preaching and in reasoning—and every approach to the natural man should be both—the Reformed theologian will ask the sinner to do what he knows the sinner of himself cannot do. The Reformed Christian is often Reformed in preaching and Arminian in reasoning. But when he is at all self-conscious in his reasoning he will seek to do in apologetics what he does in preaching. He knows that man is responsible not in spite of but just because he is not autonomous but created. He knows that the idea of analogical or covenant personality is that which alone preserves genuine significance for the thoughts and deeds of man. So he also knows that he who is dead in trespasses and sins is none the less responsible for his deadness. He knows also that the sinner in the depth of his heart knows that what is thus held before him is true. He knows he is a creature of God; he has been simply seeking to cover up this fact to himself. He knows that he has broken the law of God; he has again covered up this fact to himself. He knows that he is therefore guilty and is subject to punishment forever; this fact too he will not look in the face.

And it is precisely Reformed preaching and Reformed apologetic that tears the mask off the sinner's face and compels him to look at himself and the world for what they really are. Like a mole the natural man seeks to scurry under ground every time the facts as they really are come to his attention. He loves the darkness rather than the light. The light exposes him to himself. And precisely this neither Roman Catholic or Arminian preaching or reasoning are able to do.

As to the possibility and likelihood of the sinner's accepting the Christian position, it must be said that this is a matter of the grace of God. As the creature of God, made in the image of God, he is always accessible to God. As a rational creature he can understand that one must either accept the whole of a system of truth or reject the whole of it. He cannot understand why a position such as that of Roman Catholicism or of Arminians should challenge him. He knows right well as a rational being that only the Reformed statement of Christianity is consistent with itself and therefore challenges the non-Christian position at every point. He can understand therefore why the Reformed theologian should accept the doctrine of Scripture as the infallible Word of God. He can understand the idea of its necessity, its perspicuity, its sufficiency and its authority as being involved in the Christian position as a whole.

But while understanding them as being involved in the position of Christianity as a whole, it is precisely Christianity as a whole, and therefore each of these doctrines as part of Christianity, that are meaningless to him as long as he is not willing to drop his own assumptions of autonomy and chance.

It follows that on the question of Scripture, as on every other question, the only possible way for the Christian to reason with the non-believer is by way of presupposition. He must say to the unbeliever that unless he will accept the presuppositions and with them the interpretations of Christianity there is no coherence in human experience. That is to say, the argument must be such as to show that unless one accept the Bible for what true Protestantism says it is, the authoritative interpretation of human life and experience as a whole, it will be impossible to find meaning in anything. It is only when this presupposition is constantly kept in mind that a fruitful discussion of problems pertaining to the phenomena of Scripture and what it teaches about God in his relation to man can be discussed.

Chapter VIII

COMMON GRACE AND SCHOLASTICISM[1]

At this point it is well to consider the question of "common grace." For it is said by some Reformed theologians that the position maintained in this book does not do full justice to the knowledge and life of non-Christians because it does not assign the true place to what, since Calvin's time, has been known as *common grace.* And involved in common grace is the question of natural theology as this is taught in Roman Catholicism.

The question is whether the Christian can, at any point, approach the non-believer on a neutral basis. Abraham Kuyper applied to this question with a vigorous negative.

I

All Men Unavoidably Know God

When Kuyper gave this unequivocal negative answer, however, he did not thereby intend to deny that the unbeliever has any true knowledge in any sense of the term. Disclaiming originality Kuyper closely follows Calvin in insisting that every man knows God. Does not Paul the Apostle plainly teach this in his epistle to the Romans? Every man, said Calvin, has a sense of deity within him. Men have "in their own persons a factory where innumerable operations of God are carried on. . . ." This is revelation within men. It may be called subjective in the sense that it is mediated through the constitution of man himself. It is none the less objective to man as an ethically responsible creature of God. As ethical reactor to God's revelation man must reflect

[1] Readers who are interested in pursuing the doctrine of grace in greater detail should consult the author's *Common Grace,* and his two syllabi *Sovereign Grace Defended* and *The Heidelberg Catechism* as well as the following published booklets: *Common Grace and Witness-Bearing, Particularism and Common Grace,* and *A Letter on Common Grace* (out of print). All from the Presbyterian and Reformed Publishing Co.

upon himself as made by God in order to own that he comes from God and owes all of his praise to God.

Secondly, man has round about him the clearest possible evidence of the power and divinity of God.

> In attestation of his wondrous wisdom both the heavens and the earth present us with innumerable proofs, not only of those more recondite proofs which astronomy, medicine, and all the natural sciences, are designed to illustrate, but proofs which force themselves on the notice of the most illiterate peasant, who cannot open his eyes without beholding them.[2]

Thus the knowledge of God is inherent in man. It is there by virtue of his creation in the image of God. This may be called innate knowledge. But as such it must be distinguished from the innate ideas of idealist philosophy. For the innate knowledge as Calvin thinks of it is based upon the idea of man's creation in the image of God. And as such it is correlative to the idea of revelation to man mediated through the facts of his environment which are also created by God. In contrast with this the innate knowledge of Descartes and idealist philosophy is based on the idea of the autonomy of man.

Following Calvin, then, Kuyper did not tone down the clarity of the revelation of God to man. In this respect he is in agreement with Warfield. Both men are equally anxious to follow Calvin as Calvin simply followed St. Paul in the idea that God has never left himself without a witness to men. He witnessed to them through every fact of the universe from the beginning of time. No rational creature can escape this witness. It is the witness of the triune God whose face is before men everywhere and all the time. Even the lost in the hereafter cannot escape the revelation of God. God made man a rational-moral creature. He will always be that. As such he is confronted with God. He is addressed by God. He exists in the relationship of covenant interaction. He is a covenant being. To not know God man would have to destroy himself. He cannot do this. There is no non-being into which man can slip in order to escape God's face and voice. The mountains will not cover him; Hades will not

[2] *Institutes*, Bk. I, Chap. V, Sec. 2.

hide him. Nothing can prevent his being confronted "with him with whom we have to do." Whenever he sees himself, he sees himself confronted with God.

Whatever may happen, whatever sin may bring about, whatever havoc it may occasion, it cannot destroy man's knowledge of God and his sense of responsibility to God. Sin would not be sin except for this ineradicable knowledge of God. Even sin as a process of ever-increasing alienation from God presupposes for its background this knowledge of God.

This knowledge is that which all men have *in common.* For the race of men is made of one blood. It stood as a unity before God in Adam. This confrontation of all men with God in Adam by supernatural revelation presupposes and is correlative to the confrontation of mankind with God by virtue of creation. If then the believer presents to the unbeliever the Bible and its system of truth as God speaking to men, he may rest assured that there is a response in the heart of every man to whom he thus speaks. This response may be, and often is, unfavorable. Men will reject the claims of God but, none the less, they will own them as legitimate. That is, they will in their hearts, when they cannot suppress them, own these claims. There are no atheists, least of all in the hereafter. Metaphysically speaking then, both parties, believers and unbelievers, have all things in common; they have God in common, they have every fact in the universe in common. And they know they have them in common. All men know God, the true God, the only God. They have not merely a capacity for knowing him but actually do know him.

Thus there is not and can never be an absolute separation between God and man. Man is always accessible to God. There can be no *absolute* antithesis in this sense of the term. In this respect Protestant theology, and in particular Reformed theology, stands over against the *analogia entis* idea of Romanist theology. On a Romanist basis man might, as it were, escape from the face of God. He might fall entirely into the realm of non-being. He is so near to it to begin with that he is always in danger of falling into it. From the outset of his existence it took supernatural grace to keep him from falling into it. There is therefore on the basis of Romanism no inescapable revelation of God within the constitution of man.

And what is true of God's revelation mediated through man is true also with respect to God's revelation to man mediated through the facts of the universe about him. According to Romanism these too do not clearly and inescapably reveal God to man. They too are too near the realm of non-being to reveal God clearly. Thus the Romanist principle of discontinuity is out of accord with the teaching of the apostle Paul with respect to the inescapable knowledge that all men have of God. There is no true commonness of knowledge on this basis between men. For each man may individually slip into non-being. Thus no believer can approach an unbeliever knowing that the unbeliever *must* respond to him in terms of a common relationship that both sustain to God.

And where there is no true basis for a common knowledge there is no true basis for the unity of science. Only in Protestant thought, and more particularly in Reformed thought, with its insistence that God controls whatsoever comes to pass, and with its insistence that every man as man is an addressee of God, is there unity of science. On this basis only the unity of science is guaranteed. Every man can contribute to the progress of science. Every man must contribute to it. It is his task to do so. And he cannot help but fulfill his task even if it be against his will.

It is on this sort of basis that Kuyper and Bavinck alike maintained the basic unity of science. God is certain to attain his end with mankind. In the face of Satan, he will cause men to develop and bring to fruition the potentialities that he himself has deposited within the universe. Whether willingly or unwillingly, whether conspicuously or inconspicuously, all men, and Satan too, contribute to the realization of the purpose of God with man and his universe. The last and final song of the redeemed is the song of creation and its glorious consummation (Rev. 4:11).

But from what has been said it has already become apparent that it is through Christ that the unity of science is to be attained. To no good purpose do we speculate on what might have been if Adam had not sinned. To be sure, it is well to use this idea of what might have happened as a limiting concept in the Christian sense of the term. When Adam was confronted with the choice of obedience and disobedience it was a real choice that was given him. But this is not to say that God had not determined from before the creation of the world what would actually take place. In the last analysis only that could take place which, according to the ultimate will of God, was going to take place. Only that was possible in the ultimate sense which God had determined. And God had determined that through Christ as Redeemer mankind would accomplish the task assigned it. Only on the basis of the work of Christ, then, does the unity of science actually exist and will it be actually consummated. True, the work of Christ must be thought of as immediately and directly effecting the salvation of men. But in saving men and in saving mankind Christ saves science. The unity of science may therefore be said to be Christological in a secondary sense.

II

Natural Theology

On a Romanist basis this Christological basis of the unity of science cannot be and is not maintained. On their basis the Christ could not and did not accomplish one finished act of world salvation. Only in a universe that is unified by the plan of God can there be a once-for-all and finished act of redemption, affecting the whole race of man. And only on the basis of a world in which every fact testifies of God can there be a Word of God that testifies of itself as interpreting every other fact.

The unity of science as Romanism conceives of it is not a unity based upon the plan of God inclusive of all things and upon the work of Christ as saving all things. Rome's principle of discontinuity allows for no exclusive confrontation of man with God, for no sin that is exclusively self-conscious opposition to God and for no redemption that is in principle the complete return to and service of God.

Positively the Romanist idea of the unity of science rests upon a principle of continuity that involves the virtual denial of the difference between the Creator and the creature. Romanism has taken over the non-Christian, more especially the Aristotelian, notion of the unity of science. According to this notion all knowledge is of universals. All knowledge is based upon the assumption of some measure of identity of being manifesting itself in both God and man. If Christ is to be fitted into this idea he must be thought of as a universal ideal. He must virtually be reduced to a principle of unity in reality. Christianity then is not "accidental" and restorative in Kuyper's sense of the term; it is merely supplementative to the natural. The natural and the supernatural, the created and the soteriological are only gradationally distinct from one another.

But to understand the Romanist idea of the unity of science one must take the two principles, that of discontinuity and that of continuity, together. These must be taken as correlative of one another. And when they are taken as correlative of one another the idea of the unity of science involves an ever receding ideal of the identity of thought, whether human or divine, with reality as a whole. The ideal is ever receding because reality is utterly discontinuous. The ideal, if realized, would destroy the unity of science because then all the facts investigated would have lost their individuality in one abstract blank being. But the ideal cannot be realized. And the reason for this is that the principle of discontinuity or individuality employed is a wholly irrational one. In other words, the facts to be investigated do not form a part of any system at all. It is useless to speak of their essence since no one can know what their essence is. No one could ever find a fact and know in what way it differed from other facts.

It is true, of course, that the Aristotelian character of the Romanist position is mitigated by the teachings of the church with respect to man's creation by God. That is, the Romanist position holds to the principles as outlined only in the fields of natural revelation, and philosophy. In these fields it owns "the legitimate autonomy of reason." Even so Romanist theology is itself adjusted to the idea of the autonomy of reason in the field of the natural revelation. The total result is that no intelligible or tenable philosophy of the unity of science is offered.

It follows too that Romanism has no adequate challenge for modern thought and its notion of the unity of science. It is of some importance to see what this modern idea is. It is, in short, but a continuation of the Greek idea. But it is more relentless and consistent in working out the Greek idea. To be sure, there is an important difference between the "objective" approach of ancient and the "subjective" approach of modern philosophy. But from the Christian point of view both are still subjective. Modern thought is more consistently subjective than was ancient thought. In the case of Kant's philosophy the human subject is frankly made the source of unity in human experience and therefore the source of unity in science. This was involved in the fall of man. And it was inherent in Greek philosophy, in that of Plato and of Aristotle no less than in that of the Sophists. But in modern times man has boldly asserted that he can identify himself first before he speaks of God. He will identify God after he has first identified himself. And this is not merely a methodological matter, due to the fact that man must psychologically think of himself first before he can think of God. It is a matter of ultimate metaphysics. It is the idea that man is ultimate. Man as ultimate can and must identify himself in terms of himself. He must therefore also virtually use the law of contradiction as a means by which to determine what is possible and what is impossible in reality.

It was necessary to say this much by way of introducing the difference between Reformed men on the question of common grace. It would seem clear that any doctrine of common grace that is to be held by Reformed men must be in accord with and a part of the main body of Reformed doctrine. In particular one can scarcely claim to hold intelligently to Calvin's doctrine of common grace unless one sees it in relation to the whole of Calvin's theology, and in particular unless one sees it as it stands in relation to Calvin's doctrine of the clarity of God's revelation to man through man himself. More particularly still, the difference between Calvin's views on man's creation in the image of God and the Romanist view of man as participant in the same being with God is of basic significance for the question of common grace.

It has already been indicated that this difference has a direct bearing both upon the idea of what is properly called natural nd what is properly called redemptive. For Calvin creation itself is directly and clearly revelational of the creative and sustaining activity of God. Man is therefore naturally in contact with the expressed will of God. For the supernatural revelation of God to Adam was natural to him. This supernatural revelation is part of the normal or natural state of affairs for man. For Romanism the natural for man is that which is participant in the same being with God. At the same time that which is participant in the same being with God is near to non-being and tends to slip back into non-being.

What then is the redemptive for Calvin? And what is it for Romanism? To answer this question a previous question must first be considered. As there are differing views of the natural, so there are differing views of evil or sin. For Calvin sin is self-conscious rebellion on the part of the creature against his Creator and Benefactor. Even those who have sinned in Adam but not after the similitude of Adam are covenant breakers. They are responsible with Adam for the pre-redemptive supernatural revelation as it was conjoined to original natural revelation. For Romanism sin is only partly disobedience to God; it is also slipping back into non-being. With Calvin the idea of sin is exclusively ethical; with Rome sin as ethical is in large part reduced to a metaphysical lack. It is of the utmost importance to lay great stress on the ethical character of Reformation theology as over against Romanist theology. Reformed theology differs from Evangelicalism in the fact that it holds tenaciously to this ethical character of Christianity, while evangelicalism tends to veer to the idea of sin as metaphysical defect. With its conception of the human will as in part autonomous, evangelicalism naturally tends to the idea of Romanism.

For Calvin redemption is exclusively ethical. Sin did not lower man in the scale of being. Sin did not take away from man any of the natural powers that God had given him. Sin did not tend to destroy the metaphysical situation. To be sure, sin had physical effects. It brought disease and death into the world. But the idea that the created world would have been destroyed by sin is an abstraction. It was not God's intention that it should. Hence it was from the beginning ultimately impossible that it should. The created world has no tendency to slip back into non-being. The fact that it needs each moment to be sustained by God does not prove that it has such a tendency. This fact only shows its actually dependent character. God intended from the beginning to uphold the universe as dependent upon himself.

In particular sin did not destroy any of the powers that God gave man at the beginning when he endowed him with his image. To be sure, here too there have been weakening results. But man still has eyes with which to observe and logical ability with which to order and arrange the things that he observes. So far from sin being inherently destructive of the metaphysical situation, it is rather true that the continuation of this situation is the presupposition of sin in its ethical character.

For Romanism redemption is therefore at least in part metaphysical. For Romanism the natural tended even at the outset, before the fall, toward non-being. It therefore needed the supernatural in order to draw it upward away from non-being. The supernatural must from the beginning remedy a defect inherent in the natural. The supernatural is therefore something that lifts man up in the scale of being. The tendency to slip into non-being is, on the Romanist view, a real possibility. It is an ultimate possibility. Romanism uses the notion of abstract possibility as an aspect of its theory of being. So then the redemptive is still largely what the original supernatural was, viz., a counteracting agent against the tendency of finite being to slip into non-being. Redemption thus is not "accidental," it is not primarily ethical. The distinction between nature and grace as used in Romanist thinking and the distinction between nature and grace as used in Reformation thinking are therefore quite different in meaning.

To set the doctrine of common grace in the proper perspective therefore requires setting off Reformed theology as a whole from Romanist and also from evangelical thinking. On a Romanist basis even special grace is largely thought of along the lines of lifting man in the scale of being. On its basis common grace would therefore be only gradationally different from special or saving grace. No other than gradational differences are possible once one holds to the human will as in some measure autonomous, and once one holds to the idea of man as participant in the same being with God. The idea of saving grace is then the offering to all men or at least to groups of men the real or ultimate possibility of salvation along with the equally ultimate possibility of destruction. In no case can God overcome completely the tendency of finite being to slip into non-being.

What holds for Romanism on this point also holds to some

extent for evangelicalism. Here too saving grace is limited by abstract possibility and therefore by man's ultimate ability to resist the will or pleading of the Spirit of God. The idea of grace is in part reduced from its high ethical concept to one of metaphysical gradation.

On the basis of the Reformed view, however, saving grace is conceived of on wholly ethical lines. The metaphysical presupposition of conceiving the idea of grace thus exclusively along ethical lines is the fact that God controls whatsoever comes to pass. This rules out all abstract possibilities. It involves that man is always confronted with the revelation of God's will. It means that when he sinned, man sinned against this known revelation of God. Man is responsible for sin, and he alone is responsible for sin. When man sins he is therefore *wholly* depraved. There was no excuse for his sinning in the fact that his being, as finite, was inherently defective, or in the fact that God's will for him was not wholly clear. On the other hand, it was God's will that sin should come into the world. He wished to enhance his glory by means of its punishment and removal.

But to hold strictly to man's utter responsibility for sin and yet to the fact that it was God's ultimate intention that it should come into the world through man, requires that one think analogically. And thinking analogically is thinking concretely. It means thinking from the analogical system of truth revealed in Scripture. It involves accepting that which is apparently, though not really, contradictory. All the concepts offered in Scripture therefore are supplemental of one another. It is not possible to begin with one doctrine, and deduce from that one doctrine certain other doctrines that must "logically follow from it," except one at the same time keep in mind that there are other doctrines that are, of necessity, in apparent contradiction to the first doctrine from which the beginning was made.

III

Differences Between Reformed Theologians

The difference between Reformed theologians on the question of common grace may now be noted. There are those who do not think it necessary to distinguish thus sharply between the

Romanist and the Reformed conception of things in order to have a true conception of common grace and of the purpose it serves in connection with the problem of the unity of science. Dr. S. J. Ridderbos specifically denies the necessity of doing the sort of thing that has been done so far in this chapter. He does so in a booklet dealing with various criticisms of Dr. Abraham Kuyper's concept of common grace. The title of the booklet is *Rondom het Gemene-Gratie-Probleem* (Kampen 1949). In this pamphlet Ridderbos criticized the present writer's views on common grace set forth in a brief publication under that title (Philadelphia 1947). As this criticism represents quite clearly a point of view held by other Reformed theologians besides Ridderbos, it will be dealt with briefly here.

The present writer undertook in his booklet to meet the challenge of Etienne Gilson, a great modern Romanist apologist, which he made to the Calvinistic idea of the *sensus deitatis*. This was done in connection with Bavinck's conception of the *cognitio dei insita.*

> The question to be considered here is that of the *koinai ennoiai*, the *notiones impressae*, the *cognitationes insitae*. It is but natural that Roman Catholic theology, which holds that the natural reason can discover certain truths about God, should hold that there are ideas about God that are wholly common to the believer and the non-believer. Gilson expresses this point of view when he argues that we can discover the same truths that Aristotle discovered, by the same reason unaided by special revelation. Gilson further argues that Calvin, in holding to an "impression of divinity" or "common notion" or "innate idea" or "religious aptitude" in man, and in saying that "experience" attests the fact that God has placed in all men an innate seed of religion, virtually holds to the same position as that to which the Roman Catholic holds. He thinks the Calvinist faces an antinomy in connection with his view on this point.
>
> > At first sight, it would seem that there could not be a better solution. But it is still true that this knowledge is confronted by the problem just as certainly as is the rational certitude which the Thomistic proofs of the existence of God claim to attain. Either it is a natural

certitude, in which the right to criticize the Catholic position and to suppress pure philosophy is lost; or it is a supernatural certitude, in which case it would become impossible to find a place for that natural knowledge of God, which is exactly what one was pretending to conserve.[3]

The question now is whether the innate knowledge of which Bavinck speaks is of such a nature as to be able to escape the dilemma before which Gilson places the Calvinistic position. We believe Gilson is fair enough in demanding that Reformed theology shall come to a self-conscious defense of its notion of natural theology in general. It cannot fairly limit itself to *diminishing the area* or *reducing somewhat the value* of the natural theology of Roman Catholic theology. As long as the natural theology of the Reformed theologian is still the same in kind as that of the Roman Catholic theologian, he will find it difficult to escape the dilemma with which Gilson confronts it.[4]

The question was then asked whether Kuyper and Bavinck, great modern exponents of Calvin's views, have been wholly successful in setting off their thought clearly on the idea of *innate knowledge* and *common notions* from that of Romanism. The answer given is that they are not. Though they insist that true natural theology is that which interprets nature in the light of Scripture they have sometimes employed the notions of brute fact and of abstract universals (p. 52). How does this appear in the question of innate knowledge? It appears in the fact that the idea of innate knowledge as Calvin sees it is clearly based upon the idea of man in God's creation. As such it is correlative to the idea of *cognition dei acquisita*, the gathering together of facts that are also assumed to be created by God. Of course, both Kuyper and Bavinck agree with this view of Calvin. They even set off this notion clearly from the idea of innate knowledge which rests upon the concept of man as ultimate, and from the idea of acquired knowledge as it derives from the idea of Chance. But though they do this, they also at times adopt in their process

[3] *Christianity and Philosophy*, p. 41.

[4] Van Til: *Common Grace*, Philadelphia, 1947, pp. 51, 52.

of reasoning the non-Christian principles of continuity and of discontinuity.

When they do this they seek for *common notions* between believers and unbelievers that are not exclusively based upon the idea of the *sensus deitatis.* They then ignore the difference between the idea of fact and logic as it springs from the position that is based upon the notion of the autonomous man, and the idea of fact and logic which springs from the position that is based upon the notion of the ontological trinity.

Yet the idea of fact as it is based upon the notion of the autonomous man is that of utterly irrational differentiation. And the notion of logic as it is based upon the idea of man as autonomous is that of system that is above and inclusive of the distinction between God and man. A Reformed theologian will need to follow Kuyper and Bavinck when they call us back to Calvin in this matter. For the idea of common notions as based upon Romanism is largely that which is based upon the concept of human autonomy. With the acceptance of the Romanist idea of common notions Christianity has lost its uniqueness. For then the natural man is given the right to interpret the words of Scripture in terms of a system that it can exhaustively penetrate. On the other hand the natural man is assumed to be right when he takes for granted that the facts do not at all convey to man the revelation of God. For facts are then irrational in character. In short, the natural man is then given the right to do what Kuyper says he will surely do when confronted with the Bible and its system of truth, namely, reduce it to naturalistic proportions.

Against this type of argument Ridderbos contends that it was a mistake to accept the challenge of Gilson.[5] The difference between Romanism and the Reformed faith must be sought in that the former does *not* and the latter does teach the doctrine of common grace. The Reformed position with respect to the knowledge of sinful man differs both qualitatively and quantitatively from the teaching of Romanism on the same subject because of the doctrine of common grace.

First, he says, there is the qualitative difference. For Romanism the idea of natural knowledge is natural without quali-

[5] *Rondom Het Gemene-Gratie-Probleem,* Kampen, 1949, p. 42.

fication. Romanism does not believe in the doctrine of total depravity. It therefore thinks that the sinner, though wounded through sin, still is naturally able to know God.

On the other hand Reformed theology does believe in total depravity. In consequence, Reformed theology teaches that man by nature has no knowledge of God or of morality at all. For Romanism natural knowledge of God springs from a human situation which is not totally despoiled by sin.

> If in spite of this according to the Scriptures and the Confession there are remnants of a true knowledge of God to be seen in man, then this must be explained in terms of common grace, through which God has restrained human depravity.[6]

If we speak exactly, he adds, we should therefore place quotation marks about the phrase, "natural knowledge of God." It might better be called "common grace knowledge."

In addition to this qualitative distinction between the Reformed position and that of Romanism there is, says Ridderbos, a quantitative one. The Reformed Confessions speak of *small* remnants of the knowledge of God and of morality possessed by the natural man. And these small remnants must be upheld by common grace. Not holding to total depravity and not holding to common grace, Romanism works out a natural theology of full proportions.

Of these two points, the qualitative and the quantitative difference between the Reformed Faith and Romanism, the former is certainly for Ridderbos the more important. The difference in quantity is due to the difference in quality.

The question now is whether Ridderbos succeeds in signalizing the qualitative difference between Romanism and the Reformed faith by simply inserting the ideas of total depravity and of common grace into a complex of doctrines assumed to be essentially the same for both. Can Romanist theology and philosophy be repaired by thus inserting a block of material here and there into an edifice that is otherwise left unmolested? Can the ideas of total depravity and common grace be woven into the main motif of Romanism, that of *analogia entis*? It is that which

[6] *Idem*, p. 40.

must be done if one refuses to accept and answer the challenge of Gilson referred to above. Protestants, and especially followers of Calvin, can scarcely afford to allow the legitimacy of the idea that finite being has a tendency to slip back into non-being. Yet it is this which Ridderbos virtually does when he asserts that, were it not for common grace, every last bit of natural knowledge of God and of morality would have disappeared. He argues that except for the restraining force of common grace God's voice even in general revelation would have been silenced altogether.

But how could the voice of God's revelation in man be silenced altogether unless man himself were destroyed? Will not men in the abode of the lost have knowledge of God and of morality? Is it not precisely because they then have all too clear a knowledge of God and of morality that they suffer before the face of God? To say so is fully in line with Calvin's views. It is even of the essence of his view that men are what they are as inherently knowers of God. Yet evil spirits and the lost receive no common grace. Common grace is an attitude of favor of God toward men as men, as creatures made by himself in his own image. Common grace is the giving of good gifts to men though they have sinned against him, that they might repent and mend their evil ways. Common grace provides for the doing of relatively good deeds by sinful men who are kept from working out to its full fruition the principle of total depravity within them. Common grace thus is a means by which God accomplishes through men his purpose in displaying his glory in the created world, in history, before the judgment day. So there is no common grace in hell.

Of course Ridderbos knows all this very well. He asserts it plainly. Yet he insists that the whole of general revelation must be suspended from common grace. And he insists that the whole of general revelation would disappear except for common grace. When he then faces the fact that Satan and the lost cannot be thought of as recipients of common grace he avers that even in their case there is a restraining force of God that keeps them confronted with the general revelation of God.

It is this last point that shows conclusively that Ridderbos thinks of the idea of finite, rational creatures as slipping back into the realm of non-being as a serious possibility. Man needs a restraining force, in addition to ordinary providence, in order to keep from falling into non-being. This restraining force is, in the nature of the case, not ethical in character. It does not intend to restrain the working of the sinful principle in man. It is not the means by which the potentialities of creation are to be brought to light. It is simply and purely metaphysical in character. Without this restraining force Satan and the lost would escape the punishment of God; they would escape him because they would be no more. Sin is therefore a force which, unless restrained, would lead to the destruction of finite rational creatures themselves. Sin is no longer an exclusively ethical opposition on the part of creatures of God against the will of God. For sin then presupposes a measure of autonomy in man by which he can destroy his own being and with it the revelation of God. Why else should it be necessary for God to introduce a force after the entrance of sin for the maintenance of created reality?

Now for Ridderbos common grace does in the course of human history what this metaphysical restraining force does in hell. To be sure common grace *also* does more than that. It *also* gives good gifts to men, makes them love the truth in a sense, causes them to produce civil righteousness. But the point now of importance is that for Ridderbos common grace in history and the restraining force in hell both maintain the general revelation of God to man. In history this force is gracious in character; after history is finished this is no longer the case.

Thus, both the doctrine of total depravity and the doctrine of common grace are in some measure unintentionally adjusted to the Romanist idea of the analogy of being. There is no escaping this so long as one thinks of Protestantism, and especially of the Reformed Faith, as merely adding some building blocks to the edifice which is in part constructed along Romanist lines. Then there is no maintaining of the exclusively ethical character of Reformation theology. To maintain this ethical character one needs, with Calvin, to presuppose the idea that man is inherently and inescapably, in history and after the consummation of history, in the realm of the blest and in the realm of the damned, in his very being revelational of the will of God. It is only thus that sin retains its ethical nature. It is only thus that sin can be total depravity both in extension and in intension. It is only thus that the fruition of sin can be tasted in the realm of the lost, for only thus is sin seen to be sin against the original gracious revelation of God to mankind.

Only by presupposing this utterly revelational character of man is it possible to maintain the exclusively ethical character of saving or special grace. Christ came to save men from sin. Did he come in part, at least, to maintain the metaphysical *status quo*? Surely not. Sin is exclusively ethical hostility to God. It is this ethical hostility to God that Christ came to remove. To be sure, sin must be spoken of as in intent destructive of the work of God. And since the work of Christ is indispensable as the only means by which the work of God through man in history could be accomplished, this work of Christ is itself a part of the providence of God. In this respect the work of Christ may be said to be "essential" to the plan of God. At the same time this work is "accidental" in Kuyper's use of the term. For it is *only* because of sin as ethical hostility to God that the work of Christ "became" "essential." These two notions are supplementary of one another. They limit one another.

Once more, only by presupposing the ultimately revelational character of man in the way that Calvin, following Paul and opposing Aquinas, does, is it possible to maintain the exclusively ethical character of the doctrine of common grace. And only by maintaining its exclusively ethical character can common grace be properly related to saving grace. When both are interpreted in exclusively ethical terms then both are seen on the one hand to be "accidental" and on the other hand to be "essential." They are then both seen to be "accidental" in opposition to the Romanist idea that supernatural grace is naturally necessary and "essential" to man as a finite being. And they are then both seen to be "essential" against the Romanist idea that finite existence may slip back into non-being. In other words only by maintaining Calvin's doctrine of the sense of deity, as involved in the idea of the exhaustively revelational character of man as man, is it possible to maintain the distinctively Protestant, and more especially the distinctively Reformed, principles of discontinuity and of continuity over against these principles in Roman Catholic theology.

A word must now be said about the idea of "common notions" referred to in the quotation given above. The present writer made a distinction between notions that are psychologically and metaphysically, that is revelationally, common to all men, and common notions that are ethically and epistemologically common. The reason for this distinction lies in the difference between a view that is based upon the concept of the creation of man in the image of God and who thus has within him the ineradicable knowledge of God, and a view that is based upon man as participant with God in one general being. All men have common notions about God; all men naturally have knowledge of God. In this sense there is, as Calvin points out on the basis of Paul's letter to the Romans, a natural knowledge of God and with it of truth and morality.

It is this actual possession of the knowledge of God that is the indispensable presupposition of man's ethical opposition to God. There could be no *absolute ethical antithesis* to God on the part of Satan and fallen man unless they are self-consciously setting their own common notions, derived from the folly of sin, against the common notions that are concreated with them. Paul speaks of sinful man as suppressing within him the knowledge of God that he has. How does he do this? He does this by assuming his own ultimacy. For with this idea of his own ultimacy goes the idea that God and man are aspects of the same reality. They are then a part of a Reality that is on the one hand utterly discontinuous with itself, a Reality in which Chance is king, and on the other hand a Reality that is in principle exhaustively determnied by its own internal relations and is in principle exhaustively known to man and God alike. It is these notions of human autonomy, of irrational discontinuity and of rationalistic continuity that are the *common notions* of sinful or apostate mankind.

Or else what does the doctrine of total depravity mean?

If these common notions were allowed to come to fruition the mandate given to man by God at the beginning of history could not and would not be fulfilled. There would be no possibility even of finding a single fact in a universe of Chance. Individual men would have no common notions with other men, they would not even be able to distinguish themselves from other men. Observation of facts would be impossible because the idea of a fact is, on this basis, unintelligible. And if facts were found they could not be brought into a pattern. How could logic ever be said to have any bearing upon reality in a universe of Chance? But if it were granted to have a bearing, this logic would be inherently destructive of the facts of reality and of their individuality. For their identity would be lost in one abstract blank, in some such way as Parmenides said that they would be. There would be no God distinct from man. There would be no creation out of nothing. There would be no Fall. There would be no historic Christianity. There would be one common blur.

Kuyper has well brought out the fact that the natural man, working on the principles of his adoption must, to be logical, deny all that Christianity stands for.

It is this fact, that the natural man, using his principles and working on his assumptions, must be hostile in principle at every point to the Christian philosophy of life, that was stressed in the writer's little book, *Common Grace*. That all men have all things in common metaphysically and psychologically, was definitely asserted, and further, that the natural man has epistemologically nothing in common with the Christian. And this latter assertion was quailfied by saying that this is so only *in principle*. For it is not till after the consummation of history that men are left wholly to themselves. Till then the Spirit of God continues to strive with men that they might forsake their evil ways. Till then God in his common grace, in his long-suffering forbearance, gives men rain and sunshine and all the good things of life that they might repent. The primary attitude of God to men as men is that of goodness. It is against this goodness expressing itself in the abundance of good gifts that man sins. And even then God prevents the principle of sin from coming to full fruition. He restrains the wrath of man. He enables him by this restraint to cooperate with the redeemed of God in the development of the work he gave man to do.

But all this does not in the least reduce the fact that as far as the principle of the natural man is concerned, it is *absolutely* or utterly, not partly, opposed to God. That principle is Satanic. It is exclusively hostile to God. If it could it would destroy the work and plan of God. So far then as men self-consciously work from this principle they have no notion in common with the believer. Their epistemology is informed by their ethical hostility to God.

But in the course of history the natural man is not fully self-conscious of his own position. The prodigal cannot altogether stifle his father's voice. There is a conflict of notions within him. But he himself is not fully and self-consciously aware of this conflict within him. He has within him the knowledge of God by virtue of his creation in the image of God. But this idea of God is suppressed by his false principle, the principle of autonomy. This principle of autonomy is, in turn, suppressed by the restraining power of God's common grace. Thus the ideas with which he daily works do not proceed consistently either from the one principle or from the other.

Ridderbos also says that the natural man's ideas of God and of morality are vague. But for him this vagueness is not due to the fact of the conflict just now discussed. He has no interest in distinguishing clearly between the knowledge of the natural man that comes from his creation and his knowledge as it is implied in the idea of autonomy. He thinks it is a mistake to distinguish between common notions derived from the image of God in man and common notions that proceed from the idea of autonomy. Thus he cannot take the principle of autonomy in its full seriousness of opposition to the truth. Thus too he cannot account for the unity of science upon clearly Christian principles alone.

That such is the case may be briefly indicated with respect to two matters mentioned by Ridderbos himself.

In the first place there is the question of the non-Christian's contribution to the progress of science. In the second place there is the question of the theistic proofs. Is it not obviously true that non-Christian scientists have contributed largely to the progress of science? Can they not weigh? Can they not count? Can they not see? Do they not have logical powers as good as those of the believer? Did not Abraham Kuyper, the great protagonist of the idea of a twofold science, the science of regenerate and the science of non-regenerate men, himself maintain that in the field of externals and in the field of formal thought the subjective element of regeneration need not and should not be taken into account? How then can one say that epistemologically the believer and the non-believer have nothing in common?

In reply it may be said that only if sin and salvation be thought of along metaphysical rather than along ethical lines is it possible that such questions can arise. If sin is seen to be ethical alienation only, and salvation as ethical restoration only, then the question of weighing and measuring or that of logical reasoning is, of course, equal on both sides. All men, whatever their ethical relation to God, can equally use the natural gifts of God. How could men abuse the gift of God if they could not even use it? And what an easy way of escape for sinners it would be if the result of their folly was nothing more serious than the loss of their natural powers, and with it the loss of responsibility. The presupposition of a modern war is that both parties to it shall be equally able to use the weapons of such a war.

Moreover, only if both parties, the unbeliever and the believer, have equal natural ability to use the gifts of God can there be an all-inclusive antithesis between them. The argument between Christians and non-Christians involves every fact in the universe. If it does not involve every fact it does not involve any fact. If one fact can be interpreted correctly on the assumption of human autonomy then all facts can. If the Christian is to be able to show the non-Christian objectively that Christianity is true and that those who reject it do so because they hold to that which is false, this must be done everywhere or else it is not really done anywhere.

Still further, it is when we presuppose with Calvin that all men inherently know the truth, because they and the universe about them are made by God, and then if we assert with Calvin that all men are spiritually at enmity against God so that they are anxious always and everywhere to suppress the truth, that we can also speak with Calvin of God's common grace by which men are able to cooperate with believers in building the structure of science. As far as natural ability is concerned the lost can and do know the truth and could contribute to the structure of science except for the fact that for them it is too late. At the consummation of the age the lost will be compelled to own that their efforts to build the structure of science in terms of human autonomy, of chance and determinism, or irrationalism and rationalism, was not an ethically honest effort. Not that they were, while building, wholly self-conscious of their own ethical hostility.

They were restrained from being fully self-conscious by common grace. They were restrained by common grace, employing the pressure of God's presence in his revelation to men upon them. With the prodigal son they saw something of the folly of their way while yet they were ethically unable to do anything but walk that way to the bitter end.

It is thus in the mixed situation that results because of the factors mentioned, (1) that every man knows God naturally (2) that every sinner is in principle anxiously striving to efface that knowledge of God and (3) that every sinner is in this world still the object of the striving of the Spirit calling him back to God, that cooperation between believers and unbelievers is possible. Men on both sides can, by virtue of the gifts of God that they enjoy, contribute to science. The question of ethical hostility does not enter in at this point. Not merely weighing and measuring, but the argument for the existence of God and for the truth of Christianity, can as readily be observed to be true by non-Christians as by Christians. Satan knows all too well that God exists and that Christ was victor over him on Calvary. But the actual situation in history involves the other factors mentioned. Thus there is *nowhere* an area where the second factor, that of man's ethical hostility to God, does not also come into the picture. This factor is not so clearly in evidence when men deal with external things; it is more clearly in evidence when they deal with the directly religious question of the truth of Christianity. But it is none the less present everywhere. It is present in the field of weighing and measuring, in the field of externals as well as in the field of more directly religious import. It is present here in that the natural man attempts to impose his false philosophy of fact upon the things that he weighs and measures. This is not theoretically the case so long as he uses these facts for non-scientific purposes. It is even then practically the case. Even then he does not seek to obey Paul's injunction to men to the effect that whether they eat or drink they should do all things to the glory of God. But it is theoretically the case when they seek to work scientifically. In that case non-believers use a non-rationalistic principle of individuation. They assume that the facts they weigh and measure are not created and controlled by God. They assume this with respect to *every* fact. Thus they assume that God does not speak to men through these facts. On the other hand they assume that the powers of logic given them by their creator are not so given them. They virtually assume that by these powers they can determine what is possible and what is impossible.

It is this irrationalist-rationalist idea of fact that appears, with variations, in the writers on the philosophy of science. Generally speaking they follow the lead of Kant's philosophy of fact and of logic. There is for them first the abstract possibility of *any* sort of fact existing. Facts in this sense have no determinable nature. They belong in Kant's noumenal realm. They are unknown and unknowable. This idea is directly and completely destructive of the doctrines of creation and providence. Secondly the facts that are known, that is those that somehow come into contact with the human mind, are known by virtue of the original ordering effect of the human mind upon the raw stuff of experience. These are the facts of science. They are *taken* as much as given. What they are depends not upon the ultimate determinative character of God but upon the ultimate determinative character of man, who virtually takes the place of God. Every fact then that has scientific standing is such only if it does not reveal God, but does reveal man as ultimate. No other facts are allowed as being facts unless they are as raw material generalized into a system that keeps out God. They are "statistically standardized correlations of existential changes." Existential changes as such are irrational. But they are standardized by the original, not derivative, organizing action of man as autonomous. Only then are they facts with scientific standing. It is thus that in the very act of the observation of facts the non-Christian does, so far as he works according to his principle, do what Kuyper says the natural man always does, namely, suppress the truth of God into naturalistic categories.

But the third factor must still come into play. The natural man does not thus self-consciously work from his principles. There is operative within him the sense of deity; he cannot efface it without effacing himself. And the significance of this metaphysical situation is again and again brought home to him by the striving of God's Spirit through common grace. In consequence he cannot but see that God is good; that he has been long-suffering with him in his sins, that the Father is calling him back. God is really good to all men. He deals with them as a class. As such they are the recipients of his *good* gifts to them. And as such he makes men conscious of his goodness, of his desire that sinners should turn unto him. To be sure their salvation and their conversion is not an ultimate possibility. It is not that any more than the idea of Adam's not falling into sin was an ultimate possibility in the plan of God. Both are significantly real challenges to men as men and the second in particular is a significant challenge to sinners as sinners, though neither were meant as ultimate possibilities by God.

And by the striving of the Spirit men cannot be wholly insensitive to this goodness of God. Their hostility is curbed in some measure. They cannot but love that which is honest and noble and true. They have many virtues that often make them better neighbors than Christians themselves are. And as such they can *cooperate* with believers in seeking the truth in science. They can contribute by virtue of their metaphysical constitution; they can cooperate by virtue of the ethical restraint of common grace.

Thus it is that the idea of the unity of science is conceived of along Christological lines. For common grace is then itself conceived of along Christological lines. All men have not only the ability to know but actually know the truth. This is so even in the case of those who do not know all the truth that they would need to know in order to be saved. All men know that God exists and is their judge. Secondly, all men have become sinners through Adam's fall. All men therefore suppress the truth that they know. This suppression is perfect in principle. It is due to hatred of God; it is due to deadness in sin. Sinners use the principle of Chance back of all things and the idea of exhaustive rationalization as the legitimate aim of science. If the universe were actually what these men assume it to be according to their principle, there would be no science. Science is possible and actual only because the non-believer's principle is not true and the believer's principle is true. Only because God has created the universe and does control it by his providence, is there such a thing as science at all. Thus the unity of science cannot be built on "common notions" that are common between believers and non-believers because their difference in principle has not been taken into consideration. Common grace is not a gift of God whereby his own challenge to repentance unto men who have sinned against him is temporarily being blurred.

Common grace must rather serve the challenge of God to men to repentance. It must be a tool by means of which the believer as the servant of Christ can challenge the unbeliever to repentance. Believers can objectively show to unbelievers that unity of science can be attained only on the Christian theistic basis. It is the idea of God's controlling whatsoever comes to pass that forms the foundation of science. And no one can or does believe that idea unless by the sovereign grace of God through Christ he has repented from his sin. Thus it is Christianity that furnishes the basis of the structure of science.

If men will not repent and accept Christianity then they will still contribute to the structure of science. But then their contributions will be in spite of themselves as ethically responsible beings. It will be through themselves as creatures of God but it will be in spite of them as alienated from God. If they would enjoy the fruits of their labors they must, by the grace of God, come into the fold of God.

A word may now be said about the theistic proofs. The difference of opinion regarding them between Reformed men is the same in nature as the difference with respect to the idea of "common notions" and "facts." There are those who, like Ridderbos, want to ignore the difference between common notions that are common metaphysically and therefore psychologically and common notions that spring from either the root idea of autonomy or from the idea of regeneration. There are those who, like Ridderbos, want to ignore the difference between a Christian and a non-Christian philosophy of fact in certain limited areas of interpretation. They would use the idea of common grace in the interest of an area of commonness with little or no difference.

This position, it has been shown, leads away from Calvin and back to Thomas Aquinas. It is no wonder that Ridderbos, and they who believe like him, also has a view of the theistic proofs that involves a return to a natural theology of the Romanist sort. And this too he seeks to accomplish through the idea of common grace. He does not, indeed, discuss the matter of theistic proofs more than in passing form. But he says in effect that, as the result of ignoring the distinctions between common notions psychologically and common notions epistemologically conceived, it is possible to regard the proofs as having value as witnesses to God. They are not then to be regarded as having mathematical cogency but they are means by which the Christian position can be defended before the "natural reason" as well as any other position can.

> Because Van Til denies, that believers and unbelievers have anything in common epistemologically, he cannot appreciate the "proofs" as being witnesses. But when with Bavinck one allows for a certain epistemological commonness, then one can put the question as to what one can accomplish in this territory with the proofs for the existence of God. And then one will come to the conclusion, that nothing can be mathematically demonstrated in this field, but that the Christian position can be defended before the "natural reason" as well as that of others.[7]

A few remarks must suffice in this connection. The proofs may be formulated either on a Christian or on a non-Christian basis. They are formulated on a Christian basis if, with Calvin, they rest clearly upon the ideas of creation and providence. They then appeal to what the natural man, because he is a creature of God, actually does know to be true. They are bound to find immediate response of inward assent in the natural man. He cannot help but own to himself that God does exist.

When the proofs are thus formulated they have absolute probative force. They are not demonstrable in the sense that this word is often taken. As often taken, the idea of demonstration is that of exhaustive penetration by the mind of man; pure deduction of one conclusion after another from an original premise that is obvious. Such a notion of demonstration does not comport with the Christian system. That system is analogical. Man cannot penetrate through the relations of the Creator to the creature. But this does not in the least reduce the probative force of the proofs. Man is internally certain of God's existence only because his sense of deity is correlative to the revelation of God about him. And all the revelation of God is clear.

[7] *Idem*, p. 47.

If then they are used as witnesses it is because they have absolute probative force. They could not be used as witnesses if they had no probative force. To what God would they witness unless to the true and only living God? And if they witness to the true God they must witness to him as being what he is. And he is that One who cannot but exist. And when he is seen to be such the world is, in the same act, seen of necessity to be existing as the creation of God.

Thus the Christian-theistic position must be shown to be not *as defensible as* some other position; it must rather be shown to be *the position which alone does not annihilate intelligent human experience.*

In other words Ridderbos tones down the objective claims of God upon men by saying that there is no absolute probative force in the proofs for the existence of God. This is in line with the idea of seeking common notions in some twilight zone of semi-neutrality between believers and unbelievers. And this is also in line with the idea that there is an area of factual interpretation where the difference between autonomy and regeneration need not to be taken into account. This is in line, in short, with the Romanist notion of natural theology which holds that man does justice by the evidence if he concludes that God *probably* exists. But all this is out of line with Calvin's *Institutes* which stress with greatest possible force that the revelation of God to man is so clear that it has absolute compelling force objectively.

On the other hand the position of Ridderbos virtually allows that the proofs have some probative force even when they are not clearly founded upon a Christian basis. He says that the Christian position can *as well* be defended as any other. But even if it be said that Christianity is more probably true than is the non-Christian position this is still to allow that objectively something can be said for the truth of the non-Christian position. Something objectively valid can be said for idol worship as well as for worship of the true God. In other words on his general approach Ridderbos cannot show negatively that if one interprets life on the assumption of human autonomy there is no meaning to human experience.

Thus lowering the objective claims of the gospel, thus reducing the challenge of God and his servants upon sinful men by allowing that the principles of these sinful men have a measure of objective validity in them, is the natural result of the doctrine of common grace advocated by Ridderbos.

Herewith we are led back to the question of Scripture as identifying itself as the Word of God and of the system of truth set forth in Scripture as that in terms of which alone human experience in all of its aspects has meaning. The ideas of natural theology, discussed in the preceding chapter, and the idea of common grace, discussed in this chapter, must themselves be interpreted in terms of this self-attesting Scripture. If they are used independently of Scripture in order by means of them to effect a common territory of quasi- or complete neutrality between those who believe in God and those who do not, they are apologetically worse than useless. For then they make it impossible to distinguish clearly between the Christian and the non-Christian position. And in doing so the non-believer is not clearly shown why he should forsake his position. If it be allowed that he can interpret any aspect of experience in terms of his principles without destroying the very idea of intelligibility, he has a full right to claim that there is then no reason why he cannot in terms of his principles interpret the whole of experience. "Ye are my witnesses." That is the word of the covenant God to those he has redeemed. They are such and can be such only if they bear witness to a God who cannot do otherwise than bear witness of himself by means of himself. Christians can bear witness of this God only if they humbly but boldly make the claim that only on the presupposition of the existence of this God and of the universe in all its aspects as the revelation of this God is there any footing and verge for the interpretative efforts of man.

CHAPTER IX

ARGUMENT BY PRESUPPOSITION

In the preceding chapters it has been our contention that the Christian position cannot be "proved" by the traditional method of apologetics. The traditional method of apologetics was devised by Roman Catholic theologians and fits their theology.

Protestant apologetics starts by listening with loving obedience to God who identifies himself to man in Christ as his creator and redeemer. Christ's voice is, in the nature of the case, the voice of authority. Believers accept his Word for what it is by the inward work of the Holy Spirit, bearing witness by and with the Word in their hearts.

A truly Protestant apologetic must therefore make its beginning from the presupposition that the triune God, Father, Son and Holy Spirit, speaks to him with absolute authority in Scripture.

Does this imply the end of all reasoning? Only he who assumes, with the Romanist, that it is possible to find a firm foundation for human predication on some form or other of non-Christian thought, can claim that it does. But once we have followed the development of non-Christian thought and motivation, and have found that it always leads toward the destruction of predication, we think otherwise. For then it appears that we could never ourselves, as believers, have seen and acknowledged the futility of reasoning on non-Christian foundations unless we were already standing on Christian foundations.

Every form of intellectual argument rests, in the last analysis, upon one or the other of two basic presuppositions. The non-Christian's process of reasoning rests upon the presupposition that man is the final or ultimate reference point in human predication. The Christian's process of reasoning rests upon the presupposition that God, speaking through Christ by his Spirit in the infallible Word, is the final or ultimate reference point in human predication.

The unqualified acceptance of the authority of Christ speaking in Scripture, so far from excluding the possibility of fruitful discussion with unbelievers, is rather the only possible foundation for it. If reality were the sort of thing that non-Christian thinking assumes it to be, something not created and not controlled by God, then there would be no possibility of human knowledge of it at all. And if the human person were the sort of thing that non-Christian thinking assumes it to be, something sprung by chance from chance, then there would be no possibility of it knowing the world at all. It is just because the world and man are, as the Scriptures teach, created for one another and directed toward their goal through redemption by Christ, that human predication is possible. And by the same token reasoning with unbelievers is possible and fruitful for believers just so far as believers remain true to their own basic presupposition. True to this presupposition they can, *for argument's sake,* place themselves with the unbeliever on his presupposition, in order then to show him that he cannot even raise an intelligible objection against the Christian view. For in objecting to the Christian view he has to presuppose its truth.

It is well, however, that we listen to the objections made against this position by one who is himself an adherent of the Reformed Faith, and one who claims to follow the methodology of Charles Hodge and of B. B. Warfield. In his magazine, *The Bible Today,* Dr. J. Oliver Buswell, Jr. wrote a lengthy analysis and criticism of the views of the present writer. What follows in this chapter is a quotation at length from my reply to his strictures. The reply takes the form of direct address to Dr. Buswell.

The God of the Bible Differs From All Other Gods

In speaking of the God of the Bible it is, I believe, of the utmost importance that we speak of him first as he is in himself prior to his relation to the created world and man. Reformed theologians therefore distinguish between the ontological and the economical Trinity, the former referring to the three persons of the Godhead in their internal relations to one another, the latter referring to the works of this triune God with respect to the created universe. With respect to the ontological Trinity I try to follow Calvin in stressing that there is no subordination of essence as between the three persons. As Warfield points out when speaking of Calvin's doctrine of the Trinity " . . . the Father, the Son, the Spirit is each this one God, the entire divine essence being in each"; (*Calvin and Calvinism,* p. 232). In the syllabi to which you refer and with which you are familiar, I have spoken of the equal ultimacy of the one and the many or of unity and diversity in the Godhead. I use this philosophical language in order the better to be able to contrast the Biblical idea of the Trinity with philosophical theories that are based upon human experience as ultimate. When philosophers speak of the one and many problems they are simply seeking for unity in the diversity of human experience. In order to bring out that it is Christianity alone that has that for which men are looking but cannot find I use the terminology of philosophy, always making plain that my meaning is exclusively derived from the Bible as the word of

God. "In the Bible alone do we hear of such a God. Such a God, to be known at all, cannot be known otherwise than by virtue of his own voluntary revelation. He must therefore be known for what he is, and known to the extent that he is known, by authority alone" (*Common Grace,* p. 8).

Take now these two points together (a) that I have consistently stressed the necessity of asking what God is in himself prior to his relation to the created universe and (b) that I have consistently opposed all subordinationism within the self-contained Trinity and it will appear why I have also consistently opposed correlativism between God and the universe and therefore correlativism between God and man. By correlativism I understand a mutually interdependent relationship like that of husband and wife or the convex and the concave side of a disk. I know of no more pointed way of opposing all forms of identity philosophy and all forms of dialectical philosophy and theology. I have also spoken of this self-contained Trinity as "our concrete universal." Judging merely by the sound of this term you charge me with holding Hegelianism. I specify clearly that my God is precisely that which the Hegelian says God is not and yet you insist that I am a Hegelian.

I have further said that in God, as he exists in himself, apart from his relation to the world, thought and being are coterminous. Are they not? Is God's consciousness not exhaustively aware of his being? Would you believe with Brightman that there is a "given" element in God? God is light and in him is no darkness at all.

God's Decree Controls All Things

I further hold that the self-sufficient triune God "from all eternity did, by the most wise and holy counsel of his own will, freely and unchangeably ordain whatsoever comes to pass—." This is what I mean when I say that God is the ultimate cause back of all things. In this terminology I am merely reproducing Calvin's argument against Pighius in *The Eternal Predestination of God.* (See Henry Cole, *Calvin's Calvinism.*) Calvin speaks of *remote* and *proximate* causes. I simply use the word *ultimate* instead of *remote.* I do not think there is any essential difference between Calvin's usage of the word *remote* and my usage of the word *ultimate*.

In various works Calvin had maintained the all-inclusiveness of the decree of God. This, Pighius had argued, was in effect to make God the author of sin. Calvin denies vigorously that he makes God the author of sin. "I have with equal constancy, asserted that the eternal death to which man rendered himself subject so proceeded from his own fault that God cannot, in any way, be considered the author of it" (*Calvin's Calvinism*, p. 127). Here Calvin makes the distinction between remote and proximate causes. As the proximate cause of sin man is guilty before God. "But now, removing as I do from God all the *proximate cause* of the act in the Fall of man, I thereby remove from him also all the *blame* of the act leaving man alone under the sin and the guilt" (*Idem*, p. 128). But Pighius argues that if man is the responsible cause of his sin, then God's eternal reprobation must logically be denied. He identifies Calvin's conception of proximate cause with *the cause*, that is the *only* cause. To this Calvin replies again by means of his distinction between remote and proximate causes. There could be no responsible proximate cause unless there were also an all-comprehensive remote cause. He clinches his point by indicating that the doctrine of free grace cannot be maintained except upon the presupposition of a remote or ultimate cause back of the proximate cause. "If the wickedness of man be still urged as the *cause* of the difference between the elect and the non-elect, this wickedness might indeed be made to appear more powerful than the grace of God which he shows toward the elect, if that solemn truth did not stand in the way of such an argument: 'I will have mercy on whom I will have mercy'" (*Idem*, p. 80). Dealing with the blindness of sinners referred to in Acts 28:25, 26, Calvin says: "Some persons will here erroneously and ignorantly conclude that *the cause* and beginning of this obduracy in the Jews was their malicious wickedness. Just as if there were no deeper and more occult *cause* of the wickedness itself, namely, the original corruption of nature! And as if they did not remain sunk in this corruption *because*, being reprobated by the secret counsel of God before they were born, they were left undelivered!" (*Idem*, p. 81). Speaking still further of the cause of the sinner's blindness and of the Evangelist John's exposition of the famous Isaiah passage on this subject Calvin says: "Now, most certainly John does not here give us to understand that the Jews were prevented from believing by their sinfulness. For though this be quite true in one sense, yet *the cause* of their not believing must be traced to a far higher source. The secret and eternal purpose and counsel of God must be viewed as the original cause of their blindness and unbelief" (*Idem*, p. 81). Again he adds: "The unbelief of the world, therefore, ought not to astonish us, if even the wisest and most acute of men fail to believe. Hence, unless we would elude the plain and confessed meaning of the Evangelist, that few receive the gospel, we must fully conclude that *the cause* is *the will of God*; and that the outward sound of that gospel strikes the ear in vain until God is pleased to touch them by the heart within" (*Idem*, p. 82).

When therefore you object to my saying that "God is the ultimate cause back of whatsoever comes to pass" you will also need to reject Calvin's distinction between proximate and remote causes. I was simply reproducing Calvin's argument against Pighius. With Pighius you will have to say that man's deeds of wickedness are *the cause*, the *only* or *final* cause of his eternal state. And therewith you have, as Calvin points out, virtually denied the doctrine of the sovereign grace of God in the case of the elect. I do not think that you can show how Ephesians 1:11 which says that God "worketh all things after the counsel of his own will" is a "very different statement" from saying that God is the ultimate or remote cause back of all things, without falling into Arminianism.

I was much surprised when you objected to my simple reproduction of Calvin's argument. I could not imagine that as a Calvinist you would hold with Pighius against Calvin. So I looked up your own discussion of freedom in your book, "*Sin and Atonement*." In your argument against determinism you assert: "We hold that there is genuine and absolute freedom within certain areas of human life, a freedom for which God himself in his infinite foreknowledge holds man absolutely responsible" (p. 49). Then, speaking of your own choice of becoming a violinist or a missionary you add: "There was a period of time when the decision though foreknown of God was still indeterminate—" (*Idem*, p. 50). In opposing determinism you do not carefully distinguish between fatalism and Calvinism. You do not mention foreordination but only foreknowledge. You speak of man having "absolute freedom" in certain areas, and of the result as being "indeterminate" without saying that it was indeterminate only in the sense that you as a man did not know the outcome. Add all this to your peremptory rejection of my reproduction of Calvin's argument and the question cannot be repressed to what extent you would hold to Calvin's position rather than to that of Pighius.

Do you think Charles Hodge's "great chapter distinguishing between necessity and certainty, showing that complete certainty is not dependent upon the idea of necessity" is out of agreement with Calvin's doctrine of God as the *remote* cause of all things? If you can show it to be such it will surely be "anathema" to me; if you cannot show it to be such why should you object to my statement that God's decree is the *ultimate* though not the immediate cause of all things? Hodge says: "It may, however, be remarked that there is no difficulty attending the doctrine of foreordination which does not attach to that of foreknowledge. The latter supposes the certainty of free acts, and the former secures their certainty" (*Systematic Theology,* II, p. 301). Or again, being the cause of all things God knows everything by knowing himself; all things possible, by the knowledge of his power, and all things actual by the knowledge of his own purposes" (*Idem I,* p. 398). Again, "The futurition of events, according to the Scriptures, depends on the foreordination of God who foreordains whatever comes to pass" (*Idem I,* p. 400).

Your readers must certainly have been amazed at hearing that I unequivocally teach that God is the author of sin. You assert: "To say that Calvin knew that his opponent could 'rightly insist that God is the cause of sin,' is a direct contradiction of the statement, based upon many scores of Scripture passages, that 'neither is God the author of sin'" (p. 76). What did I actually say? "If God is the ultimate cause back of whatsoever comes to pass, Pighius can, on his basis, rightly insist that God is the author of sin" (*Common Grace,* p. 66). First you misquote me. You quote me as saying: *on this basis* while I say *on his* basis. Then in your reproduction of my argument you omit this all-important phrase *on his basis.* Omitting that phrase makes me say the exact opposite of what I actually said. Pighius denies the validity of the distinction between remote and proximate causes. Accordingly he holds that a proximate cause in Calvin's sense of the term is no *real* cause and that the only real cause of sin *on Calvin's basis* must be God. Is he logically inconsistent *with his own assumption* when he reasoned thus? He is not. Calvin does not say that he is. He points to no flaw in Pighius' reasoning. Instead he points to the necessity of introducing the distinction between remote and proximate causes. Then and then only, Calvin argues, is it really possible to establish the exclusive responsibility of man for sin. For then, and then only, is the freedom of man really established and are secondary causes given a true foundation.[1]

In this connection you further assert: "It is of course characteristic of the school of thought to which Dr. Van Til belongs to deny the possibility of any distinction between God's permissive decrees and his compelling decrees" (p. 46). Was there any necessity for thus lumping me with a "school of thought" and asserting or suggesting that as a member of such a school I must hold so and so when as a matter of fact I do speak of the permission of God with respect to sin? (See the Syllabus on *Introduction to Theology, Vol. II,* p. 217.) But I am anxious that what God permits be not set in contrast over against that which God foreordains. In that case the will of man would again be thought of as the final or ultimate cause of its own acts and therewith God's grace be denied. (The reader may find Calvin's evaluation of the idea of God's permission of sin in *Calvin's Calvinism,* p. 244.) Are your "permissive decrees" in no sense "compelling decrees"? Would you deny the ultimate efficiency of God in order to make room for the entrance of sin? If you are not to make your distinction between permissive and compelling decrees to fall into a virtual argument for an Arminian conception of the freedom of the will how can you avoid saying with Calvin that "whatsoever men do, they do according to the *eternal will and secret purpose of God*"? (*Idem,* p. 205.)

The same school of thought to which I am supposed to belong is accustomed, you say, "to stop in the ninth chapter of Romans with the great and profound truth of the twentieth verse,

[1] The reader is referred to *The Bible Today* (Vol. 42, No. 7) for Dr. Buswell's remarks on this point.

O man, who art thou that repliest against God'" without going on to the twenty-second verse in which Paul "so simply explains" why God brought Pharaoh into existence (p. 46). Well I am not in the habit of stopping with the twentieth verse any more than was Calvin. But neither do I think that the twentieth verse gives a merely arbitrary statement about God while the twenty-second verse gives a more profound reason for God's dealings with Pharaoh. In complete contrast with Calvin's approach (see *Calvin's Calvinism,* p. 246) you assert, while speaking of the passages of Romans 9:20, 21 and 9:22, 23: "I do wish to emphasize very forcefully that the Apostle Paul does not stop with the first merely arbitrary answer. He goes forward to suggest a further and a much more profound analysis of God's plan of redemption" (*What is God,* p. 53). I do not think the will of God is an arbitrary reason. I believe with Calvin that God's will "is and must be, the highest rule of all equity" (*Op cit.,* p. 190). I do not think that the explanation given in the twenty-second verse is offered as more profound or more ultimate than the point made in verse twenty. "Taking, then, an honest and sober review of the whole of this high and Divine matter," says Calvin, "the plain and indubitable conclusion will be that *the will of God* is the one principal and all-high *cause* of all things in heaven and earth" (*Idem,* p. 246). Or again, "But as the will of God is the surest rule of all righteousness, that will ought ever to be to us the principal reason, yea—if I may so speak—the reason of all reasons!" (*Idem,* p. 247.) But Calvin desires that his distinction between proximate and remote causes be always observed. It is because his adversaries have failed to make this distinction which he considers so essential that they have done him grave injustice. "Our adversaries load us with illiberal and disgraceful calumny, when they cast it in our teeth that we make God the author of sin, by maintaining that his will is the cause of all things that are done" (*Idem,* p. 251). Making the distinction between proximate and remote causes enables Calvin to do full justice to the longsuffering of God without giving up the decree of God as basic to whatsoever comes to pass.[2]

[2] Calvin's distinction between God the remote or ultimate Cause and man the immediate or proximate cause answers my present critics as it did Pighius and Dr. Buswell.

On the question of creation I believe that it pleased God "for the manifestation of the glory of his eternal power, wisdom, and goodness, in the beginning, to create, or make of nothing, the world, and all things therein, whether visible or invisible, in the space of six days and all very good." This doctrine of creation fits in with the doctrine of the ontological trinity. If God is fully self-contained then there was no sort of half existence and no sort of non-being that had any power over against him. There was therefore no impersonal law of logic that told God what he could do and there was no sort of stuff that had as much even as refractory power over against God when he decided to create the world.

I have not merely held but have also frequently defended this doctrine. I have defended it not merely against those who openly reject it or assert it to be impossible on the basis of logic as was the case with Parmenides. I have defended it against those who assumed the existence of some sort of limiting power next to God. I have in particular defended it against all forms of modern dialecticism, whether Hegelian or Barthian.

For all that you charge me with holding to something like a Platonic realism. You first assert that I mean by "autonomous man" "man as an actually existing substantive entity" (p. 56). Then you add that you fear that I do not believe in man as being created as such an entity. As a matter of fact I have frequently explained that by the term "autonomous man" I mean the idea of a man who *virtually* denies his createdness. As created in paradise man was a distinct ontological entity over against God. As made perfect he recognized that God his creator was also his lawgiver. Of his own accord, according to the law of his own being as God had made him, he was therefore a covenant keeper. But with the entrance of sin man was no longer willing to obey the law of his maker. He became a covenant breaker. He sought to be a law unto himself, that is, he sought to be autonomous. Speaking of my meaning of the word autonomous you say: "I do not think he means eternal or uncreated." But why can I not mean "uncreated" when I assert that I do? I do not say that all men openly assert that they are non-created. What I have asserted time and again is that men *virtually* assume or presuppose that they are non-created. If they do not assume or presuppose that they are created then what else are they doing than assuming or presupposing that they are not created and therefore are not responsible to their creator? Is this too broad and sweeping a statement to make about all sinners? The daily newspaper is unintelligible on any other basis. There are those who worship and serve the creature and there are those who worship and serve the Creator. This is the simple differentiation with which I am concerned. I try to call men back to the recognition of the fact that they are creatures of God by challenging their false assumption of their non-createdness, their autonomy or ultimacy.

A word may here be said about the relation of the ontological Trinity to temporal creation. You assert the following: "The doctrine of paradox comes to its extreme expression in the words . . . 'we have, in our doctrines of the ontological Trinity and temporal creation cut ourselves loose once and for all from correlativism between God and man'" (p. 47). Then you criticize my rejection of correlativism as though in rejecting it I were rejecting the idea of man's relatedness to and dependence upon God. Was there any need for giving my words such a construction? Even the sentence following upon the one you quote shows that I am arguing for the God of the Bible who is back of history, who has his plan for history against those who speak of a comprehensive reality which includes God and man in one whole. Does it follow that I reject the Bible with its doctrine of God's creation of man and the world because I reject the teaching which connects God *necessarily* with the world or makes him a principle within the world?

At this point I may say a brief word on your statement, "Van Til holds that holiness and truth are created by the *will* of God" (p. 53). But I have neither said nor implied any such thing anywhere. You refer to pp. 6, 7, 65, of *Common Grace*. On p. 6, I am arguing against Platonic realism. Does that make me a nominalist? If I reject one error must I hold to an opposite error? I find nothing on p. 7 that has any bearing on the subject unless in your mind it is the sentence, "Romanism and Arminianism have virtually allowed that God's counsel need not always and everywhere be taken as our principle of individuation." Perhaps you object to this because you hold that man has been created "to be the *ultimate cause* of the acts for which he is morally responsible" (*What is God,* p. 38). Even so is there anything in what I say here or anywhere else that justifies you in saying that I hold that God's will acts independently of his character? On p. 65 I quote Calvin to the effect that the will of God is "the highest rule of righteousness." Do you disagree with Calvin? Do you want to by-pass the will of God in order thus to reach God's character? Is Calvin also a nominalist?

Sin and Its Implications

As far as I know my mind I hold sin to be that which the Confession and catechisms say it is. This involves the historicity of the Genesis account.

I have defended that time and again, particularly against Barth, Brunner and Niebuhr. It involves, I believe, also the covenant theology. God dealt with every man that was to come into the world through Adam the first man as their representative. Even when they do not yet exist as historical individuals men are thought of by God and treated by God through Adam the first historically existent man. So in the passage you quote I speak of all men as existing in Adam their common representative. You yourself say, "I sinned in Adam specifically and precisely because he, an individual, represented me—stood as the federal and representative head of all mankind in this original act of sin" (p. 57). Do I say anything else? You say, "I sinned in Adam." Did you then not in some sense exist in Adam? When I first say of sinners that in paradise "they do not yet exist" obviously I mean as "historical individuals." When then I add in the next sentences, "yet they do exist. They exist in Adam as their common representative," you speak of this as Platonic realism. I could say the same thing of your position not merely for as good a reason but for the same reason. You yourself quote Genesis 2:15-17 and then add: "In this passage we see humanity in the image of God in 'knowledge, righteousness, and holiness,' given the opportunity of exercising free will," (*Sin and Atonement,* p. 23). Is this also Platonic realism?

You even go so far as to say: "The reader will remember that, for Van Til, Adam is not an individual but 'mankind'" (p.

59). You have not the least bit of justification for making such a charge. You admit that I believe in the infallibility of the Bible. How could I believe in that unless I believed the historicity of the Genesis story? You claim to be familiar with the contents of my class syllabi as well as with what I have published. The article on "Nature and Scripture" in *The Infallible Word* is utterly unintelligible without the assumption of the historicity of the story of Adam as an individual in paradise. How could I speak of Adam as representing man in paradise unless I thought of Adam as the first individual man that lived? I have defended the historicity of the Genesis account on more than one occasion, against Barth, against Hegel and against Niebuhr. Even in the little pamphlet on *Why I Believe in God* I explained that in my infancy a "formula was read over me at my baptism which solemnly asserted that I had been conceived and born in sin, the idea being that my parents, like all men, had inherited sin from Adam, the first man and the representative of the human race," adding a little further on that though later made acquainted with the arguments for evolution and higher criticism I had not in the least given up the faith of my childhood.

As to *Common Grace* its whole argument is surcharged with the historicity of the story of the Bible.

Even in the immediate context of the words you quote I speak of the relation of the *earlier* and the *later* in history. "To set the problem before us as clearly as possible, we do well to think of it in connection with Adam in paradise. Would it be possible to maintain that only by the later revelation of God's final purpose could anything be known of his attitude toward man? Then Adam would at the beginning have known nothing of God's attitude toward him. No revelation of God's final purpose had yet been made. The whole future, as far as Adam's knowledge was concerned, was conditioned by his obedience or disobedience" (p. 71). From this point on I begin speaking about *man*. "Man was originally created good." Even so I continue to mention Adam as an historical individual, and speak of his "representative act of obedience or disobedience." How could I speak of Adam as engaged in paradise in a *representative* act if I were identifying him with mankind? Then on page 72 I go on to speak of the elect and the non-elect and of what they have in common. The argument is that *in paradise*, at the beginning of history Adam acted for all of them representatively. They have had things done with respect to them by their common representative. I am speaking of Adam in paradise at the beginning of history, when they did not themselves exist as historical individuals. On page 73 the argument goes on to the effect that the original situation was an historically unfinished situation. "Whether Adam (the Adam who existed historically in paradise) was to obey or disobey, the situation would be changed." Is it wrong after all this to say: "We need not hesitate to affirm, then, that in the beginning God loved mankind in general. That was before mankind had sinned against God. A little later God hated mankind in general. That was after mankind had sinned against God" (p. 74). Is it wrong to say, "When man first sinned he did not know God as fully as we know him now, but he did know God for what he is, as far as he knew him at all. And it was *mankind*, not some individual elect or reprobate person that sinned against God"? Have not all men who appeared or will appear as historical individuals after Adam sinned in Adam their common representative in paradise?

Christ and His Work

My reason for stressing this matter is that together with all orthodox believers I have frequently argued, as you know, that the historicity of Christianity cannot be maintained unless the historicity of the Old Testament and in particular the historicity of the Genesis account be also maintained. But then, having been "deeply mired in Hegelian idealistic pantheism" and holding to God as the "concrete universal" I should, to be consistent, you argue, also deny the uniqueness of Christ. "What becomes of the incarnation?" (p. 49.) But I hold to temporal creation and to the incarnation in the orthodox sense of the term not because of an inconsistency but because it is taught in Scripture. At the same time the doctrines of the self-sufficient God, of temporal creation and of the incarnation are not inconsistent with one another. They are all part of the one system of doctrine of Holy Writ.

Charles Hodge with whose statement of the Reformed faith you say you agree "with great delight in almost every point" begins his chapter under the above given title by indicating what is not involved in the question. He says (a) that it does not in the first place, concern "the nature of Christ's work," (b) that it does not concern "the value of Christ's satisfaction. That Augustinians admit to be infinite," (c) that it "does not concern the suitableness of the atonement. What was suitable for one was suitable for all," (d) that it "does not concern the actual application of the redemption purchased by Christ. The parties to this controversy are agreed that some only, and not all of mankind, are to be actually saved" (*Systematic Theology, II*, pp. 544, 545). He concludes his introductory section by saying, "The simple question is, had the death of Christ a reference to the elect which it had not for other men? Did he come into the world to secure the salvation of those given to him by the Father, so that the other effects of his work are merely incidental to what was done for the attainment of that object" (*Idem*, p. 546).

He goes on to argue that God from eternity "determined to save one portion of the human race and not another." He says that it seems to be contradictory to say "that the Father sent his Son to die for those whom he had predetermined not to save, as truly as, and in the same sense that he gave him up for those whom he had chosen to make the heirs of salvation" (*Idem*, p. 548). He points to Ephesians 5:25 where Christ is said to have laid down his life for his Church. He points to John 15:13 where Christ is said to have laid down his life for his friends. He points to John 11:52 where the whole mission of Christ is summed up in the task of gathering together in one the children of God that are scattered abroad. Then he adds: "When mankind are divided into two classes, the Church and the world, the friends and the enemies of God, the sheep and the goats, whatever is affirmed distinctly of the one class is impliedly denied of the other" (*Idem*, p. 549).

You assert that my "unqualified statement that 'Christ has not died for all men' is intolerable" (p. 47). But I was again simply reproducing Calvin's argument against Pighius. Pighius had argued that one who believed in the doctrine of election could not consistently also believe in the genuineness of the general offer of salvation to all men. Calvin replies that he believes in both. Moreover, he offers his distinction between remote and proximate cause as the reason why he can hold to both *without* contradiction. Christ has not died for all men, in the sense of intending actually to save them all. But the "special reference" of Christ's work (as Charles Hodge calls it) with respect to the elect does not make void the *general* call to repentance. From the immediate context of the words you object to it appears that as Calvin argued against Pighius I am arguing against those who deny common grace *for* the genuineness of the general reference of Christ's work. My statement therefore is (a) not unqualified, (b) is part of an argument which *defends* rather than rejects the importance of what Hodge calls the "merely incidental" effects of Christ's work, (c) is designed to oppose the idea that the doctrines of Christianity which seem to unbelievers to be contradictory are really contradictory. If my position is intolerable to you that of Hodge must be also.

Apologetics

Coming now to a brief statement of the method of defense that I use for the propagation of what I believe and how it differs from the traditional method I may note first that you have not, for all the length of your article, anywhere given a connected picture of my argument. Yet you at once characterize it in contrast with your own as being "negative and universal." Without the least bit of qualification I am said to deny "that there is common ground of reasoning between those who accept Christian presuppositions and engage in the spread of the gospel, and those who do not accept Christian presuppositions and reject the gospel" (p. 41). The facts are far otherwise.

I am, to be sure, opposed to the traditional method of apologetics as this has found its most fundamental expression in the *Summae* of Thomas Aquinas the Roman Catholic and in Bishop Butler the Arminian. I seek to oppose Roman Catholicism and Arminianism in Apologetics as I seek to oppose it in theology. Does that make my main thesis universally negative? I think there is a better and more truly Biblical way of reasoning with and winning unbelievers than the Romanist Arminian method permits.

To begin with then I take what the Bible says about God and his relation to the universe as unquestionably true on its own authority. The Bible requires men to believe that he exists apart from and above the world and that he by his plan controls whatever takes place in the world. Everything in the created universe therefore displays the fact that it is controlled by God, that it is what it is by virtue of the place that it occupies in the plan of God. The objective evidence for the existence of God and of the comprehensive governance of the world by God is therefore so plain that he who runs may read. Men cannot get away from this evidence. They see it round about them. They see it within them. Their own constitution so clearly evinces the facts of God's creation of them and control over them that there is no man who can possibly escape observing it. If he is self-conscious at all he is also God-conscious. No matter how men may try they cannot hide from themselves the fact of their own createdness. Whether men engage in inductive study with respect to the facts of nature about them or engage in analysis of their own self-consciousness they are always face to face with God their maker. Calvin stresses these matters greatly on the basis of Paul's teachings in Romans.

In maintaining the essential clarity of all of the created universe as revelational of God's existence and his plan Calvin is nothing daunted even by the fact of sin and its consequences. If there has been any "obscuration" in the revelation situation on account of sin this sin is in any case the fault of man. If in Adam, the first man, who acted for me representatively, I have scratched the mirror of God's general revelation round about and within me, I know at bottom that it is I who have scratched it. Men ought therefore, says Calvin, to conclude that when some individual sin is not punished immediately it will be punished later. Their consciences operate on this basis.

One thing should be particularly stressed in this connection. It is the fact that man today is sinful because of what happened at the beginning of history. "We are told that man could never have had any fruition of God through the revelation that came to him through nature as operating by itself. There was superadded to God's revelation in nature another revelation, a supernaturally communicated positive revelation. Natural revelation, we are virtually told, was from the outset incorporated into the idea of a covenant relationship of God with man. Thus every dimension of created existence, even the lowest, was enveloped in a form of exhaustively personal relationship between God and man. The 'ateleological' not less than the 'teleological,' the 'mechanical' no less than the 'spiritual,' was covenantal in character" (*The Infallible Word,* p. 259). Even in paradise, therefore, supernatural revelation was immediately conjoined with natural revelation. Revelation in and about man was therefore never meant to function by itself. "It was from the beginning insufficient without its supernatural concomitant. It was inherently a limiting notion" (*Idem,* p. 267).

Having taken these two, revelation in the created universe, both within and about man, and revelation by way of supernatural positive communication as aspects of revelation as originally given to man, we can see that natural revelation is even after the fall perspicuous in character. "The perspicuity of God's revelation in nature depends for its very meaning upon the fact that it is an aspect of the total and totally voluntary revelation of a God who is self-contained" (*Idem,* p. 269). God has an all comprehensive plan for the universe. "He has planned all the relationships between all the aspects of created being. He has planned the end from the beginning. All created reality therefore actually displays this plan. It is, in consequence, inherently rational" (*Idem,* p. 269).

At this point we may add the fact of Scriptural revelation. God has condescended to reveal himself and his plan in it to sinners. It is the same God who speaks in Scripture and in nature. But in Scripture he speaks of his grace to such as have broken his covenant, to such as have set aside his original revelation to them. And as the original revelation of God to man was clear so is the revelation of grace in Scripture. "The Scriptures as the finished product of God's supernatural and saving revelation to man have their own evidence in themselves" (*Idem,* p. 271).

In all of this there is one thing that stands out. It is that man has no excuse whatsoever for not accepting the revelation of God whether in nature, including man and his surroundings, or in Scripture. God's revelation is always clear.

The first and most basic point on which my approach differs from the traditional one is therefore that: (a) I start more frankly from the Bible as the source from which as an absolutely authoritative revelation I take my whole interpretation of life. Roman Catholicism also appeals to Scripture but in practice makes its authority void. Its final appeal is to the church and that is, in effect, to human experience. Even Arminianism rejects certain Scripture doctrines (e.g., election) because it cannot logically harmonize them with the general offer of salvation. (b) I stress the *objective clarity* of God's revelation of himself wherever it appears. Both Thomas Aquinas and Butler contend that men have done justice by the evidence if they conclude that God *probably* exists. (I have discussed the views of Aquinas in *The Infallible Word* and those of Butler in the *Syllabus on Evidences.*) I consider this a compromise of simple and fundamental Biblical truth. It is an insult to the living God to say that his revelation of himself so lacks in clarity that man, himself through and through revelation of God, does justice by it when he says that God *probably* exists. "The argument for the existence of God and for the truth of Christianity is objectively valid. We should not tone down the validity of this argument to the probability level. The argument may be poorly stated, and may never be adequately stated. But in itself the argument is absolutely sound. Christianity is the only reasonable position to hold. It is not merely as reasonable as other positions, or a bit more reasonable than other positions; it alone is the natural and reasonable position for man to take. By stating the argument as clearly as we can, we may be the agents of the Holy Spirit in pressing the claims of God upon men. If we drop to the level of the merely probable truthfulness of Christian theism, we, to that extent, lower the claims of God upon men" (*Common Grace,* p. 62). Accordingly I do not reject "the theistic proofs" but merely insist on formulating them in such a way as not to compromise the doctrines of Scripture. "That is to say, if the theistic proof is constructed as it ought to be constructed, it is objectively valid, whatever the attitude of those to whom it comes may be"

(*Idem,* p. 49). (c) With Calvin I find the point of contact for the presentation of the gospel to non-Christians in the fact that they are made in the image of God and as such have the ineradicable sense of deity within them. Their own consciousness is inherently and exclusively revelational of God to themselves. No man can help knowing God for in knowing himself he knows God. His self-consciousness is totally devoid of content unless, as Calvin puts it at the beginning of his Institutes, man knows himself as a creature before God. There are "no atheistic men because no man can deny the revelational activity of the true God within him" (*Common Grace,* p. 55). Man's own interpretative activity, whether of the more or less extended type, whether in ratiocination or intuition, is no doubt the most penetrating means by which the Holy Spirit presses the claims of God upon man" (*Idem,* p. 62). Even man's negative ethical reaction to God's revelation within his own psychological constitution is revelational of God. His conscience troubles him when he disobeys; he knows deep down in his heart that he is disobeying his creator. There is no escape from God for any human being. Every human being is by virtue of his being made in the image of God accessible to God. And as such he is accessible to one who without compromise presses upon him the claims of God. Every man has capacity to reason logically. He can intellectually understand what the Christian position claims to be. Conjoined with this is the moral sense that he knows he is doing wrong when he interprets human experience without reference to his creator. I am therefore in the fullest agreement with Professor Murray when, in the quotation you give of him, he speaks of the natural man as having an "*apprehension of the truth of the gospel* that is *prior* to faith and repentance." But I could not thus speak with assurance that the natural man could have any such apprehension of the truth of the gospel if I held with the traditional view of Apologetics that man's self-consciousness is something that is intelligible without reference to God-consciousness. If man's self-consciousness did not actually depend upon his God-consciousness there would be no meaning to Romans 1:20. Each man would live in a world by himself. No man could even have that intellectual cognition of the gospel which is the prerequisite of saving faith. In short if the universe were not what the Calvinist, following Paul, says it is, it would not be a *universe*. There would be no system of truth. And if the mind of man were not what Calvin, following Paul, says it is, it could not even intellectually follow an argument for the idea that the universe is a *universe*. All arguments for such a universe would come to him as outside that universe.

Yet it is the very essence of the positions of Aquinas and Butler that human self-consciousness is intelligible without God-consciousness. Both make it their point of departure in reasoning with the non-believers that we must, at least in the area of things natural, stand on the ground of neutrality with them. And it is of the essence of all non-believing philosophy that self-consciousness is taken as intelligible by itself without reference to God. Moreover the very theology of both Romanism and Arminianism, as already noted, requires a measure of subtraction of the self-consciousness of men from its creaturely place. (d) Implied in the previous points is the fact that I do not artificially separate induction from deduction, or reasoning about the facts of nature from reasoning in *a priori* analytical fashion about the nature of human-consciousness. I do not artifically abstract or separate them from one another. On the contrary I see induction and analytical reasoning as part of one process of interpretation. I would therefore engage in historical apologetics. (I do not personally do a great deal of this because my colleagues in the other departments of the Seminary in which I teach are doing it better than I could do it.) Every bit of historical investigation, whether it be in the directly Biblical field, archaeology, or in general history, is bound to confirm the truth of the claims of the Christian position. But I would not talk endlessly about facts and more facts without ever challenging the non-believer's philosophy of fact. A really fruitful historical apologetic argues that every fact *is* and *must be* such as proves the truth of the Christian theistic position.

A fair presentation of my method of approach should certainly have included these basic elements that underlie everything else. (See the syllabi on *Apologetics* and *Introduction to Theology*, Vol. I.)

It is only in the light of this positive approach that my statements to the effect that epistemologically believers and non-believers have nothing in common can be seen for what it is. Even in *Common Grace* it is evident that by the sinner's epistemological reaction I mean his reaction as an ethically responsible creature of God. Does the sinner react properly to the revelation of God that surrounds him, that is within him and that comes to him from Scripture? As I have followed Calvin closely in stressing the fact that men *ought* to believe in God inasmuch as the evidence for his existence is abundantly plain, so I have also closely followed Calvin in saying that no sinner reacts properly to God's revelation. Is this too sweeping a statement? It is simply the doctrine of total depravity. All sinners are covenant breakers. They have an axe to grind. They do not want to keep God in remembrance. They keep under the knowledge of God that is within them. That is they try as best they can to keep under this knowledge for fear they should look into the face of their judge. And since God's face appears in every fact of the universe they oppose God's revelation everywhere. They do not want to see the facts of nature for what they are; they do not want to see themselves for what they are. Therefore they assume the non-createdness of themselves and of the facts and the laws of nature round about them. Even though they make great protestations of serving God they yet serve and worship the creature more than the Creator. They try to make themselves believe that God and man are aspects of one universe. They interpret all things immanentistically. Shall we in the interest of a point of contact admit that man can interpret anything correctly if he virtually leaves God out of the picture? Shall we who wish to prove that nothing can be explained without God first admit some things at least can be explained without him? On the contrary we shall show that all explanations without God are futile. Only when we do this do we appeal to that knowledge of God within men which they seek to suppress. This is what I mean by presupposing God for the possibility of intelligent predication.

You ask what person is consistent with his own principles. Well I have consistently argued that no one is and that least of all the non-Christian is. I have even argued in the very booklet that you review that if men were consistent they would be end products and that then there would be no more reasoning with them. However since sinners are not consistent, and have what is from their point of view an old man within them they can engage in science and in the general interpretation of the created universe and bring to light much truth. It is because the prodigal is not yet at the swine trough and therefore still has of the substance of the Father in his pockets that he can do that and discover that, which for the matter of it, is true and usable for the Christian. Why did you omit this all important element in what I teach? In a booklet largely written in the defense of the idea of "commonness" as between believers and unbelievers against those who deny it you find nothing but the opposite. If your contention is that I have said precisely the opposite of what I wanted to say you should in fairness at least have discussed the points just now discussed.

What then more particularly do I mean by saying that epistemologically the believer and the non-believer have nothing in common? I mean that every sinner looks through colored glasses. And these colored glasses are cemented to his face. He assumes that self-consciousness is intelligible without God-consciousness. He assumes that consciousness of facts is intelligible without consciousness of God. He assumes that consciousness of laws is intelligible without God. And he interprets all the facts and all the laws that are presented to him in terms of these assumptions. This is not to forget that he also, according to the old man within him, knows that God exists. But as a covenant breaker he seeks to suppress this. And I am now speaking of him as the covenant breaker. Neither do I forget that no man is actually fully consistent in working according to these assumptions. The non-believer does not fully live up to the new man within him which in his case is the man who worships the creature above all else, any more than does the Christian fully live up to the new man within him, which in his case is the man who worships the Creator above all else. But as it is my duty as a Christian to ask my fellow Christians as well as myself to suppress the old man within them, so it is my duty to ask non-believers to suppress not the old man but the new man within them.

The necessity for this can be observed every time there is some popular article on religion in one of the magazines. There was a questionnaire sent out recently by one of them asking a certain number of people whether they believed in God. By far the greater number of them said that they did. But from further questions asked it appeared that only a very small number believed in the God of the Bible, the Creator and Judge of men. Yet they said that they believed in God. From such an article it is apparent that every sinner has the sense of deity and therefore knows God as his Creator and Judge. But from such an article it is also apparent that *every* sinner seeks in one way or another to deny this. They are therefore without God in the world. They must, as Charles Hodge so well points out, be renewed *unto* knowledge (Colossians 3:10) as well as unto righteousness and holiness (Ephesians 4:24).

Now neither Aquinas nor Butler makes any such distinctions as I have made. And in that they are but consistent. They do not make the Creator-creature distinction absolutely fundamental in their own thinking. How then could they consistently ask others to do so? It is of the essence of their theology to maintain that God has made man so that he has such freedom as to be able to initiate something that is beyond the counsel of God. For them the human self therefore is supposed to be able to think of itself as intelligible and of the facts and laws of the world as manipulable and therefore intelligible apart from their relationship to God. I have already pointed out that for this reason the traditional view of apologetics has no universe and has no real point of contact in the unbeliever. If either Romanism or Arminianism were right in their view of the self-consciousness of man there could be no apologetics for Christianity at all. There would be no all-comprehensive plan of God. This much being clear it can be seen that the Romanist and the Arminian will, in consistence with their own theology, not be able to challenge the natural man's false assumptions. The traditional apologist must somehow seek for a point of contact within the thinking of the natural man as this thinking has been carried on upon false assumptions. He cannot seek to stir up the old man in opposition against the new man in the non-Christian. He makes no use of such a distinction. He will allow for gradational differences within the natural man. He will even make a great deal of these. To him therefore the passages of Paul to the effect that every man knows God and that man is made in the image of God are interpreted so as to do injustice to other equally important teaching of Scripture to the effect that the natural man knoweth not God. All this is compromising theology. It is no wonder that the Romanist and the Arminian will also follow a compromising apologetics.

The basic falseness of this apologetics appears in the virtual if not actual denial of the fact that the natural man makes false assumptions. Aquinas and Butler hold that the natural man, whom the Calvinist knows to be a covenant breaker and as such one who interprets God himself in terms of the universe, has some correct notions about God. I mean correct notions as to content, not merely as to form. Anyone who says "I believe in God," is formally correct in his statement, but the question is what does he mean by the word *God*? The traditional view assumes that the natural man has a certain measure of correct thought content when he uses the word God. In reality the natural man's "God" is always a finite God. It is his most effective tool for suppressing the sense of the true God that he cannot fully efface from the fibres of his heart.

The natural man's god is *always* enveloped within a Reality that is greater than his god and himself. He always makes Reality, inclusive of all that exists, the *All* the final subject of which he speaks. With Thales he will say *All* is water, with Anaximenes *All* is air. With others he may be a dualist or a pluralist or an atomist, a realist or a pragmatist. From the Christian point of view he still has a monistic assumption in that he makes Reality to be inclusive of God and himself. And there is not much that the traditional apologist can do about this. He has bound himself to confusion in apologetics as he has bound himself to error in theology. He must tie on to some small area of thought content that the believer and the unbeliever have in common without qualification when both are self-conscious with respect to their principle. This is tantamount to saying that those who interpret a fact as dependent upon God and those who interpret that same fact as not dependent upon God have yet said something identical about that fact.

All this is bound to lead to self-frustration on the part of the traditional apologist. Let us watch him for a moment. Think of him first as an inductivist. As such he will engage in "historical apologetics" and in the study of archaeology. In general he will deal with the "facts" of the universe in order to prove the existence of God. He cannot on his position challenge the assumption of the man he is trying to win. That man is ready for him. Think of the traditional apologist as throwing facts to his non-Christian friend as he might throw a ball. His friend receives each fact as he might a ball and throws it behind him in a bottomless pit. The apologist is exceedingly industrious. He shows the unbelieving friend all the evidence for theism. He shows all the evidence for Christianity, for instance, for the virgin birth and the resurrection of Christ. Let us think of his friend as absolutely tireless and increasingly polite. He will then receive all these facts and toss them behind him in the bottomless pit of pure possibility. "Is it not wonderful," he will say, "what strange things do happen in Reality. You seem to be a collector of oddities. As for myself I am more interested in the things that happen regularly. But I shall certainly try hard to explain the facts you mention in accord with the laws that I have found working so far. Perhaps we should say that laws are merely statistical averages and that nothing can therefore be said about any particular event ahead of its appearance. Perhaps there are very unusual things in reality. But what does this prove for the truth of your view?"

You see that the unbeliever who does not work on the presupposition of creation and providence is perfectly consistent with himself when he sees nothing to challenge his unbelief even in the fact of the resurrection of Christ. He may be surprised for a moment as a child that grows up is surprised at the strange things of life but then when he has grown up he realizes that "such is life." Sad to say the traditional Christian apologist has not even asked his unbelieving friend to see the facts for what they really are. He has not presented the facts at all. That is he has not presented the facts as they are according to the Christian way of looking at them and the Christian way of looking at them is the true way of looking at them. Every fact in the universe is what it is by virtue of the place that it has in the plan of God. Man cannot comprehensively know that plan. But he does know that there is such a plan. He must therefore present the facts of theism and of Christianity, of Christian theism, as proving Christian theism because they are intelligible as facts in terms of it and in terms of it alone.

But this is also in effect to say that the Christian apologist should never seek to be an inductivist only. He should present his philosophy of fact with his facts. He does not need to handle less facts in doing so. He will handle the same facts but he will handle them as they ought to be handled.

Now look at the traditional apologist when he is not an inductivist but an *a priori* reasoner. He will first show his fellow worker, the inductivist, that he defeats his own purposes. He will show that he who does not challenge the assumptions of his non-Christian friends has placed himself on a decline which inevitably leads down from Locke through Berkeley to Hume, the skeptic. Then for his own foundation he will appeal to some internal ineffable principles, to some *a priori* like that of Plato or of Descartes. He will appeal to the law of contradiction either positively or negatively and boldly challenge the facts to meet the requirements of logic. Then he will add that the facts of Christianity pass the examination *summa cum laude*. Well, they do. And in passing the examination they invariably pass out of existence too. He can only prove the immortality of the soul if with Plato he is willing to prove also that man is divine. He can only prove the universe to have order if with the Stoics he is also willing to say that God is merely its principle of order. With the Hegelian idealists such as Bradley and Bosanquet or Royce he will prove all the facts of the Bible to be true by weaving them into aspects of a Universe that allows for them as well as for their opposites.

But usually the traditional apologist is neither a pure inductivist nor a pure *a priorist*. Of necessity he has to be both. When engaged in inductive argument about facts he will therefore talk about these facts as proving the existence of God. If anything exists at all, he will say, something absolute *must* exist. But when he thus talks about what *must* exist and when he refuses even to admit that non-believers have false assumptions about their *musts*, let alone being willing to challenge them on the subject, he has in reality granted that the non-believer's conception about the relation of human logic to facts is correct. It does not occur to him that on any but the Christian theistic basis there is no possible connection of logic with facts at all. When the non-Christian, not working on the foundation of creation and providence, talks about *musts* in relation to *facts* he is beating the air. His logic is merely the exercise of a revolving door in a void, moving nothing from nowhere into the void. But instead of pointing out this fact to the unbeliever the traditional apologist appeals to this non-believer as though by his immanentistic method he could very well interpret many things correctly.

That this traditionalist type of apologetics is particularly impotent in our day I have shown in my review of Dr. Richardson's and Dr. Carnell's books on Apologetics. Dr. Richardson is a modernist. But he says he holds to the uniqueness of the facts of Christianity. At the same time he holds that this holding to the uniqueness of Christianity and its facts is not inconsistent with holding to a form of coherence that is placed upon human experience as its foundation. Dr. Carnell is an orthodox believer. To an extent he has even tried to escape from the weaknesses of the traditional method of apologetic argument. But he merely rejects its inductivist form. By and large he falls back into traditional methodology. And just to that extent he has no valid argument against Richardson. To the extent that he admits the type of coherence which Richardson holds to be valid he has to give up the uniqueness of the events of Christianity as he himself holds them. On the other hand, to the extent that he holds to the uniqueness of events the way Richardson holds to them, to that extent he has to give up the coherence to which he himself as an orthodox Christian should hold. (See *The Westminster Theological Journal,* November, 1948.)

Your own handling of the question of the immutability of God exhibits exactly the same difficulty. You speak of the dynamical self-consistency of God as a concept that will make it quite easy to see how God's immutability can be consistent with the genuine significance of facts in the course of history. But to the extent that you explain how the immutability of God can be consistent with the actuality of historical change you explain it away. You go so far as to define that very immutability in terms of God's constancy of relationship to the created temporal universe. "God's immutability consists in his perfectly unified plan in dealing with the world, which he created, God's absoluteness is in his perfectly consistent relatedness" (*What is God?* p. 32). Now if God's immutability is not first to be spoken of as an attribute that pertains to the character of God as he is in himself apart from his relation to the universe, then there is no problem any more because one of the factors of the problem has been denied. To the extent that you have explained you have also destroyed the fact to be explained. And to speak of self-consistency after first reducing the self to a relationship is meaningless. On the other hand you do not really hold to the identity of the being of God in himself with his relationship to the world. That is also plain from your general discussion of God. But then if you are to speak to an unbeliever with respect to the God who is really self-contained and ask him to think of this God along the lines of his own procedure, without challenging the assumptions that underlie that procedure, then he will simply say that such a God is so wholly beyond his experience that he can make nothing of him and that such a God is therefore meaningless to him. To this you can on your method offer him no adequate answer.

The general conclusion then is that on the traditional method it is impossible to set one position clearly over against the other so that the two may be compared for what they are. Certainly there can be no confrontation of two opposing positions if it cannot be pointed out on what they oppose each other. On the traditional basis of reasoning the unbeliever is not so much as given an opportunity of seeing with any adequacy how the position he is asked to accept differs from his own.

But all this comes from following the Roman Catholic, Thomas Aquinas, or the Arminian, Butler. If one follows Calvin there are no such troubles. Then one begins with the fact that the world is what the Bible says it is. One then makes the claims of God upon men without apologies though always *suaviter in modo*. One knows that there is hidden underneath the surface display of every man a sense of deity. One therefore gives that sense of deity an opportunity to rise in rebellion against the oppression under which it suffers by the new man of the covenant breaker. One makes no deal with this new man. One shows that on his assumptions all things are meaningless. Science would be impossible; knowledge of anything in any field would be impossible. No fact could be distinguished from any other fact. No law could be said to be law with respect to facts. The whole manipulation of factual experience would be like the idling of a motor that is not in gear. Thus every fact—not *some* facts—every fact *clearly* and not probably proves the truth of Christian theism. If Christian theism is not true then nothing is true. Is the God of the Bible satisfied if his servants say anything less?

And have I, following such a method, departed radically from the tradition of Kuyper and Bavinck? On the contrary I have learned all this primarily from them. It is Kuyper's *Encyclopedia* that has, more than any other work in modern times, brought out the fact of the difference between the approach of the believer and of the unbeliever. It is Bavinck's monumental work which set a natural theology frankly oriented to Scripture squarely over against that of Romanism which is based on neutral reason. It is Bavinck who taught me that the proofs for God as usually formulated on the traditional method prove a finite god. I have indeed had the temerity to maintain that these great Reformed theologians have in some points not been quite true to their own principles. But when I have done so I have usually tried to point out that when they did so and to the extent that they did so they had departed from Calvin.

Chapter X

THE DEFENSE OF CHRISTIANITY

Everything that has been said so far has bearing upon the question of apologetics. How shall Christians win unbelievers to an acceptance of Christian truth? Kuyper speaks much of the fact that, since the entrance of sin, truth must be set over against error. Satan is the prince of darkness. He instigated Adam to make alliance with him over against God. But God in his grace sent his Son to establish the kingdom of righteousness and truth.

There is a global war on between Christ and Satan. All men are participants in this war. They all wear uniforms; they are all for or against God. There are, that is, two principles opposed to one another. But those who fight for truth must fight with spiritual weapons only. Their opposition to Satan is in the interest of winning converts to the love of God in Christ.

There are those who do not like such martial terminology. But how can we avoid martial terminology and be true to the Bible? Is not Modernism and neo-Modernism preaching a gospel of love that makes no ultimate distinction between truth and falsehood? Did not Paul warn us to put on the whole armour of God in order to be able to stand against the wiles of the devil? Was Christ's assertion that he came not to bring peace but a sword out of accord with his love for sinners?

Christians must present the truth in terms of God the Creator, of man his creature and also of this man's rebellion against God. Romanism and Evangelicalism do not want to think of the fall of man as having immediate significance for an argument between a Christian and a non-Christian. The Reformed view of theology alone takes the Bible story of Adam's representation seriously. Hence the Reformed view alone appreciates fully the significance of the fall of man for Apologetics.

The Reformed apologetic, therefore, does not take for granted, as does the Romanist and the Evangelical, that because men have "common notions" about God by virtue of their creation in God's image, that sinners and saints also have common notions when they are epistemologically self-conscious. The Reformed apologetic, following Calvin, will distinguish between what was true for Adam, then what is true for the sinner, the natural man, and after that what is true for the saint, the regenerated man.

After we have begun with the Adamic consciousness, and then turned to the unregenerate consciousness, we must next consider the *regenerate consciousness*. The regenerate consciousness is the Adamic consciousness *restored* and *supplemented*, but restored and supplemented in principle or standing only.

In the first place, the regenerated consciousness is the Adamic consciousness *restored*. It recognizes afresh its own *derivative* character. It is able to do so only because God has regenerated it and thus made it confess its ethical depravity. God has *quickened* what was the natural man so that he now lives. The regenerate man can discern and do that which is spiritually good because it is God who works in him both to will and to do. In the second place, the regenerated consciousness is the Adamic consciousness *supplemented*. Adam was in the position of *posse peccare*, while the restored are in the position of *non posse peccare*. "Whosoever is begotten of God doeth no sin, because his seed abideth in him; and he *cannot* sin because he is begotten of God" (I John 3:9).

In the third place the regenerate consciousness is restored in principle but not in degree. The struggle of Romans VII remains the struggle of every Christian till the day of his death. "If we say that we have no sin we deceive ourselves, and the truth is not in us" (I John 1:8).

If we keep all these distinctions between the Adamic, the non-regenerate, and the regenerate consciousness in mind, we can approach the question as to the place of reason in theology.

I

The Place of Reason in Theology

In the first place, we can no longer figure with the Adamic consciousness as actually existing at the present time. We deal only with the non-regenerate and the regenerate consciousness. But the true meaning of the fallen and the regenerate consciousness cannot be maintained unless back of both lies the history of Adam and his fall. This does not mean that it is a matter of indifference whether or not we take the Genesis narrative with respect to Adam as historical. It is only if we do take this narrative as historical that a sound theology can be maintained. Adam's sin was the wilful transgression of man to the known revelation of God. If we deny the historicity of the Genesis narrative we shall be compelled to reduce man's responsibility for sin so drastically that in reality nothing remains of it. Man's "sinfulness" is then virtually identical with "fate." Accordingly such theologians as Otto Piper[1] and Nels F. S. Ferre[2] who virtually reduce the Genesis narrative to the status of myth, find themselves compelled to deny also the historic Christian views of sin, of Christ, and of the atonement.

In the second place, we cannot speak of human reason in general, or of the human consciousness in general, except in the objective sense explained above. And as such we may call it a limiting concept in the Christian sense of the term. In other words, it is a concept that should never be employed to do duty by itself. All men have a sense of deity, but there is no man

[1] *God in History,* New York, 1939, p. xx, p. 58.

[2] *The Christian Faith,* New York, 1942 and *Evil and the Christian Faith,* New York, n.d.

who has not at the same time also something else that at once colors his sense of deity. All men are either in covenant with Satan or in covenant with God. The former invariably seek to suppress and therefore always misinterpret the general sense of deity within them. The latter invariably seek to relate that general sense of diety to the revelation of God in Christ.

While therefore it is of the utmost consequence to recognize the fact of a "common consciousness" of God as the revelational pressure of God on man, it is of no less importance to note that, in so far as men are aware of their most basic alliances, they are wholly for or wholly against God at every point of interest to man.

In the third place, when we deal with the non-regenerate consciousness, we must think of it as it is according to its adopted monistic assumption. Hence we cannot grant that it has *any right to judge* in matters of theology, or, for the matter of that, in anything else. The Scriptures nowhere appeal to the unregenerated reason as to a qualified judge. On the contrary, Scripture says over and over that the unregenerate reason is entirely unqualified to judge. When Scripture says: "Come, let us reason together," it often speaks to the people of God, and, if it does speak to others, it never regards them as equal with God or as really competent to judge. The unregenerate man has knowledge of God, that is of the revelation of God within him, the sense of deity which he seeks to suppress. Scripture does appeal to this sense of deity in man, but it does so and can do so only by denying that man, when acting on his adopted monistic assumption, has any ability or right to judge of what is true or false, right or wrong.

In the fourth place, though Scripture does not appeal to the natural man as to a competent judge and though it considers the natural man as blind to spiritual things, the Scriptures continue to hold man responsible for his blindness.

In the fifth place, Scripture teaches us to speak and preach to, as well as to reason with blind men, because God, in whose name we speak and reason, can cause the blind to see. Jesus told Lazarus while dead to arise and come forth from the grave. The prophet preached to the dead bones in the valley till they took on flesh. So our reasoning and our preaching is not in vain inasmuch as God in Christ reasons and preaches through us. Once we were blind; God reasoned with us, perhaps through some human agency, and we saw.

I shall quote part of a summary of the type of argument I have constantly used. It appeared in *His* (April, 1948) magazine of the Inter-Varsity Fellowship, as an answer to Professor William Pepperell Montague's article, "Does the Universe Have a Mind?" in the *Saturday Review of Literature* of September 6, 1947.

"Does the universe show any evidence in its behavior of being created and benign?" (*S.R.L.*, p. 31.) "To this time-honored theological question the answer must be a flat negative. Nature is tooth and claw, and life so constituted that each creature can preserve its existence only by devouring other creatures. If there is a God, he is either not omnipotent or not good, in any sense of the word 'good' that the human conscience can sanction."

That the position taken by Montague is fairly typical of the attitude of many modern philosophers and scientists needs no proof. Even when men do not express themselves as vigorously as does Montague, their attitude toward Christianity and its claims is frequently the same as his. It is therefore imperative that Christians investigate their own attitude toward such a criticism carefully.

When Christians look at evil and suffering, they say that it is the result of the sin of man (Romans 5:12). They add that the nature of sin is therefore lack of conformity to and transgression of the will of God. They assert further that God "hath appointed a day, in the which he will judge the world in righteousness by that man whom he hath ordained; whereof he hath given assurance unto all men, in that he hath raised him from the dead" (Acts 17:31). Christians interpret the "fact" of evil, therefore, in the light of a story. And the story they get from the Bible, which they claim to be the Word of God. Moreover, what is true of the fact of evil is true of every other fact. Christians interpret every fact in the light of the same story. For them the nature of every fact in this world is determined by the place it occupies in the story. The story they cannot get from any other source than supernatural revelation.

The Christian finds that his conscience agrees to the truth of the story. He holds that those who deny the truth of the story have an axe to grind. They do not want the story to be true; they do not want the facts to be what the story says they are. They "protest too much." And by protesting too much they testify, in spite of themselves, that their conscience does not tell them that the story is untrue. Their conscience tells them the reverse of what they say it does.

The Christian finds, further, that logic agrees with the story. Human logic agrees with the story, because it derives its meaning from the story. The facts of the world are what the story says they are; if logic would deal with facts rather than fancies it must itself, together with the facts, be a part of the story. By logic man must seek for coherence in his experience of the story. The story tells him that "seed time and harvest, and cold and heat, and summer and winter, and day and night shall not cease." Hence scientific predictions can be made. But the story also tells him that the final judgment will come in God's time. Accordingly, these scientific predictions are contingent upon the maintenance of the course and constitution of nature by God.

Consider now what Montague has to say. He observes the "facts" of nature and says they are not what the Christian says they are. Involved in this mere looking at the facts is the assertion that they *cannot* be what the Christian says they are. Merely by looking at the facts Montague virtually claims to know what *did not* happen in the past and what *cannot* happen in the future. By mere observation of facts, he knows that there has been no creation or fall and that there will be no judgment. The merest statement of fact about any fact of nature, as Montague sees it, involves and is virtually identical with an *a priori* universal negative judgment about all possibility.

On Montague's position then the observation of facts is virtually identical with exhaustive insight into their nature. It is only on the basis of exhaustive insight into the nature of facts that one can determine just what they can or cannot be. And exhaustive insight presupposes absolute control. In other words, on Montague's scheme of things the mind of man must, for all practical purposes, take the place of God in the Christian scheme of things. To talk about what can or cannot exist according to logic is but to swing a sword in the sky unless it is first determined at what point logic meets reality. According to the Christian story, logic and reality meet first of all in the mind and being of God. God's being is exhaustively rational. Then God creates and rules the universe according to his plan. Even the evil of this world happens according to this plan. The only substitute for this Christian scheme of things is to assert or assume that logic and reality meet originally in the mind of man. The final point of reference in all predication must ultimately rest in some mind, divine or human. It is either the self-contained God of Christianity or the would-be autonomous man that must be and is presupposed as the final reference point in every sentence that any man utters.

We would therefore ask Montague how it is that he, as a mere man claims what is tantamount to absolute *a priori* or analytical knowledge of all possibility. But if we should ask him this, he would, of course disclaim any such thing. He would disown the attempt of Parmenides to equate all being with what can without contradiction be said about it by man. Neither has he any place for a first cause. "It seems rather that the thing or principle responsible for the origin of nature as we find it was a power of fecundity, self-repetition or increase and that the only hope of ascribing to it *mind* or *life* would depend on showing that those categories are interpretable as later phases, 'emergent' yet inevitable developments of the principle of development itself."[3]

But how then, we now inquire of Montague, is it that you can make universal negative propositions about all possibility if for you, according to your own assertions, possibility and even reality is something that exists prior to any mind and any logical assertion about it? If we hear a motor roar in a new Buick car while the car does not move, we assume that the driver merely

[3] Article on "The Trinity" in *Religious Realism*, New York, 1931, p. 497.

does not want the car to move. He could put the motor in gear at any time and the car would go. But when we see him take the motor out of the car and drop it in the middle of the Pacific Ocean with the avowed intention of making things move, we are not impressed.

The Christian and the non-Christian may then be compared to one another in some such way as follows:

1. Both make presuppositions about the nature of reality:

    a. The Christian presupposes the self-contained God and his plan for the universe.

    b. The non-Christian presupposes "Chaos and Old Night."

2. Neither can, as finite beings, by means of logic legislate what reality should be.

    a. Knowing this the Christian observes facts and arranges them logically in self-conscious subjection to the plan of God revealed in Scripture.

    b. Knowing this the non-Christian none the less constantly attempts the impossible.

        1. Negatively he says in effect that reality is not rationally constituted at all and that the Christian story therefore cannot be true. This is involved in his idea of "facts" as springing from "Chaos and Old Night."

        2. Positively he assumes that reality is after all rationally constituted and answers exhaustively to his logical manipulations. This is involved in his idea that any "cosmic mind" or God that is to be tolerated must be manipulable by categories devised by man without reference to "him" or "it."

3. Each claims that his position is "in accordance with the facts of experience."

    a. The Christian claims this because he interprets the facts and his experience of them in terms of his presupposition. The "uniformity of nature" and his knowledge of that uniformity both rest for him upon the plan of God. The coherence of his experience he takes to be analogical to the absolute coherence of God.

b. The non-Christian also interprets the facts in terms of his presuppositions. One of these presuppositions is that of ultimate non-rationality. On such a basis any fact would have a nature that is different in all respects from all other facts. Here is "Chaos and Old Night" with a vengeance. The second of these presuppositions is the rationality of all reality in terms of the reach of logic as manipulated by man. On such a basis the nature of any fact would be identical with the nature of every other fact. In practice the procedure of the non-Christian is that of keeping in careful balance the utter equivocism involved in his first and the utter univocism involved in his second presupposition. In any case the non-Christian can never so much as discover any fact. On his principles he knows nothing of its nature. But when he has discovered what he cannot discover he can tell us everything about it. On his principles he knows everything if he knows anything.

4. Each claims that his position is "in accord with the demands of logic."

a. The Christian claims this because he interprets the reach of logic as manipulated by man in terms of his story and therefore in terms of his presupposition of God. The story tells him that nature is made subject to man and both subject to God and his purpose. Thus his logic is in gear with reality but it does not claim to control the possible.

b. The non-Christian claims this, but cannot put any intelligible meaning into the claim. If he works according to his presupposition about the ultimate non-rationality of facts, there is no such thing as validity to logic. All logic is then *de facto* and therewith void. If he works according to his presupposition about the ultimate legislative character of logic as manipulated by man, then there are no facts that can be related to one another by logic. All facts are then reduced to logic; logic has validity but a validity that is purely formal.

5. Each claims that with respect to the problem of evil his position is in accord with conscience.

a. The Christian claims this because he interprets his moral consciousness, as an aspect of his total experience, in terms of his presuppositions. He knows that the judge of the whole earth must do right. All the facts and problems of evil and sin take their meaning from and find their solution in terms of the story of Scripture. The approvals and disapprovals of his conscience take their meaning from this story and from this story alone.

b. The non-Christian claims this because he takes his conscience to be its own ultimate point of reference. Evil has not come into the world because of man's disobedience; it is therefore metaphysically ultimate. Evil cannot be distinguished from good; what is, ought to be. Assuming that good could be distinguished from evil, there is no right to expect that the one will ever be victorious over the other. If those who think they are good succeed in making what they think is "good" to prevail upon earth, it can only be the suppression of the "good" of others who also think they are "good." Thus power politics would forever replace all ethical distinctions.

The sort of argument outlined above differs from the traditional method of apologetics, the apologetics of "old Princeton." This apologetics was derived via Butler's famous *Analogy* from the scholastic position. How do the two positions differ?

I shall indicate this in a general way by quoting a part of a series of articles on "Defending the Faith" which appeared in the *Torch and Trumpet*.[4]

[4]Vol. I, No. 1, pp. 16 ff.; Vol. I, No. 2, pp. 17 ff.; Vol. I, No. 3, pp. 16 ff.; Vol. I, No. 4, pp. 16 ff.; and Vol. II, No. 5, pp. 18 ff.

II

Defending the Faith

In this series of articles our concern will be to discover some of the main features of the Reformed approach in Christian Apologetics.

While seeking light on this question, let us turn first to the inaugural address of the late Dr. Valentine Hepp of the Free University of Amsterdam. The title of this address is *Reformed Apologetic.*[5] Hepp says that a Reformed Christian must naturally be Reformed in his approach to the problem of Apologetics. Men and women do not walk about first as human beings and afterward as men and women. No more can a Reformed Christian first appear as a Christian and later as a Reformed Christian. A Reformed Christian is a Reformed Christian from the outset. If Hepp is right, then the Reformed Christian will have a distinctively Reformed approach when he is trying to win "Mr. Black" to become a Christian. He wants "Mr. Black" to become at once a Reformed Christian, not first a Christian and then a Reformed Christian. "Mr. Black" must become a Reformed Christian not in two but in one transaction.

The late Dr. Benjamin Breckinridge Warfield once said that Calvinism or the Reformed Faith is Christianity come to its own. Warfield did not like to identify Calvinism with the so-called "five points of Calvinism": total depravity, unconditional election, limited atonement, irresistible grace, and perseverance of the saints. Historically at least, Warfield asserts, these five points were but the "theological obverse" of the "five points of Arminianism." The "five points of Calvinism" are but so many branches of the tree of Calvinism.

Looked at as a unit, Calvinism represents the "vision of God in his majesty." Regarded a little more particularly, Calvinism implies three things. "In it, objectively speaking, theism comes to its rights; subjectively speaking, the religious relation attains its purity; soteriologically speaking, evangelical religion finds at

[5] *Gereformeerde Apologetiek,* Kampen, 1922.

length its full expression and its secure stability."[6] Amplifying this statement Warfield says: "I think it is important to insist that Calvinism is not a specific variety of theistic thought, religious experience, evangelical faith, but just the perfect manifestation of these things. . . . There is but one kind of theism, religion, evangelicalism; and if there are several constructions laying claim to these names they differ from one another not as correlative species of a more inclusive genus, but only as more or less good or bad specimens of the same thing differ from one another."[7]

If Warfield is right, then our conclusion must be the same as that based on Hepp's remarks. The Reformed Faith is theism come to its own. If there be other theisms they are not true theisms. How could they be? Are there several true Gods? There is but one true God; there is therefore but one true theism, namely, Christian theism, the theism of the Bible. There is but one God, the God triune of the Scriptures. And it is the vision of this God "in his majesty" that constitutes the essence of the Reformed Faith. It is to the recognition of this God as wholly sovereign that the Reformed Christian would win "Mr. Black."

Two general conclusions of a negative nature may now be drawn. First, the Reformed apologist cannot cooperate with the Romanist in the establishment of the existence of God. The theism of Roman Catholic theology is not "theism come to its own"; it is a vague, general sort of theism. It is a theism in which the God of Christianity and the god of Greek philosophy, particularly the Unmoved Mover of Aristotle, are ground together into a common mixture. The theism of Romanist theology is a theism heavily freighted with pagan elements of thought. If such a theism were proved to be true, then the Christian theism of the Reformed Christian would be proved to be untrue. If with the Romanist we "prove" the existence of *a* god, then we have disproved the existence of *the* God of Christianity. It is only a perverted type of theism which is "proved" by Romanist theologians.

[6] B. B. Warfield: *Calvin as a Theologian and Calvinism Today* (pamphlet), Philadelphia, 1909, p. 23.

[7] *Idem*, p. 24.

The second major negative conclusion to be drawn from the remarks of Hepp and Warfield is that the Reformed apologist cannot cooperate with the "evangelical" in providing the truth of Evangelicalism. By Evangelicalism we mean what Warfield meant when he spoke of it as identical with general non-Reformed Protestantism (cf. his *The Plan of Salvation*).

This second negative conclusion follows directly from the first. The evangelical *does* want to cooperate with the Romanist in proving the truth of theism. He argues that Protestants have many doctrines in common with Romanists, and that the existence of God is the most basic of them. Why then he asks in amazement, cannot Protestants cooperate with Romanists in proving the truth of theism? Why not have the Romanist help us build the first story of the house of Christian theism? After they have helped us build the first story of our house, we can dismiss them with thanks for their services and proceed to build the second story, the story of Protestantism, ourselves.

The answer to this is that if Romanists have helped us in building the first story of our house, then the whole house will tumble into ruins. It has already been noted that when they build the first story of their house the Romanists mix a great deal of the clay of paganism with the iron of Christianity. The concrete blocks may be those of Christianity, but the cement is nothing other than the sand of paganism. Woe to the Protestant who seeks to build his Protestantism as a second story upon a supposedly theistic foundation, and a first story built by Romanism or by Protestants in conjunction with Romanists. Only a defective Protestantism can be built upon the perverted theism of the Romanist type. For, as Warfield puts it, the precise characterization of Evangelicalism is that which describes it as a defective Protestantism. Warfield's point is that Evangelicalism is inconsistent Protestantism. It has carried into its system certain foreign elements—elements ultimately derived by way of Romanism from paganism.

"But," someone will exclaim, "look where you have brought us! To what extremes you have gone! Not to speak of Romanists, are we not even to cooperate with Evangelicals? I know many Evangelicals who are much better Christians than are many Calvinists." But this is not the issue. The question is not as to who are Christians and who are going to heaven. We are not judging men's hearts. Many Evangelicals are no doubt better Calvinists in practice than other men who are officially known as Calvinists.

The point is that we are now speaking of theological systems. When Warfield makes the high claim that Calvinism is "nothing more or less than the hope of the world," he is speaking of the Reformed system of theology and of the Reformed point of view in general. Other types of theology are supernaturalistic in patches. To some extent they yield to the idea of autosoterism, to the idea that man to some degree is saved by his own effort. Therefore, argues Warfield, "Calvinism is just Christianity." But then, by precisely the same reasoning, *Reformed apologetics is the hope of the world.*

A further objection may be met here: Have not certain Reformed theologians been willing in some measure to cooperate with Romanists in defending theism and with evangelicals in defending evangelicalism, in order, after that, to defend the specific doctrines of Calvinism? Are they all wrong and are you alone right?

The answer to this objection is not easy. It would require separate and extensive discussion to do it justice. There is, no doubt, some measure of truth in the contention that at least some Reformed theologians have been willing to follow the method of cooperation first and distinctiveness afterward. Over against this stands the fact that other Reformed theologians, seeing, as they thought, the compromising result of such a method, have argued that the very idea of apologetics as a positive theological discipline is out of accord with the principles of the Reformed Faith. Or again, some have argued that apologetics must at most be given a very small task in the way of warding off the attacks of the enemy. The difference between Warfield and Kuyper on the question of apologetics is well known. Are we to be reprimanded in advance for not agreeing with Kuyper? Or for not agreeing with Warfield? Let us rather seek to listen to both Warfield and Kuyper and also to Calvin, and then do the best we can as we ask just what the genius of the Reformed Faith requires of us. Is there anything else that anyone today *can* do?

A third party is anxious to ask a question here. Are all the efforts of evangelical apologists then to no avail? Are we to make no use whatsoever of the research done by them in such fields as Biblical history and archaeology, to mention nothing more?

Let us reply to these questions with other questions. Reformed theologians do not cooperate with Arminian theologians in the preaching of the gospel. Do they therefore conclude that all Arminian preaching is to no avail? God uses even defective preaching to accomplish his purposes; so God also uses defective reasoning to bring men to himself. And as for the results of evangelical scholarship, the Reformed apologist should gratefully employ all that is true and good in it. What is true and good in it derives from the measure of Calvinism any form of Christianity contains. But when it comes to the master plan of procedure, the Reformed apologist must go his own way; and it is only of the master plan that we speak when we deal with the question of apologetics in general. Solomon made use even of the Sidonians when building the temple of the Lord, but he did not give them membership on his building committee.

A fourth party now asks: "Granting all this for the sake of argument, can you tell us in a few words wherein you think the main difference consists between a Reformed and a Romanist or evangelical apologetics?"

Here, indeed, is the heart of the matter. It is not easy to answer this question. But let us try to deal with it as best we can in a general way before going on to further specific points.

The basic difference between the two types of apologetics is to be found, we believe, in the primary assumption that each party makes. The Romanist-evangelical type of apologetics assumes that man can first know much about himself and the universe and *afterward* ask whether God exists and Christianity is true. The Reformed apologist assumes that nothing can be known by man about himself or the universe unless God exists and Christianity is true.

It will be observed that it is this very difference that exists between the two types of theology, the Romanist-evangelical and the Reformed. The former type of theology assumes that it first knows what human freedom is from "experience." It then adjusts the doctrines of Scripture concerning God and Christianity to its notion of freedom derived from experience. The Reformed type of theology *begins* with Scriptures and defines human freedom in terms of its principles alone.

It is natural that this difference which is basic in the two types of theology should also be basic in the two types of apologetics. Thomas Aquinas, the Roman Catholic, and Bishop Butler, the Arminian, both talk a great deal about the nature of man and of reality as a whole before they approach the question of the existence of God or of the truth of Christianity. At least, they assume much about the nature of man and of reality as a whole *while* they are speaking about the possibility of the existence of God or of the truth of Christianity. Over against them stands Calvin. He will not say one word about man or about the universe except in the light of the revelation of God as given in Scripture. The very first page of *The Institutes* is eloquent testimony to this fact.

Otherwise expressed, it may be said that the Reformed apologist *does* while the Romanist-evangelical apologist *does not* make the Creator-creature distinction basic in all that he says about anything. His argument is that unless this distinction is made basic to all that man says about anything, then whatever man says is fundamentally untrue. The natural man, who assumes that he himself and the facts about him are not created, therefore assumes what is basically false. Everything he says about himself and the universe will be colored by this assumption. It is therefore impossible to grant that he is right, basically right, in what he says about any fact. If he says what is right in detail about any fact, this is *in spite of*, not *because of* his basically false assumption.

Since the Romanist-evangelical apologist *does not* make the Creator-creature distinction basic to the very first thing that he says about man or the universe, he is willing to join hands with the natural man, and together with him "discover" many "truths" about man and the universe. He will make common ground with the unbeliever as in science or in philosophy they investigate together the nature of Reality as a whole. He will agree with the natural man as he speaks about "being in general," and only afterward argue against the unbeliever for the necessity of introducing the Creator-creature distinction. So Butler agrees with the deists on their view of the "course and constitution" of nature, and afterward tries to persuade them that they ought *also* to believe in Christ.

Of course, the reason why the one type of apologetics *does* and the other *does not* wish to make the Creator-creature distinction basic at the outset of all predication is to be found in the differing conceptions of sin. The natural man does not want to make the Creator-creature distinction basic in his thought. The sinner does not want to recognize the fact that he is a creature of God, and as such responsible to God, and because of his sin under the judgment of God. This is to be expected. But why should Christians who have confessed their sins to God, who have therefore recognized him as Creator and Lord, and especially why should evangelicals who confess that they hold to the Bible as their only infallible rule of authority, not wish to bring their *every* thought captive to the obedience of Christ. In other words, how do you account for the fact that evangelicals carry into their theology and into their apologetics so much foreign material? It is, of course, because of their defective view of sin. In fact, their defective view of sin is itself of foreign origin. More must be said about this subject later.

III

The Believer Meets the Unbeliever

To see clearly what is meant, think of a dentist. You go to him with a "bad tooth." Does he take care of your tooth in two operations? To be sure, you may have to come back to have him finish the job. But it is one job he is doing. He takes all the decayed matter out before he fills the cavity. Well, Mr. Black is the man with the toothache, and you, as a Reformed Christian, are the dentist. Would you first convert him to Evangelicalism and then to the Reformed Faith? Then you would be like a dentist who would today take half the decayed matter out and fill the cavity, and tomorrow or next week take out the rest of the decayed matter and fill the cavity again. Or, rather, you would be like the dentist who takes part of the decayed matter out, fills the cavity, and then lets the patient go until a long time later he returns complaining again of a toothache.

Indeed, it is no fun to have the dentist drill deep into your tooth. And it is the last and deepest drilling that hurts most. So Mr. Black is likely to feel more at home in the office of the "evangelical" dentist than in the office of the "Reformed" dentist. Will the latter have any customers? He is likely to fear that he will not. He is ever tempted, therefore, to advertise that he is cooperating with all good "conservatives" in all good dentistry, but that he has a specialty which it would be very nice for people to see him about.

Let us now ask by what means we may diagnose Mr. Black. For that purpose we use the X-ray machine. Whence do you know your misery? Out of the law, the revealed will of God, answers the Reformed Christian. Let us call him Mr. White. It is by means of the Bible, not by personal experience, that he turns the light on himself, as well as on Mr. Black. He does not appeal to "experience" or to "reason" or to "history" or to anything else as his source of information in the way that he appeals to the Bible. He may appeal to experience, but his appeal will be to experience as seen in the light of the Bible. So he may appeal to reason or to history, but, again, only as they are to be seen in the light of the Bible. He does not even look for *corroboration* for the teachings of Scripture from experience, reason or history except insofar as these are themselves first seen in the light of the Bible. For him the Bible, and therefore the God of the Bible, is like the sun from which the light that is given by oil lamps, gas lamps and electric lights is derived.

Quite different is the attitude of the "evangelical" or conservative." Let us call him Mr. Grey. Mr. Grey uses the Bible, experience, reason or logic as equally independent sources of information about his own and therefore about Mr. Black's predicament. I did not say that for Mr. Grey the Bible, experience and reason are *equally* important. Indeed they are not. He knows that the Bible is by far the most important. But he none the less constantly appeals to "the facts of experience" and to "logic" without first dealing with the very idea of fact and with the idea of logic in terms of the Scripture.

The difference is basic. When Mr. White diagnoses Mr.

Black's case he takes as his X-ray machine the Bible only. When Mr. Grey diagnoses Mr. Black's case he first takes the X-ray machine of experience, then the X-ray machine of logic, and finally his biggest X-ray machine, the Bible. In fact, he may take these in any order. Each of them is an independent source of information.

Let us first look briefly at a typical sample of procedure generally followed in conservative or evangelical circles today. Let us, in other words, note how Mr. Grey proceeds with an analysis of Mr. Black. And let us at the same time see how Mr. Grey would win Mr. Black to an acceptance of Christianity. We take for this purpose a series of articles which appeared in the January, February and March, 1950, issues of *Moody Monthly*, published by the Moody Bible Institute in Chicago. Edward John Carnell, Ph.D., author of *An Introduction to Christian Apologetics* and Professor of Apologetics at Fuller Theological Seminary, Pasadena, California, wrote this series. Carnell's writings are among the best that appear in evangelical circles. In fact, in his book Carnell frequently argues as we would expect a Reformed apologist to argue. By and large, however, he represents the evangelical rather than the Reformed method in Apologetics.

When Mr. Carnell instructs his readers "How Every Christian Can Defend His Faith," he first appeals to facts and to logic as independent sources of information about the truth of Christianity. Of course, he must bring in the Bible even at this point. But the Bible is brought in only as a book of information about the fact of what has historically been called Christianity. It is not from the beginning brought in as God's Word. It must be shown to Mr. Black to be the Word of God by means of "facts" and "logic." Carnell would thus avoid at all costs the charge of reasoning in a circle. He does not want Mr. Black to point the finger at him and say: "You prove that the Bible is true by an appeal to the Bible itself. That is circular reasoning. How can any person with any respect for logic accept such a method of proof?"

Carnell would escape such a charge by showing that the facts of experience, such as all men recognize, and logic, such as all men must use, point to the truth of Scripture. This is what he says: "If you are of a philosophic turn, you can point to the remarkable way in which Christianity fits in with the moral sense inherent in every human being, or the influence of Christ on our ethics, customs, literature, art and music. Finally, you can draw upon your own experience in speaking of the reality of answered prayer and the witness of the Spirit in your own heart. . . . If the person is impressed with this evidence, turn at once to the gospel. Read crucial passages and permit the Spirit to work on the inner recesses of his heart. Remember that apologetics is merely a preparation. After the ground has been broken, proceed immediately with sowing and watering.[8]

It is assumed in this argument that Mr. Black agrees with the "evangelical," Mr. Grey, on the character of the "moral sense" of man. This may be true, but then it is true because Mr. Grey has himself not taken his information about the moral sense of man exclusively from Scripture. If with Mr. White he had taken his conception of the moral nature of man from the Bible, then he would hold that Mr. Black, as totally depraved will, of course, misinterpret his own moral nature. True, Christianity is in accord with the moral nature of man. But this is so only because the moral nature of man is first in accord with what the Bible says it is, that is, originally created perfect, but now wholly corrupted in its desires through the fall of man.

If you are reasoning with a naturalist, Carnell advises his readers, ask him why when a child throws a rock through his window, he chases the child and not the rock. Presumably even a naturalist knows that the child, not the rock, is free and therefore responsible. "A bottle of water cannot ought; it must. When once the free spirit of man is proved, the moral argument—the existence of a God who imposes moral obligations—can form the bridge from man to God."[9]

Here the fundamental difference between Mr. Grey's and Mr. White's approach to Mr. Black appears. The difference lies in the different notions of the free will of man. Or, it may be said, the difference is with respect to the nature of man as such. Mr. White would define man, and therefore his freedom, in terms of Scripture alone. He would therefore begin with the fact that man is the creature of God. And this implies that man's freedom

[8] *Moody Monthly,* January 1950, p. 313.
[9] *Idem,* p. 343.

is a derivative freedom. It is a freedom that is not and cannot be wholly ultimate, that is, self-dependent. Mr. White knows that Mr. Black would not agree with him in this analysis of man and of his freedom. He knows that Mr. Black would not agree with him on this any more than he would agree on the Biblical idea of total depravity.

Mr. Grey, on the other hand, must at all costs have "a point of contact" in the system of thought of Mr. Black, who is typical of the natural man; just as Mr. Grey is afraid of being charged with circular reasoning, so he is also afraid of being charged with talking about something that is "outside of experience." And so he is driven to talk in general about the "free spirit of man." Of course, Mr. Black need have no objections from his point of view in allowing for the "free spirit of man." That is at bottom what he holds even when he is a naturalist. His whole position is based upon the idea of man as a free spirit, that is, a spirit that is not subject to the law of his Creator God. And Carnell does not distinguish between the Biblical doctrine of freedom, as based upon and involved in the fact of man's creation, and the doctrine of freedom, in the sense of autonomy, which makes man a law unto himself.

Of course, Mr. Black will be greatly impressed with such an argument as Mr. Grey has presented to him for the truth of Christianity. In fact, if Christianity is thus shown to be in accord with the moral nature of man, as Mr. Black himself sees that moral nature, then Mr. Black does not need to be converted at all to accept Christianity. He only needs to accept something additional to what he has always believed. He has been shown how nice it would be to have a second story built on top of the house which he has already built according to his own plans.

To be sure, the Evangelical intends no such thing. Least of all does Carnell intend such a thing. But why then does not the "Evangelical" see that by presenting the non-Christian with Evangelicalism rather than with the Reformed Faith he must compromise the Christian religion? And why does he not also see that in doing what he does the non-Christian is not really challenged either by fact or by logic? For facts and logic which are not themselves first seen in the light of Christianity have, in the nature of the case, no power in them to challenge the unbeliever to change his position. Facts and logic, not based upon the creation doctrine and not placed in the context of the doctrine of God's all-embracing Providence, are without relation to one another and therefore wholly meaningless.

It is this fact which must be shown to Mr. Black. The folly of holding to any view of life except that which is frankly based upon the Bible as the absolute authority for man must be pointed out to him. Only then are we doing what Paul did when he said: "Where is the wise? where is the scribe? where is the disputer of this world? hath not God made foolish the wisdom of the world?" (I Corinthians 1:20.)

As a Reformed Christian Mr. White therefore cannot cooperate with Mr. Grey in his analysis of Mr. Black. This fact may appear more clearly if we turn to see how Mr. Black appears when he is analyzed by Mr. White in terms of the Bible alone.

Now, according to Mr. White's analysis, Mr. Black is not a murderer. He is not necessarily a drunkard or a dope addict. He lives in one of the suburbs. He is every whit a gentleman. He gives to the Red Cross and to the Red Feather campaigns. He was a boy scout; he is a member of a lodge; he is very much civic minded; now and then his name is mentioned in the papers as an asset to the community. But we know that he is spiritually dead. He is filled with the spirit of error. Perhaps he is a member of a "fine church" in the community, but nevertheless he is one of a "people that do err in their heart" (Psalms 95:10). He lives in a stupor (Romans 11:8). To him the wisdom of God is foolishness. The truth about God, and about himself in relation to God, is obnoxious to him. He does not want to hear of it. He seeks to close eyes and ears to those who give witness of the truth. He is, in short, utterly self-deceived.

Actually, Mr. Black is certain that he looks at life in the only proper way. Even if he has doubts as to the truth of what he believes, he does not see how any sensible or rational man could believe or do otherwise. If he has doubts it is because no one can be fully sure of himself. If he has fears it is because fear is to be expected in the hazardous situation in which modern man lives. If he sees men's minds break down he thinks this is to be expected under current conditions of stress and strain. If he sees grown men act like children he says that they were once beasts. Everything, including the "abnormal" is to him "normal."

In all this Mr. Black has obviously taken for granted that what the Bible says about the world and himself is not true. He has *taken this for granted.* He may never have argued the point. He has cemented yellow spectacles to his own eyes. He cannot remove them because he will not remove them. He is blind and loves to be blind.

Do not think that Mr. Black has an easy time of it. He is the man who always "kicks against the pricks." His conscience troubles him all the time. Deep down in his heart he knows that what the Bible says about him and about the world is true. Even if he has never heard of the Bible he knows that he is a creature of God and that he has broken the law of God (Romans 1:19, 20; 2:14, 15). When the prodigal son left his father's house he could not immediately efface from his memory the look and the voice of his father. How that look and that voice came back to him when he was at the swine trough! How hard he had tried to live as though the money with which he so freely entertained his "friends" had not come from his father! When asked where he came from he would answer that he came "from the other side." He did not want to be reminded of his past. Yet he could not forget it. It required a constant act of suppression to forget the past. But that very act of suppression itself keeps alive the memory of the past.

So also with Mr. Black. He daily changes the truth of God into a lie. He daily worships and serves the creature more than the Creator. He daily holds the truth in unrighteousness (Romans 1:18). But what a time he has with himself! He may try to sear his conscience as with a hot iron. He may seek to escape the influence of all those who witness to the truth. But he can never escape himself as witness bearer to the truth.

His conscience keeps telling him: "Mr. Black, you are a fugitive from justice. You have run away from home, from your father's bountiful love. You are an ingrate, a sneak, a rascal! You shall not escape meeting justice at last. The father still feeds you. Yet you despise the riches of his goodness and forbearance and longsuffering; not recognizing that the goodness of God is calculated to lead you to repentance (Romans 2:4).

Why do you kick against the pricks? Why do you stifle the voice of your conscience? Why do you use the wonderful intellect that God has given you as a tool for the suppression of the voice of God which speaks to you through yourself and through your environment? Why do you build your house on sand instead of on rock? Can you be sure that no storm is ever coming? Are you omniscient? Are you omnipotent? You say that nobody knows whether God exists or whether Christianity is true. You say that nobody knows this because man is finite. Yet you assume that God cannot exist and that Christianity cannot be true. You assume that no judgment will ever come. You must be omniscient to know that. And yet you have just said that all man declares about "the beyond" must be based upon his brief span of existence in this world of time and chance. How, then, if you have taken for granted that chance is one of the basic ingredients of all human experience, can you at the same time say what *can* or *cannot* be in all time to come? You certainly have made a fool of yourself, Mr. Black," says Mr. Black to himself. "You reject the claims of truth which you know to be the truth, and you do that in terms of the lie which really you know to be the lie."

It is not always that Mr. Black is thus aware of the fact that he lives like the prodigal who would eat of the things the swine did eat, but who knows he cannot because he is a human being. He is not always thus aware of his folly—in part at least, because of the failure of evangelicals, and particularly because of the failure of Reformed Christians to stir him up to a realization of his folly. The Evangelical does not want to stir him up thus. It is in the nature of his own theology not to stir him up to a realization of this basic depth of folly. But the Reformed Christian should, on his basis, want to stir up Mr. Black to an appreciation of the folly of his ways.

However, when the Reformed Christian, Mr. White, is to any extent aware of the richness of his own position and actually has the courage to challenge Mr. Black by presenting to him the picture of himself as taken through the X-ray machine called the Bible, he faces the charge of "circular reasoning" and of finding no "point of contact" with experience. And he will also be subject to the criticism of the evangelical for speaking as if

Christianity were irrational and for failing to reach the man in the street.

Thus we seem to be in a bad predicament. There is a basic difference of policy between Mr. White and Mr. Grey as to how to deal with Mr. Black. Mr. Grey thinks that Mr. Black is not really such a bad fellow. It is possible, he thinks, to live with Mr. Black in the same world. And he is pretty strong. So it is best to make a compromise peace with him. That seems to be the way of the wise and practical politician. On the other hand, Mr. White thinks that it is impossible permanently to live in the same world with Mr. Black. Mr. Black, he says, must therefore be placed before the requirement of absolute and unconditional surrender. And surely it would be out of the question for Mr. White first to make a compromise peace with Mr. Black and then, after all, to require unconditional surrender! But what then about this charge of circular reasoning and about this charge of having no point of contact with the unbeliever?

IV

A Consistent Witness

The one main question to which we are addressing ourselves in this series of articles is whether Christians holding to the Reformed faith should also hold to *a specifically Reformed method* when they are engaged in the defense of the faith.

This broad question does not pertain merely to the "five points of Calvinism." When Lutherans or Arminians attack these great doctrines (total depravity, unconditional election, limited atonement, irresistible grace, perseverance of the saints) we, as Calvinists, are quick to defend them. We believe that these five points are directly based upon Scripture. But the question now under discussion is whether, in the defense of *any* Christian doctrine, Reformed Christians should use a method all their own.

People easily give a negative reply to this question. Do we not have many doctrines in common with all evangelicals? Don't all orthodox Protestants hold to the substitutionary atonement of Christ? More particularly, what about the simple statements of fact recorded in Scripture? How could anyone if he believes such statements at all, take them otherwise than as simple statements of fact? How could anyone have a specifically Reformed doctrine of such a fact as the resurrection of Christ? If together with Evangelicals we accept certain simple truths and facts of Scripture at face value, how then can we be said to have a separate method of defense of such doctrines?

Yet it can readily be shown that this negative answer cannot be maintained. Take, for example, the doctrine of the atonement. The Arminian doctrine of the atonement is not the same as the Reformed doctrine of the atonement. Both the Arminian and the Calvinist assert that they believe in the substitutionary atonement. But the Arminian conception of the substitutionary atonement is colored, and as Calvinists we believe discolored, by the view of "free will." According to the Arminian view, man has absolute or ultimate power to accept or to reject the salvation offered him. This implies that the salvation offered to man is merely the *possibility* of salvation.

To illustrate: suppose I deposit one million dollars to your account in your bank. It is still altogether up to you to believe that such wealth is yours, and to use it to cover the floor of your house with Persian rugs in place of the old threadbare rugs now there. Thus, in the Arminian scheme, the very possibility of things no longer depends exclusively upon God, but, in some areas at least, upon man. What Christ did *for* us is made to depend for its effectiveness upon what is done *by* us. It is no longer right to say that with God all things are possible.

It is obvious, therefore, that Arminians have taken into their Protestantism a good bit of the leaven of Roman Catholicism. Arminianism is less radical, less consistent in its Protestantism than it should be. And what is true of Arminianism is true also, though in a lesser degree, of orthodox Lutheranism.

Now Mr. Grey, the Evangelical, seems to have a relatively easy time of it when he seeks to win Mr. Black, the unbeliever, to an acceptance of "the substitutionary atonement." He can stand on "common ground" with Mr. Black on this matter of what is possible and what is impossible. Listen to Mr. Grey as he talks with Mr. Black.

"Mr. Black, have you accepted Christ as your personal

Savior? Do you believe that he died on the cross as your substitute? If you do not, you will surely be lost forever."

"Well now," replies Mr. Black, "I've just had a visit from Mr. White on the same subject. You two seem to have a 'common witness' on this matter. Both of you believe that God exists, that he has created the world, that the first man, Adam, sinned, and that we are all to be sent to hell because of what that first man did, and so forth. All this is too fatalistic for me. If I am a creature, as you say I am, then I have no ultimate power of my own and therefore am not free. And if I am not free, then I am not responsible. So, if I am going to hell, it will be simply because your 'god' has determined that I should. You orthodox Christians kill morality and all humanitarian progress. I will have none of it. Good-by!"

"But wait a second," says Mr. Grey, in great haste. "I do not have a common witness with the Calvinist. I have a common witness with you against the Calvinist when it comes to all that determinism that you mention. Of course you are free. You are absolutely free to accept or to reject the atonement that is offered to you. I offer the atonement through Christ only as a possibility. You yourself must make it an actuality for yourself. I agree with you over against the Calvinist in saying that 'possibility' is wider than the will of God. I would not for a moment say with the Calvinist that God's counsel determines 'whatsoever comes to pass.'

"Besides, even less extreme Calvinists like J. Oliver Buswell, Jr., virtually agree with both of us. Listen to what Buswell says: 'Nevertheless, our moral choices are choices in which we are ourselves ultimate causes.' Buswell himself wants to go beyond the 'merely arbitrary answer' in Romans 9:20, 21, which speaks of the potter and the clay, to the 'much more profound analysis of God's plan of redemption' in Romans 9:22-24, in which Paul pictures Pharaoh as '. . . one who, according to the foreknowledge of God, would rebel against God.'"[10]

"Do I understand then," replies Mr. Black, "that you Evangelicals and even the more moderate Calvinists are opposed to the determinism of the regular, old-style Calvinists of the his-

[10] *What is God?* Grand Rapids, 1937, pp. 50, 53, 54.

toric Reformed Confessions? I am glad to hear that. To say that all things have been fixed from all eternity by God is terrible! It makes me shudder! What would happen to all morality and decency if all men believed such a teaching? But now you Evangelicals have joined us in holding that 'possibility' is independent of the will of God. You have thus with all good people and with all modern and neo-modern theologians, like Barth, made possible the salvation of all men.

"That means, of course, that salvation is possible too for those who have never heard of Jesus of Nazareth. Salvation is therefore possible without an acceptance of your substitutionary atonement through this Jesus, of whom you speak. You certainly would not want to say with the Calvinists that God has determined the bounds of all nations and individuals and has thus, after all, determined that some men, millions of them, in fact, should never hear this gospel.

"Besides, if possibility is independent of God, as you Evangelicals and moderate Calvinists teach, then I need not be afraid of hell. It is then quite possible that there is no hell. Hell, you will then agree, is that torture of a man's conscience which he experiences when he fails to live up to his own moral ideals. So I do not think that I shall bother just yet about accepting Christ as my personal Savior. There is plenty of time."

Poor Mr. Grey. He really wanted to say something about having a common testimony with the Calvinists after all. At the bottom of his heart he knew that Mr. White, the Calvinist, and not Mr. Black, the unbeliever, was his real friend. But he had made a common witness with Mr. Black against the supposed determinism of the Calvinist. So it was difficult for him to turn about face and also make a common testimony with Mr. White against Mr. Black. He had nothing intelligible to say. His method of defending his faith had forced him to admit that Mr. Black was basically right. He had not given Mr. Black an opportunity of knowing what he was supposed to accept, but his testimony had confirmed Mr. Black in his belief that there was no need of his accepting Christ at all.

It is true, of course, that in practice Mr. Grey is much better in his theology and in his method of representing the gospel than he is here said to be. But that is because in practice every Evangelical who really loves his Lord is a Calvinist at heart. How could he really pray to God for help if he believed that there was a possibility that God could not help? In their hearts all true Christians believe that God controls "whatsoever comes to pass." But the Calvinist cannot have a common witness for the substitutionary atonement with "evangelicals" who first make a common witness with the unbeliever against him on the all-determining question whether God controls all things that happen.

It must always be remembered that the first requirement for effective witnessing is that the position to which witness is given be intelligible. Evangelicalism, when consistently carried out, destroys this intelligibility.

The second requirement for effective witnessing is that he to whom the witness is given must be shown why he should forsake his own position and accept that which is offered him. Evangelicalism, when consistently carried out, also destroys the reason why the unbeliever should accept the gospel. Why should the unbeliever change his position if he is not shown that it is wrong? And, in particular, why should he change if the one who asks him to change is actually encouraging him in thinking that he is right? The Calvinist will need to have a better method of defending the doctrine of the atonement, for example, than that of the Evangelical.

We have dealt with the doctrine of the atonement. That led us into the involved question whether God is the source of possibility, or whether possibility is the source of God. It has been shown that the "evangelical" or Arminian fundamentalist holds to a position which requires him to make both of these contradictory assertions at once. But how about the realm of fact? Do you also hold, I am asked, that we need to seek for a specifically Reformed method of defending the facts of Christianity? Take the resurrection of Christ as an example—why can there be no common witness on the part of the Evangelical and the Calvinist to such a fact as that?

Once more Mr. Grey, the Evangelical, punches the doorbell at Mr. Black's home. Mr. Black answers to admit him.

"I am here again, Mr. Black," begins Grey, "because I am still anxious to have you accept Christ as your personal Savior.

When I spoke to you the other time about the atonement you got me into deep water. We got all tangled up on the question of 'possibility.'

"But now I have something far simpler. I want to deal with simple facts. I want to show you that the resurrection of Jesus from the dead is as truly a fact as any that you can mention. To use the words of Wilbur Smith, himself a Calvinist but opposed to the idea of a distinctively Reformed method for the defense of the faith: 'The *meaning* of the resurrection is a theological matter, but the fact of the resurrection is a historical matter; the nature of the resurrection body of Jesus may be a mystery, but the fact that the body disappeared from the tomb is a matter to be decided upon by historical evidence.'[11] And the historical evidence for the resurrection is the kind of evidence that you as a scientist would desire.

"Smith writes in the same book: 'About a year ago, after studying over a long period of time this entire problem of our Lord's resurrection, and having written some hundreds of pages upon it at different times, I was suddenly arrested by the thought that the very kind of evidence which modern science, and even psychologists, are so insistent upon for determining the reality of any object under consideration is the kind of evidence that we have presented to us in the gospels regarding the resurrection of the Lord Jesus, namely, the things that are seen with the human eye, touched with the human hand, and heard by the human ear. This is what we call empirical evidence. It would almost seem as if parts of the gospel records of the resurrection were actually written for such a day as ours when empiricism so dominates our thinking.'[12]

"Now I think that Smith is quite right in thus distinguishing sharply between the *fact* and the *meaning* of the resurrection. And I am now only asking you to accept the fact of the resurrection. There is the clearest possible empirical evidence for this fact. The living Jesus was touched with human hands and seen with human eyes of sensible men after he had been crucified and put into the tomb. Surely you ought to believe in the resurrec-

[11] *Therefore Stand*, Boston, 1945, p. 386.
[12] *Idem*, pp. 389, 390.

tion of Christ as a historical fact. And to believe in the resurrected Christ is to be saved."

"But hold on a second," says Mr. Black, "Your friend the Calvinist, Mr. White, has been ahead of you again. He was here last night and spoke of the same thing. However, he did not thus distinguish between the fact and the meaning of the resurrection. At least, he did not for a moment want to separate the fact of the resurrection from the system of Christianity in terms of which it gets its meaning. He spoke of Jesus Christ, the Son of God, as rising from the dead. He spoke of the Son of God through whom the world was made and through whom the world is sustained, as having risen from the dead. And when I asked him how this God could die and rise from the dead, he said that God did not die and rise from the dead but that the second person of the Trinity had taken to himself a human nature, and that it was in this human nature that he died and rose again. In short, in accepting the fact of the resurrection he wanted me also to take all this abracadabra into the bargain. And I have a suspicion that you are secretly trying to have me do something similar."

"No, no," replies Mr. Grey. "I am in complete agreement with you over against the Calvinist. I have a common witness with you against him. I, too, would separate fact and system. Did I not agree with you against the Calvinist, in holding that possibility is independent of God? Well then, by the same token I hold that all kinds of facts happen apart from the plan of God. So we Evangelicals are in a position, as the Calvinists are not, of speaking with you on neutral ground. With you, we would simply talk about the facts of Christianity without bringing into the picture anything about the meaning or the significance of those facts.

"It makes me smile," continues Mr. Grey, "when I think of Mr. White coming over here trying to convert you. That poor fellow is always reasoning in circles. I suppose that such reasoning in circles goes with his determinism. He is always talking about his self-contained God. He says that all facts are what they are because of the plan of this God. Then each fact would of necessity, to be a fact at all, prove the truth of the Christian system of things and, in turn, would be proved as existing by virtue of this self-same Christian system of things. I realize full well that you, as a modern scientist and philosopher, can have no truck with such horrible, circular reasoning as that.

"It is for this reason that, as Evangelicals, we have now separated sharply between the resurrection as a historical fact and the meaning of the resurrection. I'm merely asking you to accept the *fact* of the resurrection. I am not asking you to do anything that you cannot do in full consistency with your freedom and with the 'scientific method.'"

"Well, that is delightful," replies Mr. Black. "I always felt that the Calvinists were our real foes. But I read something in the paper the other day to the effect that some Calvinist churches or individuals were proposing to make a common witness with Evangelicals for the gospel. Now I was under the impression that the gospel had something to do with being saved from hell and going to heaven. I knew that the modernists and the 'new modernists,' like Barth, do not believe in tying up the facts of history with such wild speculations. It was my opinion that 'fundamentalists' did tie up belief in historical facts, such as the death and the resurrection of Jesus, with going to heaven or to hell. So I am delighted that you, though a fundamentalist, are willing to join with the modernist and the neo-modernist in separating historical facts from such a rationalistic system as I knew Christianity was.

"Now as for accepting the resurrection of Jesus," continued Mr. Black, "as thus properly separated from the traditional system of theology, I do not in the least mind doing that. To tell you the truth, I have accepted the resurrection as a fact now for some time. The evidence for it is overwhelming. This is a strange universe. All kinds of 'miracles' happen in it. The universe is 'open.' So why should there not be some resurrections here and there? The resurrection of Jesus would be a fine item for Ripley's *Believe It or Not*. Why not send it in?"

Mr. Gray wanted to continue at this point. He wanted to speak of the common witness that he had, after all, with the Calvinist for the gospel. But it was too late. He had no "common" witness left of any sort. He had again tried to gallop off in opposite directions at the same time. He had again taken away all intelligibility from the witness that he meant to bring. He had again established Mr. Black in thinking that his own unbelieving reason was right. For it was as clear as crystal to Mr. Black, as it should have been to Mr. Grey, that belief in the fact of the resurrection, apart from the system of Christianity, amounts to belief that the Christian system is not true, is belief in the universe as run by Chance, is belief that it was not Jesus Christ, the Son of God, who rose from the dead.

To be sure, in practice the "evangelical" is much better in his witness for the resurrection of Christ than he has been presented here. But that is because every Evangelical, as a sincere Christian is at heart a Calvinist. But witnessing is a matter of the head as well as of the heart. If the world is to hear a consistent testimony for the Christian faith, it is the Calvinist who must give it. If there is not a distinctively Reformed method for the defense of every article of the Christian faith, then there is no way of clearly telling an unbeliever just how Christianity differs from his own position and why he should accept the Lord Jesus Christ as his personal Savior. We are happy and thankful, of course, for the work of witnessing done by Evangelicals. We are happy because of the fact that, in spite of their inconsistency in presenting the Christian testimony, something, often much, of the truth of the gospel shines through unto men, and they are saved.

V

The Authority of Scripture

"But how can anyone know anything about the 'Beyond'?" asks Mr. Black.

"Well, of course," replies Mr. Grey, "if you want absolute certainty such as one gets in geometry, Christianity does not offer it. We offer you only 'rational probability.' 'Christianity,' as I said in effect a moment ago when I spoke of the death of Christ, 'is founded on historical facts, which, by their very nature, cannot be demonstrated with geometric certainty. All judgments of historical particulars are at the mercy of the complexity of the time-space universe. . . . If the scientist cannot rise above rational probability in his empirical investigation, why should the Christian claim more?' And what is true of the death of Christ," adds Mr. Grey, "is, of course, also true of his resurrection. But this only shows that 'the Christian is in possession of a world-view which is making a sincere effort to come to grips with actual history.' "[13]

By speaking thus, Mr. Grey seeks for a point of contact with Mr. Black. For Mr. Black, history is something that floats on an infinitely extended and bottomless ocean of Chance. Therefore he can say that *anything* may happen. Who knows but the death and resurrection of Jesus as the Son of God might issue from this womb of Chance? Such events would have an equal chance of happening with "snarks, boojums, splinth, and gobble-de-gook." God himself may live in this realm of Chance. He is then "wholly other" than ourselves. And his revelation in history would then be wholly unique.

Now the Evangelical does not challenge this underlying philosophy of Chance as it controls the unbeliever's conception of history. He is so anxious to have the unbeliever accept the possibility of God's existence and the *fact* of the resurrection of Christ that, if necessary, he will exchange his own philosophy of fact for that of the unbeliever. Anxious to be genuinely "empirical" like the unbeliever, he will throw all the facts of Christianity into the bottomless pit of Chance. Or, rather, he will throw all these facts at the unbeliever, and the unbeliever throws them over his back into the bottomless pit of Chance.

Of course, this is the last thing that such men as Wilbur Smith, Edward J. Carnell, and J. Oliver Buswell, Jr., want to do. But in failing to challenge the philosophy of Chance that underlies the unbeliever's notion of "fact," they are in effect accepting it.

This approach of Mr. Grey is unavoidable if one holds to an Arminian theology. The Arminian view of man's free will implies that "possibility" is above God. But a "possibility" that is above God is the same thing as Chance. A God surrounded by Chance cannot speak with authority. He would be speaking into a vacuum. His voice could not be heard. And if God were surrounded by Chance, then human beings would be too. They would live in a vacuum, unable to hear either their own voices

[13] E. J. Carnell: *An Introduction to Christian Apologetics*, p. 113. For an extended critique of the apologetics of E. J. Carnell see the writer's *Case for Calvinism* (Presbyterian and Reformed Publishing Co.) and his forthcoming *The Future of Evangelicalism* (Presbyterian and Reformed Publishing Co.).

or those of others. Thus the whole of history, including all of its facts, would be without meaning.

It is this that the Reformed Christian, Mr. White, would tell Mr. Black. In the very act of presenting the resurrection of Christ or in the very act of presenting any other fact of historic Christianity, Mr. White would be presenting it as authoritatively interpreted in the Bible. He would argue that unless Mr. Black is willing to set the facts of history in the framework of the meaning authoritatively ascribed to them in the Bible, he will make gobble-de-gook of history.

If history were what Mr. Black assumes that it is, then *anything* might happen and then *nobody* would know what may happen. No one thing would then be more likely to happen than any other thing. David Hume, the great skeptic, has effectively argued that if you allow any room for Chance in your thought, then you no longer have the right to speak of probabilities. Whirl would be king. No one hypothesis would have any more relevance to facts than any other hypothesis. Did God raise Christ from the dead? Perchance he did. Did Jupiter do it? Perchance he did. What is Truth? Nobody knows. Such would be the picture of the universe if Mr. Black were right.

No comfort can be taken from the assurance of the Conservative that, since Christianity makes no higher claim than that of rational probability, "the system of Christianity can be refuted only by probability. Perhaps our loss is gain." How could one ever argue that there is a greater probability for the truth of Christianity than for the truth of its opposite if the very meaning of the word probability rests upon the idea of Chance? On this basis nature and history would be no more than a series of pointer readings pointing into the blank.

In assuming his philosophy of Chance and thus virtually saying that *nobody knows* what is back of the common objects of daily observation, Mr. Black also virtually says that the Christian view of things is wrong.

If I assert that there is a black cat in the closet, and you assert that nobody knows what is in the closet, you have virtually told me that I am wrong in my hypothesis. So when I tell Mr. Black that God exists, and he responds very graciously by saying that perhaps I am right since nobody knows what is in the "Beyond," he is virtually saying that I am wrong in my hypothesis. He is obviously thinking of such a God as could comfortably live in the realm of Chance. But the God of Scripture cannot live in the realm of Chance.

Mr. Black's response when confronted with the claims of God and his Christ, is essentially this: Nobody knows, but nevertheless your hypothesis is certainly wrong and mine is certainly right. Nobody knows whether God exists, but God certainly does not exist and Chance certainly does exist.

When Mr. Black thus virtually makes his universal negative assertion, saying in effect that God *cannot* possibly exist and that Christianity *cannot* possibly be true, he must surely be standing on something very solid. Is it on solid rock that he stands? No, he stands on water! He stands on his own "experience." But this experience, by his own assumption, rests again on Chance. Thus standing on Chance, he swings the "logician's postulate" and modestly asserts what cannot be in the "Beyond," of which he said before that nothing can be said.

Of course, what Mr. Black is doing appears very reasonable to himself. "Surely," he says, if questioned at all on the subject, "a rational man must have systematic coherence in his experience. Therefore he cannot accept as true anything that is not in accord with the law of noncontradiction. So long as you leave your God in the realm of the 'Beyond,' in the realm of the indeterminate, you may worship him by yourself alone. But as soon as you claim that your God has revealed himself in creation, in providence, or in your Scripture, so soon I shall put that revelation to a test by the principle of rational coherence.

"And by that test none of your doctrines are acceptable. All of them are contradictory. No rational man can accept any of them. If your God is eternal, then he falls outside of my experience and lives in the realm of the 'Beyond,' of the unknowable. But if he is to have anything to do with the world, then he must himself be wholly within the world. I must understand your God throughout if I am to speak intelligently of any relationship that he sustains to my world and to myself. Your idea that God is both eternal and unchangeable and yet sustains such relationships to the world as are involved in your doctrine of creation and providence, is flatly contradictory.

"For me to accept your God," continues Mr. Black, "you

must do to him what Karl Barth has done to him, namely, strip him of all the attributes that orthodox theology has assigned to him, and thus enable him to turn into the opposite of himself. With that sort of God I have a principle of unity that brings all my experience into harmony. And that God is wholly within the universe. If you offer me such a God and offer him as the simplest hypothesis with which I may, as a goal, seek to order my experience as it comes to me from the womb of Chance, then the law of noncontradiction will be satisfied. As a rational man I can settle for nothing less."

All this amounts to saying that Mr. Black, the lover of a Chance philosophy, the indeterminist, is at the same time an out-and-out determinist or fatalist. It is to say that Mr. Black, the irrationalist, who said that nobody knows what is in the "Beyond," is at the same time a flaming rationalist. For him only that can be which—so he thinks—he can exhaustively determine by logic must be. He may at first grant that anything may exist, but when he says this he at the same time says in effect that nothing can exist and have meaning for man but that which man himself can exhaustively know. Therefore, for Mr. Black, the God of Christianity cannot exist. For him the doctrine of creation cannot be true. There could be no revelation of God to man through nature and history. There can be no such thing as the resurrection of Christ.

Strangely enough, when Mr. Black thus says that God cannot exist and that the resurrection of Christ cannot be a fact, and when he also says that God may very well exist and that the resurrection of Christ may very well be a fact, he is not inconsistent with himself. For he must, to be true to his method, contradict himself in every statement that he makes about any fact whatsoever. If he does not, then he would deny either his philosophy of Chance or his philosophy of Fate. According to him, every fact that he meets has in it the two ingredients: that of Chance and that of Fate, that of the wholly unknown and that of the wholly known. Thus man makes the tools of thought, which the Creator has given him in order therewith to think God's thoughts after him on a created level, into the means by which he makes sure that God cannot exist, and therefore certainly cannot reveal himself.

When Mr. White meets Mr. Black he will make this issue

plain. He will tell Mr. Black that his methodology cannot make any fact or any group of facts intelligible to himself. Hear him as he speaks to the unbeliever:

"On your basis, Mr. Black, no fact can be identified by distinguishing it from any other fact. For all facts would be changing into their opposites all the time. All would be gobble-de-gook. At the same time, nothing could change at all; all would be one block of ice. Hath not God made foolish the wisdom of this world? He clearly has. I know you cannot see this even though it is perfectly clear. I know you have taken out your own eyes. Hence your inability to see is at the same time unwillingness to see. Pray God for forgiveness and repent."

But what will be the approach of the Conservative, Mr. Grey, on this question of logic? He will do the same sort of thing that we saw him do with respect to the question of facts. Mr. Grey will again try to please Mr. Black by saying that, of course, he will justify his appeal to the authority of the Bible by showing that the very idea of such an appeal, as well as the content of the Bible, are fully in accord with the demands of logic.

"You are quite right in holding that nothing meaningful can be said without presupposing the validity of the law of non-contradiction," says Mr. Grey.[14] " 'The conservative ardently defends a system of authority.'[15] But 'without reason to canvass the evidence of a given authority, how can one segregate a right authority from a wrong one? . . . Without systematic consistency to aid us, it appears that all we can do is to draw straws, count noses, flip coins to choose an authority. Once we *do* apply the law of contradiction, we are no longer appealing to *ipse dixit* authority, but to coherent truth.'[16] 'The Scriptures tell us to *test* the spirits (I John 4:1). This can be done only by applying the canons of truth. God cannot lie. His authority, therefore, and coherent truth are coincident at every point. Truth, not blind authority, saves us from being blind followers of the blind.'[17]

" 'Bring on your revelations!' " continues Mr. Grey. " 'Let

[14] *Idem*, p. 114.
[15] Cf. Carnell, *op. cit.*, p. 57.
[16] *Idem*, p. 71.
[17] *Idem*, p. 72.

them make peace with the law of contradiction and the facts of history, and they will deserve a rational man's assent.'[18] 'Any theology which rejects Aristotle's fourth book of the *Metaphysics* is big with the elements of its own destruction.'[19] 'If Paul were teaching that the crucified Christ were objectively foolish, in the sense that he cannot be rationally categorized, then he would have pointed to the insane and the demented as incarnations of truth.' "[20]

"Well," says Mr. Black, "this is great news indeed. I knew that the modernists were willing with us to start from human experience as the final reference point in all research. I knew that they were willing with us to start from Chance as the source of facts, in order then to manufacture such facts of nature and of history as the law of noncontradiction, based on Chance, will allow. I also knew that the new modernist, Karl Barth, is willing to make over his God so that he can change into the opposite of himself, in order that thus he may satisfy both our irrationalist philosophy of Chance and our rationalist philosophy of logic. But I did not know that there were any orthodox people who were willing to do such a thing. But you have surprised me before. You were willing to throw your resurrection into the realm of Chance in order to have me accept it. So I really should have expected that you would also be willing to make the law of noncontradiction rest upon man himself instead of upon God.

"And I am extremely happy that not only the Arminian Fundamentalists but also you less extreme or moderate Calvinists, like Buswell and Carnell, are now willing to test your own revelation by a principle that is wholly independent of that revelation. It is now only a matter of time until you will see that you have to come over on our side altogether.

"I do not like the regular Calvinists. But they are certainly quite right from their own point of view. Mr. White claims that I am a creature of God. He says that all facts are made by God and controlled by the providence of God. He says that all men have sinned against God in Adam their representative. He adds

[18] *Idem*, p. 73.
[19] *Idem*, p. 178.
[20] *Idem*, pp. 77, 78.

that therefore I am spiritually blind and morally perverse. He says all this and more on the basis of the absolute authority of Scripture. He would interpret me, my facts, and my logic in terms of the authority of that Scripture. He says I need this authority. He says I need nothing but this authority. His Scripture, he claims, is sufficient and final. And the whole thing, he claims, is clear.

"Now all this looks like plain historic Protestantism to me. I can intellectually understand the Calvinist on this matter of authority. I cannot understand you. You seem to me to want to have your cake and eat it. If you believe in Scriptural authority, then why not explain all things, man, fact, and logic in terms of it? If you want with us to live by your own authority, by the experience of the human race, then why not have done with the Bible as absolute authority? It then, at best, gives you the authority of the expert.

"In your idea of the rational man who tests all things by the facts of history and by the law of non-contradiction, you have certainly made a point of contact with us. If you carry this through, you will indeed succeed in achieving complete coincidence between your ideas and ours. And, with us, you will have achieved complete coincidence between the ideas of man and the ideas of God. But the reason for this coincidence of your ideas with ours, and for the coincidence of man's ideas with God's, is that you then have a God and a Christ who are identical with man.

"Do you not think, Mr. Grey, that this is too great a price for you to pay? I am sure that you do not thus mean to drag down your God into the Universe. I am sure that you do not thus mean to crucify your Christ afresh. But why then halt between two opinions? I do not believe Christianity, but, if I did, I think I would stand with Mr. White."

VI

Proofs for the Existence of God

When Mr. Black objects against Mr. White that unconditional surrender to the authority of Scripture is irrational, then Mr. Grey nods approval and says that, of course, the "rational man" has a perfect right to test the credibility of Scripture by logic. When the Bible speaks of God's sovereign election of some men to salvation this must mean something that fits in with his "rational nature." When Mr. Black objects to Mr. White that unconditional surrender to Scripture is rationalistic, then Mr. Grey again nods approval and says that, of course, genuine human personality has a perfect right to test the content of Scripture by experience. When the Bible speaks of God by his counsel controlling whatsoever comes to pass, this must mean something that fits in with man's freedom. God created man and gave man a share in his own freedom; men therefore participate in his being.

But what of natural or general revelation? Here surely there can be no difference, you say, between the requirements of Mr. White and Mr. Grey. Here there is no law and no promise; here there is only fact. How then can you speak of requirement at all? Here surely Mr. White can forget his "five points of Calvinism" and join Mr. Grey in taking Mr. Black through the picture gallery of this world, pointing out its beauties to him so that with them he will spontaneously exclaim, "The whole chorus of nature raises one hymn to the praises of its Creator."

Let us think of Mr. White as trying hard to forget his "five points." "Surely," he says to himself, "there can be nothing wrong with joining Mr. Grey in showing Mr. Black the wonders of God's creation. We believe in the same God, do we not? Both of us want to show Mr. Black the facts of creation so that he will believe in God. When Mr. Black says: 'I catch no meaning from all I have seen, and I pass on, quite as I came, confused and dismayed' Mr. Grey and I can together take him by plane to the Mt. Wilson observatory so he may see the starry heavens above. Surely the source of knowledge for the natural sciences is the Book of Nature, which is given to everyone. Do not the Scriptures themselves teach that there is a light in nature, per se, which cannot be, and is not, transmitted through the spectacles of the Word? If this were not so, how could the Scriptures say of those who have only the light of nature that they are without excuse?"

So the three men, Mr. White, Mr. Grey, and Mr. Black, go here and there and everywhere. Mr. White and Mr. Grey agree to share the expense. Mr. Black is their guest.

They go first to the Mt. Wilson observatory to see the starry skies above. "How wonderful, how grand!" exclaims Mr. Grey. To the marvels of the telescope they add those of the microscope. They circle the globe to see "the wonders of the world." There is no end to the "exhibits" and Mr. Black shows signs of weariness. So they sit down on the beach. Will not Mr. Black now sign on the dotted line?

As they wait for the answer, Mr. Grey spies a watch someone has lost. Holding it in his hand he says to Mr. Black: "Look round the world: contemplate the whole and every part of it: you will find it to be nothing but one great machine, subdivided into an infinite number of lesser machines, which again admit of subdivisions, to a degree beyond that which human senses and faculties can trace and explain. All these various machines, and even their minute parts, are adjusted to each other with an accuracy, which ravishes into admiration all men, who have ever contemplated them. The curious adapting of means to ends, throughout all nature, resembles exactly, though it much exceeds, the productions of human contrivance; of human designs, thought, wisdom and intelligence. Since, therefore, the effects resemble each other, we are led to infer, by all the rules of analogy, that the causes also resemble one another; and that the Author of Nature is somewhat similar to the mind of man; though possessed of much larger faculties, proportioned to the grandeur of the work, which he has executed.

"Now, Mr. Black, I don't want to put undue pressure on you. You know your own needs in your own business. But I think that as a rational being, you owe it to yourself to join the theistic party. Isn't it highly probable that there is a God?

"I'm not now asking you to become a Christian. We take things one step at a time. I'm only speaking of the Book of Nature. Of course, if there is a God and if this God should have a Son and if this Son should also reveal himself, it is not likely to be more difficult for you to believe in him than it is now to believe in the Father. But just now I am only asking you to admit that there is a great accumulation of evidence of the sort that any scientist or philosopher must admit to be valid for the existence of a God back of and above this world. You see this watch. Isn't it highly probable that a power higher than itself has made it? You know the purpose of a watch. Isn't it highly probable that the wonderful contrivances of nature serve the purpose of a God? Looking back we are naturally led to a God who is the cause of this world; looking forward we think of a God who has a purpose with this world. So far as we can observe the course and constitution of the universe there is, I think, no difficulty on your own adopted principles, against belief in a God. Why not become a theist? You do want to be on the winning side, don't you? Well, the Gallup poll of the universe indicates a tendency toward the final victory of theism."

When Mr. Grey had finished his obviously serious and eloquent plea, Mr. Black looked very thoughtful. He was clearly a gentleman. He disliked disappointing his two friends after all the generosity they had shown him. But he could not honestly see any basic difference between his own position and theirs. So he declined politely but resolutely to sign on the dotted line. He refused to be "converted" to theism. In substance he spoke as follows: "You speak of evidence of rationality and purpose in the universe. You would trace this rationality or purpose back to a rational being back of the universe who, you think, is likely to have a purpose with the universe. But who is back of your God to explain him in turn? By your own definition your God is not absolute or self-sufficient. You say that he probably exists; which means that you admit that probably he does not exist. But probability rests upon possibility. Now I think that any scientific person should come with an open mind to the observation of the facts of the universe. He ought to begin by assuming that any sort of fact may exist. And I was glad to observe that on this all important point you agree with me. Hence the only kind of God that either of us can believe in is one who may not exist. In other words, neither of us do or can believe in a God who cannot *not* exist. And it was just this sort of God, a God who is self-sufficient, and as such necessarily existent, that I thought you Christian theists believed in."

By this time Mr. White was beginning to squirm. He was beginning to realize that he had sold out the God of his theology, the sovereign God of Scripture by his silent consent to the argument of Mr. Grey. Mr. Black was right, he felt at once. Either one presupposes God back of the ideas of possibility or one presupposes that the idea of possibility is back of God. Either one says with historic Reformed theology on the basis of Scripture that what God determines and only what God determines is possible, or one says with all non-Christian forms of thought that possibility surrounds God. But for the moment Mr. White was stupefied. He could say nothing. So Mr. Black simply drew the conclusion from what he had said in the following words:

"Since you in your effort to please me have accepted my basic assumption with respect to possibility and probability it follows that your God, granted he exists, is of no use whatsoever in explaining the universe. He himself needs in turn to be explained. Let us remember the story of the Indian philosopher and his elephant. It was never more applicable than to the present subject. If the material world rests upon a similar ideal world, this ideal world must rest upon some other; and so on, without end. It were better, therefore, never to look beyond the present material world. In short, gentlemen, much as I dislike not to please you, what you offer is nothing better than what I already possess. Your God is himself surrounded by pure possibility or Chance; in what way can he help me? And how could I be responsible to him? For you, as for me, all things ultimately end in the irrational."

At this point Mr. Grey grew pale. In desperation he searched his arsenal for another argument that might convince Mr. Black. There was one that he had not used for some time. The arguments for God that he had so far used, he labeled *a posteriori* arguments. They ought, he had thought, to appeal to the "empirical" temper of the times. They started from human experience with causation and purpose and by analogy argued to the idea of a cause of and a purpose with the world as a whole. But Mr. Black had pointed out that if you start with the ideas of cause and purpose as intelligible to man without God when these concepts apply to relations within the universe, then you cannot consistently say that you need God for the idea of cause or purpose when these concepts apply to the universe as a whole. So now Mr. Grey drew out the drawer marked *a priori* argument. In public he called this the argument from finite to absolute being. "As finite creatures," he said to Mr. Black, "we have the idea of absolute being. The idea of a finite being involves of necessity the idea of an absolute being. We have the notion of an absolute being; surely there must be a reality corresponding to our idea of such a being; if not, all our ideas may be false. Surely we must hold that reality is ultimately rational and coherent and that our ideas participate in this rationality. If not how would science be possible?"

When Mr. Grey had thus delivered himself of this appeal to logic rather than to fact, then Mr. White for a moment seemed to take courage. Was not this at least to get away from the idea of a God who probably exists? Surely the "incommunicable attributes of God," of which he had been taught in his catechism classes, were all based upon and expressive of the idea of God as necessarily existing. But Mr. Black soon disillusioned him for the second time. Said he in answer to the argument from Mr. Grey, "Again I cannot see any basic difference between your position and mine. Of course, we must believe that reality is ultimately rational. And of course, we must hold that our minds participate in this rationality. But when you thus speak you thereby virtually assert that we must not believe in a God whose existence is independent of our human existence. A God whom we are to know must with us be a part of a rational system that is mutually accessible to and expressive of both. If God is necessary to you then you are also necessary to God. That is the only sort of God that is involved in your argument."

"But Mr. Black, this is terrible, this is unbearable! We do want you to believe in God. I bear witness to his existence. I will give you a Bible. Please read it! It tells you of Jesus Christ and how you may be saved by his blood. I am born again and you can be born again too if you will only believe. Please do believe in God and be saved."

Meanwhile Mr. White took new courage. He realized that he had so far made a great mistake in keeping silent during the time that Mr. Grey had presented his arguments. The arguments for the existence of God taken from the ideas of cause and purpose as set forth by Mr. Grey had led to pure irrationalism and Chance. The argument about an absolute being as set forth by Mr. Grey had led to pure rationalism and determinism. In both cases, Mr. Black had been quite right in saying that a God whose existence is problematic or a God who exists by the same necessity as does the universe is still an aspect of or simply the whole of the universe. But now he felt that perhaps Mr. Grey was right in simply witnessing to the existence of God. He thought that if the arguments used are not logically coercive they may at least be used as a means with which to witness to unbelievers. And surely witnessing to God's existence was always in order. But poor Mr. White was to be disillusioned again. For the witness bearing done by Mr. Grey was based on the assumption that the belief in God is a purely non-rational or even irrational matter.

Mr. Black's reply to the words of Mr. Grey indicated this fact all too clearly. Said Mr. Black to Mr. Grey: "I greatly appreciate your evident concern for my eternal welfare. But there are two or three questions that I would like to have you answer. In the first place I would ask whether in thus witnessing to me you thereby admit that the arguments for the existence of God have no validity? Or rather do you not thereby admit that these arguments, if they prove anything, prove that God is finite and correlative to man and therefore that your position is not basically different from mine?"

Mr. Grey did not answer because he could not answer this question otherwise than by agreeing with Mr. Black.

"In the second place," said Mr. Black, "you are now witnessing to Christ as well as to God, to Christianity as well as to theism. I suppose your argument for Christianity would be similar in nature to your argument for theism would it not? You would argue that the Jesus of the New Testament is probably the Son of God and that he quite probably died for the sins of men. But now you witness to me about your Christ. And by witnessing instead of reasoning you seem to admit that there is no objective claim for the truth of what you hold with respect to Christ. Am I right in all this?"

Again Mr. Grey made no answer. The only answer he could consistently have given would be to agree with Mr. Black.

"In the third place," said Mr. Black, "you are now witnessing not only to God the Father, to Jesus Christ the Son, but also to the Holy Spirit. You say you are born again, that you know you are saved and that at present I am lost. Now if you have had an experience of some sort it would be unscientific for me to deny it. But if you want to witness to me about your experience you must make plain to me the nature of that experience. And to do that you must do so in terms of principles that I understand. Such principles must need be accessible to all. Now if you make plain your experience to me in terms of principles that are plain to me as unregenerate, then wherein is your regeneration unique? On the other hand, if you still maintain that your experience of regeneration is unique, then can you say anything about it to me so that I may understand? And does not then your witness bearing appear to be wholly unintelligible and devoid of meaning? Thus again you cannot make any claim to the objective truth of your position.

"Summing up the whole matter, I would say in the first place, that your arguments for the existence of God have rightfully established me in my unbelief. They have shown that nothing can be said for the existence of a God who is actually the Creator and controller of the world. I would say in the second place that using such arguments as you have used for the existence of God commits you to using similar arguments for the truth of Christianity with similar fatal results for your position. In both cases you first use intellectual argument upon principles that presuppose the justice of my unbelieving position. Then when it is pointed out to you that such is the case you turn to witnessing. But then your witnessing is in the nature of the case an activity that you yourself have virtually admitted to be wholly irrational and unintelligible."

When Mr. Black had finished Mr. White was in a great distress. But it was through this very distress that at last he saw the richness of his own faith. He made no pretense to having greater intellectual power than Mr. Grey. He greatly admired the real faith and courage of Mr. Grey. But he dared keep silence no longer. His silence had been sin, he knew. Mr. Black had completely discomfited Mr. Grey so that he had not another word to say. Mr. Black was about to leave them established rather than challenged in his unbelief. And all of that in spite of the best intentions and efforts of Mr. Grey, speaking for both of them. A sense of urgent responsibility to make known the claims of the sovereign God pressed upon him. He now saw clearly first that the arguments for the existence of God as conducted by Mr. Grey, are based on the assumption that the unbeliever is right with respect to the principles in terms of which he explains all things. These principles are: (a) that man is not a creature of God but rather is ultimate and as such must properly consider himself instead of God the final reference point in explaining all things; (b) that all other things beside himself are non-created but controlled by Chance; and (c) that the power of logic that he possesses is the means by which he must determine what is possible or impossible in the universe of Chance.

At last it dawned upon Mr. White that first to admit that the principles of Mr. Black, the unbeliever, are right and then to seek to win him to the acceptance of the existence of God the Creator and judge of all men is like first admitting that the United States had historically been a province of the Soviet Union but ought at the same time to be recognized as an independent and all-controlling political power.

In the second place, Mr. White now saw clearly that a false type of reasoning for the truth of God's existence and for the truth of Christianity involves a false kind of witnessing for the existence of God and for the truth of Christianity. If one reasons for the existence of God and for the truth of Christianity on the assumption that Mr. Black's principles of explanation are valid, then one must witness on the same assumption. One must then make plain to Mr. Black, in terms of principles which Mr. Black accepts, what it means to be born again. Mr. Black will then apply the principles of modern psychology of religion to Mr. Grey's "testimony" with respect to his regeneration and show that it is something that naturally comes in the period of adolescence.

In the third place Mr. White now saw clearly that it was quite "proper" for Mr. Grey to use a method of reasoning and a method of witness-bearing that is based upon the truth of anti-Christian and anti-theistic assumptions. Mr. Grey's theology is Arminian or Lutheran. It is therefore based upon the idea that God is not wholly sovereign over man. It assumes that man's responsibility implies a measure of autonomy of the sort that is the essence and foundation of the whole of Mr. Black's thinking. It is therefore to be expected that Mr. Grey will assume that Mr. Black needs not to be challenged on his basic assumption with respect to his own assumed ultimacy or autonomy.

From now on Mr. White decided that, much as he enjoyed the company of Mr. Grey and much as he trusted his evident sincerity and basic devotion to the truth of God, yet he must go his own way in apologetics as he had, since the Reformation, gone his own way in theology. He made an appointment with Mr. Black to see him soon. He expressed to Mr. Grey his great love for him as a fellow believer, his great admiration for his fearless and persistent efforts to win men to an acceptance of truth as it is in Jesus. Then he confessed to Mr. Grey that his conscience had troubled him during the entire time of their travels with Mr. Black. He had started in good faith, thinking that Mr. Grey's efforts at argument and witnessing might win Mr. Black. He had therefore been quite willing, especially since Mr. Grey was through his constant efforts much more conversant with such things than he was, to be represented by Mr. Grey. But now he had at last come to realize that not only had the effort been utterly fruitless and self-frustrating but more than that it had been terribly dishonoring to God. How could the eternal I AM be pleased with being presented as being a god and as probably existing, as necessary for the explanation of some things but not of all things, as one who will be glad to recognize the ultimacy of his own creatures? Would the God who had in paradise required of men implicit obedience now be satisfied with a claims and counter-claims arrangement with his creatures?

From the quotations given above the reader can for himself discern why I have advocated what seems to me to be a Reformed as over against the traditional method of Apologetics. The traditional method was constructed by Roman Catholics and Arminians. It was, so to speak, made to fit Romanist or Evangelical theology. And since Roman Catholic and Evangelical theology compromises the Protestant doctrines of Scripture, of God, of man, of sin and of redemption so the traditional method of Apologetics compromises Christianity in order to win men to an acceptance of it.

The traditional method compromises the Biblical doctrine of God in not clearly distinguishing his self-existence from his relation to the world. The traditional method compromises the Biblical doctrine of God and his relation to his revelation to man by not clearly insisting that man must not seek to determine the nature of God, otherwise than from his revelation.

The traditional method compromises the Biblical doctrine of the counsel of God by not taking it as the only all-inclusive ultimate cause of whatsoever comes to pass.

The traditional method therefore compromises the *clarity* of God's revelation to man, whether this revelation comes through general or through special revelation. Created facts are not taken to be clearly revelational of God; all the facts of nature and of man are said to indicate no more than that *a* god *probably* exists.

The traditional method compromises the *necessity* of supernatural revelation in relation to natural revelation. It does so in failing to do justice to the fact that even in paradise man had to interpret natural revelation in the light of the covenantal obligations placed upon him by God through supernatural communciation. In consequence the traditional method fails to recognize the necessity of redemptive supernatural revelation as concomitant to natural revelation after the fall of man.

The traditional method compromises the *sufficiency* of redemptive supernatural revelation in Scripture inasmuch as it allows for wholly new facts to appear in Reality, new for God as well as for man.

The traditional method compromises the *authority* of Scripture by not taking it as self-attesting in the full sense of the term.

The traditional method compromises the Biblical doctrine of man's creation in the image of God by thinking of him as being "free" or ultimate rather than as analogical.

The traditional method compromises the Biblical doctrine of the covenant by not making Adam's representative action determinative for the future.

The traditional method compromises the Biblical doctrine of sin, in not thinking of it as an ethical break with

God which is complete in principle even though not in practice.

In spite of these things, this traditional method has been employed by Reformed theologians and this fact has stood in the way of the development of a distinctly Reformed apologetic.

Chapter XI

AMSTERDAM AND OLD PRINCETON

It was when Abraham Kuyper published his work on the *Encyclopedia of Sacred Theology* that B. B. Warfield wrote a review of it. Warfield was committed to the traditional method of defending Christianity. With appreciation for Kuyper as a theologian Warfield none-the-less feared that his apologetics would lead to mysticism. The old Princeton method of Apologetics was largely taken from Butler's *Analogy* as this was in turn largely taken from Thomas Aquinas. According to this method the natural man was assumed to be able:

a. to work up a natural theology that would show theism to be more probably true than any other theory of reality, and

b. to show that Christianity is more probably true than any other theory of sin and redemption.

I

Warfield and Kuyper

The difference between Warfield and Kuyper appears sharply in their different evaluation of natural theology.

What evaluation is to be placed upon the interpretation of natural revelation, internal and external, that the natural man, who operates with the principle of autonomy, has given? Can the difference between the principle of autonomy and that of Christian theism be ignored so that men can together seek to interpret natural revelation in terms of one procedure?[1]

Kuyper answers in the negative. The idea of two ultimate principles is, he insists, a contradiction in terms.

Either allow that the natural principle has within itself the legitimate powers of self-interpretation and then expect the spe-

[1] *A Christian Theory of Knowledge*, p. 156.

cial principle to be destroyed by it, or else maintain that the natural principle is in any case finite and more particularly sinful and then present the special principle to it with the demand of submission. Says Kuyper: "Since the *revelatio specialis* presupposes the fact that the operation of the natural principle has been disturbed in its healthful function through sin, it follows as a matter of course that this natural principle has lost the right of judgment. Whoever attributes this right of judgment to it recognizes it *ipso facto* as sound, and has therewith done away with the *ratio sufficiens* of special revelation."[2] Again, the power of thought may be compared to a sharp blade. If this blade is put into a mower but it is put too high, so that it cannot reach the grass there is no good result.[3]

The result is, says Kuyper, even worse than that. For the action of sinful human thought is not merely fruitless; it is destructive of the truth. Sinful man is out to destroy the special principle when it comes to him with its challenge. The natural principle takes an antithetical position over against the special principle and seeks to destroy it by means of logical manipulation.[4] The natural principle lives from *apistia*; its faith is fixed upon the creature instead of upon the Creator.[5] It will therefore use its principles of discontinuity and of continuity in order by means of them to destroy the witness of Scripture to itself. The natural man is perfectly consistent with himself and intellectually honest in doing so. He is simply true to his principle. A principle, a first premise, cannot be proved. It is the basis of proof. If proof were given of a principle it would cease to be a principle.[6] The Christian realizes that the non-Christian does not know the truth about himself and about his power of reason. He should therefore expect that the non-Christian will, from his principle, seek to destroy the special principle. He will do so by saying that the "irrational" element, that is the supernatural, is like the irrational element found everywhere. Or he will by means of his principle of continuity absorb all the claims of Scripture into a system of logical gradation.[7] When you as a

[2] *Encyclopaedie der Heilige Godgeleerdheid,* II, 335.

[3] *Idem,* p. 241. [4] *Idem,* p. 242. [5] *Idem,* p. 254. [6] *Idem,* p. 338.

[7] *Idem,* p. 339. "Zelf toch erkent ge van uw eigen standpunt, dat wie buiten φωτισμός staat, het werkelijk bestand van zijn eigen wezen, en dus ook van zijn rede, niet inziet en niet inzien kan."

Christian present the unbeliever with the fact of miracles performed this has no power of compulsion for him who because of his principle cannot even allow the possibility of miracles.[8]

Kuyper makes a special point of the necessity of holding that Scripture itself is not merely a record of but is itself revelation. One cannot separate cool atmosphere from the ice through which it comes. Without the Scripture as revelation there is no revélation. If one does not take the Scripture itself as revelation then one ends by way of Origen in the philosophy of Plato or of Aristotle.[9]

Similarly the idea of the testimony of the Spirit, too, is part of the special principle the whole of which one makes the foundation of his thought or the whole of which one rejects in the name of the natural principle.[10] With the light of Scripture it is possible for man to read nature aright. Without that light we cannot, even on the Areopagus, reach further than the unknown God.[11]

It is thus that the enlightened consciousness of the people of God stands over against the natural consciousness of the world. For the believers, Scripture is the principle of theology. As such it cannot be the conclusion of other premises, but it is *the* premise from which all other conclusions are drawn.[12]

From what has been said it is not to be concluded that Kuyper has no great appreciation of the knowledge of God that may be obtained from nature. The contrary is true. He lays the greatest possible stress upon the idea that the Bible is not a book that has fallen from heaven. There is a natural foundation for it. This natural foundation is found in the fact that the natural is itself the creation of the same God who in the special principle comes to man for his redemption. In form at least Kuyper would therefore agree with Aquinas when he says that the supernatural or spiritual does not destroy but perfects nature. But Kuyper's ideas of the natural and the supernatural are quite different from those of Aquinas. For Aquinas the natural is inherently defective: it partakes of the nature of non-being. Hence sin is partly at least to be ascribed to finitude. For Kuyper the natural, as it came from the hand of God, was perfect. To be

[8] *Idem*, p. 341.
[9] *Idem*, p. 316.
[10] *Idem*, p. 320.
[11] *Idem*, p. 332.
[12] *Idem*, p. 517.

sure, there was to be development. And historically, this development has come by way of grace. But for all that it is an "accident," something incidental to the fulfillment of the natural. Christ came into the world to save, and in saving developed to its full fruition the powers of the natural. Thus grace is not reduced to something that is to be naturally expected as a development of the natural. The gradation motif of Aquinas is replaced by the idea of grace as "accidental" as the means by which sin, which is wholly unnatural or contrary to the natural, and destructive of the natural, is removed, in order that the truly natural may thus come to expression.

The natural man, working on his principle, working from the principle of his second nature, must not be given the opportunity of destroying the "accidental" character of redemption. He would be given this opportunity if his principle of autonomy were not challenged. Working on his principle he would destroy the "accidental" character of grace altogether. He would do what Romanism has so largely done. He would seek to show that redemption is naturally to be expected by man. He would show on the other hand that the redemptive is something without determinate character in history so that every man may regard it as he pleases.

It will now be seen that what has been advocated in this syllabus has in large measure been prepared under the influence of Kuyper, or has at least to a large extent been suggested by his thinking. The interdependence of the various aspects of what Kuyper so effectively speaks of as the special principle is something that would seem to be of the essence of a sound doctrine of Scripture. It is difficult to see how else the Scriptures can be presented as self-attesting. As soon as the elements of the special principle, such as the indications of divinity, the testimony of the Spirit, or the words of Christ are set next to one another, as largely independent of one another, the natural man is given an opportunity to do his destructive work. He is then allowed to judge at least with respect to one or more of these elements. And if he is allowed to judge of the legitimacy or meaning of any one of them he may as well be given the right to judge of all of them. If the natural man is allowed the right to take the documents of the gospels as merely historically trustworthy witnesses to the Christ and his work, he will claim and can consistently claim also to be the judge of the Christ himself. For it is only if the Christ be taken as the Son of God that he can be said legitimately to identify himself. If he is not presupposed as such then his words too have no power. Then they too are absorbed in what is a hopeless relativity of history.[13]

My critics might well concern themselves with this *absolutistic* position of Kuyper's. This head-on collision between the principle of the natural man and the principle of the regenerate man, can it do anything but destroy science? Warfield thought it would. He therefore reduced Kuyper's distinction between two kinds of science to one of degree. Otherwise "there would be no science attainable at all."[14]

Warfield accordingly attributes to "right reason" the ability to interpret natural revelation with essential correctness. This "right reason" is not the reason of the Christian. It is the reason that is confronted with Christianity and possesses some criterion apart from Christianity with which to judge of the truth of Christianity.[15]

Appealing to "right reason" in the sense defined, Warfield asks it to judge in its own terms that Christianity is true.

We found the whole Christian system on the doctrine of plenary inspiration as little as we found it upon the doctrine of angelic existences. Were there no such thing as inspiration, Christianity would be true, and all its essential doctrines would be credibly witnessed to us in the generally trustworthy reports of the teaching of our Lord. . . . Inspiration is not the most fundamental of Christian doctrines, nor even the first thing we prove about the Scriptures. It is the last and crowning fact as to the Scriptures. These we first prove authentic, historically credible, generally trustworthy, before we prove them inspired.[16]

[13] *A Christian Theory of Knowledge*, pp. 156-158.

[14] Cf. Warfield's "Introduction" to Beattie's *Apologetics*, 1903.

[15] Cf. his article on "Apologetics" in the *New Schaff Herzog Encyclopedia of Religious Knowledge*, New York, 1932.

[16] "The Real Problem of Inspiration" in *The Inspiration and Authority of the Bible*, p. 210.

The result of this method of appealing to "right reason" is that theism and Christianity are shown to be only *probably* true.[17]

It is not, of course, that Warfield himself entertains any doubts about the plenary inspiration of Scripture. He was one of its greatest advocates. Nor is it that he disagrees with Calvin in maintaining the clarity of natural revelation or in holding that all men have the sense of deity. It is only that in Apologetics, Warfield wanted to operate in neutral territory with the non-believer. He thought that this was the only way to show to the unbeliever that theism and Christianity are objectively true. He sought for an objectivity that bridged the gulf between Kuyper's "natural" and special principles.

I have chosen the position of Abraham Kuyper. But I am unable to follow him when from the fact of the mutually destructive character of the two principles he concludes to the uselessness of reasoning with the natural man.

The Arminian holds that on the Reformed conception of man there is no sense to preaching. There would, the Arminian argues, be no approach to an identity of meanings between the preacher and the man "dead in trespasses and sins" to whom he preaches. The dead man cannot even count and weigh and measure. There is an absolute severance of all connection between him and the living.

For this absolute deadness of the natural man, the Arminian substitutes the notion of degrees of deadness, in order thus to establish degrees of contact with the truth. There can be no absolutely evil deed because then the will itself would be destroyed. It is ambiguous or meaningless, says the Arminian, to talk about the natural man as knowing God and yet not truly knowing God. Knowing is knowing.

[17] *Idem*, p. 218.

A man either knows or he does not know. He may know less or more, but if he does not "truly" know, he knows not at all. The Calvinist, he argues, is an absolutist who destroys the light of day.

In reply to this the Calvinist insists that there are no degrees in deadness. The natural man does not know God. But to be thus without knowledge, without living, loving, true knowledge of God, he must be one who knows God in the sense of having the sense of deity (Romans I). For the spiritual deadness of the natural man is what it is as suppression of the knowledge of God given man by virtue of creation in God's image.

Hence Warfield was quite right in maintaining that Christianity is objectively defensible. And the natural man has the ability to understand intellectually, though not spiritually, the challenge presented to him. And no challenge is presented to him unless it is shown him that on his *principle* he would destroy all truth and meaning. Then, if the Holy Spirit enlightens him spiritually, he will be born again "unto knowledge" and adopt with love the principle he was previously anxious to destroy.

II

WILLIAM BRENTON GREENE, JR. [18]

When Warfield flourished at Princeton in the field of systematic theology it was William Brenton Greene, Jr. who, for some time, occupied the Chair of Apologetics. He was the present writer's revered teacher.

In what he has written, Greene states and defends the historic Reformed position with respect to Scripture much in the way that Warfield does. Speaking of the Bible he says: "We do not obey it because it is reasonable; we believe it to be reasonable ultimately because it is 'the word' of Him who is the source of all reason" (*Christian Doctrine*, Philadelphia, 1905, p.

[18] The rest of the material of this chapter is taken from my syllabus on *A Christian Theory of Knowledge.*

12). On the other hand, and again like Warfield, Greene defends the notion that the idea of the Bible as the Word of God can be made to appear reasonable to "reason" in terms of principles which that reason, though not distinctly interpreted in Christian terms, must itself recognize as valid. In short, Greene follows the traditional method of apologetics as worked out by Bishop Butler and others. (He recommends as an excellent book on apologetics the treatise of George P. Fisher entitled, *The Grounds of Theistic and Christian Belief*. He does so in an article under the title "The Function of Reason in Christianity," in the *Presbyterian and Reformed Review*, 1895, pp. 481 ff.)

By "reason" Greene means "the cognitive faculty, that which perceives, compares, judges, and infers." This definition of reason is taken from Charles Hodge. What is the function of this reason? The answer is as follows: "Within its own sphere it may be a source and ground and measure of religious truth" (*op. cit.*, p. 481). And as it has this function in religion in general, reason has a similar function with respect to Christianity. The most important knowledge that man needs lies beyond reason. Reason must, to be sure, function within the limitations that are due to sin and to finitude. Even so it has its own independent function to perform with respect to Christianity.

What then is the function of reason "in relation to the Bible, or Inspired Word of God?" (*op. cit.*, p. 498.) The answer is:

> For all that logically precedes the Scriptures, as the being and personality of God, the need of a written revelation, etc.; we must go back to philosophy, to reason pure and simple. Even the Romanists admit this. . . . This is evidently true. Though reason is not infallible, yet antecedently to revelation, it is, as we have seen, the only instrument of investigation, the only test. Hence, Henry B. Smith has well said: "If we cannot construct the foundation and the outworks of the Christian system on impregnable grounds; if we cannot show the possibility of miracles, and of a revelation; if we cannot prove, absolutely prove . . . the existence of a wise, intelligent, personal, and providential Ruler of all things: then we are merged in infidelity, or given over to an unfounded faith. If we cannot settle these points on the field of open discussion, we cannot settle them

at all." Nor may it be said that reason's results cannot be certain, inasmuch as, since she cannot discover the truths of revelation, she cannot prove the necessity of them. A man may be too sick or too ignorant to find the remedy that he needs, and yet not be too sick or too ignorant to make known what he needs.

Reason should judge of the evidence that the Scriptures are the Word of God, and so to be received on his authority. Faith in them as such is irrational and impossible without evidence; for faith involves assent, and assent is conviction produced by evidence. . . .

Again,

Reason should distinguish among the interpretations of the Scriptures between what is above reason in the true sense of beyond it, and what is above reason in the wrong sense of out of relation to it, or contrary to it (*op. cit.*, p. 499). The other points mentioned need not concern us.

In a series of four articles on the *Metaphysics of Christian Apologetics* (in the *Presbyterian and Reformed Review*, 1898) the position taken is similar to that of the article just discussed.

The first article of this series deals with the subject of *Reality*. Says Greene:

Christian apologetics is that theological science which sets forth the proofs to the reason that Christianity is the supernatural, the authoritative, the final religion, equally for us and for all men; in a word, the absolute religion (*op. cit.*, p. 60).

And metaphysics is, "the science of first and fundamental truths." Accordingly the metaphysics of apologetics must establish to reason the basic principles not merely of truth in general but particularly those that sustain a peculiar relation to Christianity. The truths with which the metaphysics of apologetics is concerned are such truths as are "independent of the Christian revelation," while yet they are "the conditions of it and thus of its absolute vindication" (*op. cit.*, p. 62).

Such truths are four in number:

Reality, or the truth that what we call real existence implies substance, and so is not a succession of mere appearances; *Duality*, or the truth that substance is of two essentially different kinds, mind and matter; *Personality*, or the truth of the real existence of mind as intelligent, voluntary self-conscious entities; and *Immortality*, or the truth that the self-conscious mind or person is fitted for real existence independent of the body and so for life after death. These truths, as it would seem must be evident, and may all be known prior to the Christian revelation, and are all indispensable to the vindication and even to the understanding of it (*op. cit.*, p. 62).

To establish Reality as outlined above, appeal must be made to the "trustworthiness of consciousness." And the "denial of the trustworthiness of the testimony of consciousness to reality is suicidal" (*idem*, p. 81).

Under the heading of *Duality* Greene seeks to disprove first the claims of materialism. Materialism, he argues, "presupposes the mind which it would eliminate" (*idem*, p. 268). Then he seeks to disprove idealism. "Logic cannot reason out being," and "logic implies a logician" (*idem*, p. 271). Psychological idealism "outrages consciousness" (*idem*, p. 275). Thirdly he seeks to disprove idealistic materialism. "The reality of the soul is the condition of science" (*idem*, p. 282). Greene then seeks to prove Dualism positively. "Sense perception seems to imply it" (p. 284). It "has been and is the working hypothesis of the race" (p. 285). The verdict of common sense renders it *presumptively* true (p. 285). It has "inherent reasonableness." "Duality is the only theory of reality that gives to life and even to existence any true significance" (*ibid.*).

As to *Personality*, reasoning presupposes it and "is irrational without it" (p. 473). "The burden of proof rests on those who would deny personality" (p. 493). It is self-evident (p. 497).

When he deals with *Morality* Greene shows that to deny an "objective obligatory ideal" ends in absurdity (p. 680). The burden of proof is on those who would deny such an ideal (p. 681). The notion of such an ideal "meets the requirements of the case" (*ibid.*). Men have a clear and distinct "sense of rightness."

We turn now to an important article by Professor Greene on the "Supernatural." It was published in the *Biblical and Theo-*

logical Studies, which was put out in commemoration of the one hundredth anniversary of Princeton Seminary (New York, 1912).

What is meant by "the Supernatural"? It is "being that is above the sequence of *all* nature whether physical or spiritual; substance that is not caused, and that is not determined whether physically and necessarily as in the case of physical nature or rationally and freely as in the case of spiritual nature; in a word, unique reality the essence of whose uniqueness is that the reality is uncaused, self-subsistent and autonomous. We call this Supernatural the Infinite to denote the absence of limitation. We call it also the Absolute to express perfect independence both in being and action. We call it, too, the Unconditioned to emphasize freedom from necessary relation" (p. 141). "Does it exist? Does it manifest itself? What is its nature? If a person can he reveal himself immediately as such? These are the inquiries which we shall raise" (p. 141).

1. The Reality of the Supernatural

Positivism, monism and pluralism are each seen to be untenable. Should we not then take up the only remaining hypothesis, that of the Supernatural "with a presumption at least that it is true? Some world view that really explains the universe there must be, and this would seem to be the only other possible" (p. 167). "This presumption is strengthened by the fact that the Christian doctrine of the Supernatural would, if true, meet all the necessary conditions" (p. 167). "Moreover, the Christian doctrine of the Supernatural is a satisfactory hypothesis in fact as well as in logic" (p. 168). It is the only hypothesis "that has not been proved to be untenable" (p. 169). Moreover "most schools of philosophy declare for the Supernatural" (p. 169). It "is not too much to claim that philosophy on the whole declares for the reality of the Supernatural, if not in the precise form of the Christian doctrine, yet in what approximates and tends towards it. Did not our limits forbid, nothing could be easier than to illustrate and establish this statement from such masters in philosophy as Plato, Aristotle, Cicero, Bacon, Descartes, Berkeley, Kant, Hamilton, Lotze and many others" (p. 170).

Again, religion needs the idea of the Supernatural. And, lastly, the Supernatural is a necessity of thought (p. 173). Thought requires the idea of causation. Thought requires that when we think of acts we also think of an agent. Every thought of the finite presupposes the Supernatural (p. 174). In the realm of the finite our principles of thought are found to be trustworthy. "If then, these principles are thus found to be trustworthy in the sphere of the natural or finite, why should we not trust them in the sphere of the Supernatural or Infinite?" (p. 176). And the Supernatural must be the deepest reality. "If we could ground it in anything deeper and so prove its existence strictly, we should only prove that it was not the Supernatural whose existence we had proved. From its very nature the Supernatural must be incapable of formal demonstration" (p. 180).[19]

2. The Manifestation of the Supernatural

Has the Supernatural so manifested itself that "though partially, it can be and is known by us?" (p. 182). "There is no *a priori* impossibility that the Supernatural should manifest itself and should be known as manifested. Admitting that only its bare existence has been established, it does not follow that no more can be established" (p. 186). "The reality of the Supernatural cannot be known and its nature not be known also to some degree at the same time" (*ibid.*). "In knowing the existence of the Supernatural we know it as that whose nature it is to manifest itself" (p. 187). This is not to be understood monistically. "Still, Infinite Being looks toward finite being, and thus towards manifestation in it, that it can be the ground and condition of it" (p. 187).

3. The Personality of the Supernatural

a. "The Supernatural can be personal" (p. 190). Without "some such determination as that of personality the Supernatural could not *be*" (p. 192).

b. "As there must be a real Supernatural, so he must be at least personal" (p. 192).

[19] At this point, as at some others, Professor Greene virtually uses the argument from presupposition.

1. This is so because the Supernatural must be "in the nature of a first cause" (p. 192).

2. It follows from the law of "cause resemblance" (p. 193).

3. It follows also from "the law of universal development" (*ibid.*). "Whence this universal tendency of all that lives toward personality, if it be not the law of the world; and whence this law, if the Principle of the world is an impersonal one? And if personality constitutes the pre-eminence of man over the inferior creation, can this pre-eminence be wanting in the highest Being of all?" (p. 193).

c. "The Supernatural, though he must be at least personal cannot be higher than personal" (p. 194). "Personality is of all possible modes of existence the highest" (*ibid.*).

4. The Personal or Immediate Manifestation of the Supernatural

"By this we mean, such a manifestation as would be such a direct communication from the Supernatural as it is claimed that the Decalogue is; such Supernatural works as the miracles, if they were wrought, must have been; such a Supernatural act as regeneration, if it be a real act, evidently is; such a Supernatural person as Christ could not but have been, if he was as he said, both 'the Son of God,' and 'the Son of Man'"(p. 196).

In the cases under consideration, "no instruments are employed, no media intervene" (p. 196). "Could they, then, take place? This is the question of questions to the Christian. If they could not, Christianity is a lie" (p. 196). "Not only Christianity, but all higher religion is at stake" (p. 197). As sinners "we need to feel, that God himself is in the midst of us" (p. 198). "Even the impression of the Supernatural made in the creation, if it is to abide, needs to be deepened by supernatural interventions in history" (p. 198). "An effect, reason dictates, can be assigned to a particular cause only as it reproduces what is distinctive of that cause. Hence, the necessary inference is that if the Supernatural Person reveals himself, the revelation will be, at any rate, at times, both above nature and in contrast with, if not in opposition to, nature. Accordingly, were such a revelation to be throughout natural, though, as we have seen, necessarily presupposing and thus indirectly revealing the Supernatural, reason would hesitate to recognize it as really Supernatural. Though it would *be* such, it could not be certainly discriminated as such" (p. 198). "Thus belief in the personal intervention in nature, and so above and in contrast with it, of the Supernatural Person is indispensable to the highest conviction of the reality of his self-revelation. Without such interventions, the latter could not be recognized infallibly" (p. 199).

Thus we come to the specific question of miracles. Are they possible? Can they be recognized? We cannot answer these questions by *a priori* considerations. "We can argue for or against the uniformity of nature only from what nature and the Supernatural have been found to be. Antecedently, there is as much reason to infer that nature must not be uniform as that it must be uniform; and that is no reason. There is no must in the case" (p. 200). "Nor does the objector gain anything, if we concede that the uniformity of nature never has been interrupted. Were this so, we might not infer that it never could be. Induction from individual facts, however numerous or well attested, cannot give necessary truth" (p. 201). The uniformity of nature "is not a principle; it is only the name of a mode of action" (p. 201). It only says that "the same causes acting under the same conditions produce the same results. This is the only principle, the only ultimate truth, the only immutable law, in the case. What is there in this to hinder at any time the personal intervention of the Supernatural?" (p. 201.)

As a result it may be said:

1. The abstract possibility of supernatural interventions in the course of nature cannot be rationally questioned (p. 202).

2. This possibility becomes much clearer in view of the fact that the Supernatural as we have already shown, is a person and is constantly acting in and through nature (*ibid.*). A being who can use tools can certainly work with his own hands (p. 203).

3. It is probable that the Supernatural will choose to do so, This follows from the fact that he is a person (p. 203).

4. This conclusion is much strengthened by the consideration that nature would seem to have been constituted with a view to such action by the Supernatural Person (p. 203).

5. But we are not left to inferences like the above, trustworthy though these could be shown to be. We know that the Supernatural has acted in a purely personal manner (p. 204).

6. The progressive development of religion is inexplicable unless the Supernatural does continue so to manifest himself. Religion, at least in all its higher forms, presupposes, not only the possibility, or even the probability, but the fact of such personal manifestations of the Supernatural (p. 204). Can it be that religion is only the most solemn of all delusions? If so, there is no mystery so great as that of its persistence. Nothing has been able to overthrow it, yet it itself rests on nothing (p. 204).

7. This conclusion is much strengthened by the fact that the course of human development, has been interrupted and perverted by sin (*ibid.*).

8. Must not, then, directly and exclusively Supernatural works, such as we designate miracles, be expected, both to call attention to the messengers bringing the good tidings of the grace of God and to authenticate them as his ambassadors and so to attest the truth of their proclamation? (p. 205).

9. Nor may it be replied that were the Supernatural thus to intervene directly in nature, such manifestations could not be recognized as such by us. This overlooks the fact that it is the manifestation of a person to persons that is under consideration. Now personality is known immediately by personality, and more especially if there be a moral affinity between the persons (p. 206).

What then is the net result of the discussion? It is not that Christianity is thereby established as the Supernatural religion.

This must be decided by the appropriate evidence. The way, however, has been opened, and the only way, for the fair consideration of this evidence; and this has been done in that we have established the reality of the existence of the Supernatural, of his manifestation through nature, of his personality, and of the possibility and even probability of his personal intervention in nature. It is true that no one of these has been in the strict sense demonstrated. But in the nature of the case this is impossible. Himself the ground and so proof of everything, there is nothing that can be the ground and so proof of the Supernatural. Yet as the building necessarily evidences the foundation on which it rests; so all nature and especially that in it which is highest and surest, namely, reason, demands the reality in the above respects of the Supernatural. This must be granted or reason must be stultified. To have shown this is thus both the utmost that could be shown and in itself enough (p. 207).

Only a very brief survey of Greene's position has been given. His method is clearly similar to that of Warfield. There is the same concept of reason, apart from the question of its regeneration, as able to interpret general revelation with essential correctness. And there is the same ability and function ascribed to this reason with respect to determining the factuality of special revelation. When Greene begins from the abstract possibility of the existence of the Supernatural and goes on to the probability and after that to the actuality of its appearance, he employs the categories of the natural man without challenging them. He seeks to prepare men for an acceptance of the gospel by showing them that the gospel is possible, probable and actual in terms of the principles of continuity and discontinuity of the natural man.

It is this avowed insistence that apologetics must deal neutrally with such questions as the existence of God and the facts of Christianity that marks the old Princeton Apologetics. And it is this type of apologetics that is definitely rejected as being out of accord with the principles of the Reformed faith in Kuyper's *Encyclopedia of Sacred Theology*. It is difficult to see how anyone can reduce the difference between "Princeton" and "Amsterdam" to one of emphasis and speak of one historic method of apologetics used by both.

III

Floyd E. Hamilton [20]

The old Princeton approach in apologetics may be seen in easy survey in the first edition of the Reverend Floyd E. Hamilton's book, *The Basis of the Christian Faith* (New York, 1927). In his preface Hamilton says: "Special thanks are due to Dr. William Brenton Greene, Jr., former professor of Apologetics in Princeton Theological Seminary, for his assistance in revising and criticizing the whole book" (p. ix).

In the first Chapter Hamilton deals with The Human Reason.

> Befcre we can attempt to prove the existence of God or discuss the truth of Christianity, we must show that the soul exists as something distinct from the body. We must show that our reasoning processes can be trusted, and that we have a valid right to reason from our sensations to the real world back of these sensations. And we must also show that when we attempt to deal with questions such as the existence of God and the possibility of his giving a revelation to man in a Book, we are dealing with questions which properly lie within the scope of the human reason. First of all, then, we must discuss the question of the existence of the soul (*op. cit.*, p. 15).

The human mind is shown not to be a mere stream of consciousness (p. 18). "It is an active agent and not a passive substance" (p. 19).

So here we take our start. We have found and identified ourselves. "Here at any rate we have *reality*" (*ibid*).

Having identified our real selves we examine our reasoning process. We receive sensations. In receiving them our mind is not a blank.

In addition to these space and time forms, which the mind uses in the thinking process, there are certain other "mind born" or innate ideas which the mind originates upon the occasion of receiving sensations. We will mention only two ideas of this class which particularly concern us in our discussion. They are the ideas of "being" and "cause." We cannot think without un-

[20] For an extended critique of the apologetics of F. Hamilton as expressed in the fourth edition (1964) of *The Basis of the Christian Faith* see the present writer's revised *Christian Theory of Knowledge* (1967).

consciously assuming the existence of something. When we receive a sensation our mind assumes the reality of the sensation and the reality of the fact that we are receiving it. When we think, we assume the reality of at least the mind that is doing the thinking. This idea of existence is thus seen to underlie all thought, and to be a presupposition of thought. We call it by the name of "being." It is an idea not received through the senses, but originating in the mind itself upon the occasion of sensation.

When the brain receives a sensation it assumes that there is a cause of the sensation. It may not be able to tell what the cause is, but it never doubts that there is a *cause*. It is not an idea which comes into the mind through the senses, but is originated upon the occasion of sensation (pp. 21, 22).

Thus we have ourselves as the real starting point, and we have the idea of cause which serves us as a bridge between ourselves and the external world. We are now ready to express judgments about the world. "But when is a judgment trustworthy?" (p. 25.) When it is made in accordance with the laws of reasoning. Our minds and the facts they deal with must be normal. Our minds must possess the necessary facts. Our minds must not fall into logical fallacies (p. 25). If care is exercised "in checking the process of reasoning it is possible to trust the reasoning process in all ordinary circumstances" (p. 26).

Reasoning must not proceed regardless of facts. And "there are some things which are beyond the realm of reason" (p. 27). Then too our emotions must be kept in control.

> However with these limitations and imperfections guarded against there remains a wide scope of activity for the mind. The mind can take all the evidence which comes to us through the senses and reason about it, building up a splendid structure of logical truth. It has a right to take these facts which come to us through the senses and use them as stepping stones into the realm of cause lying back of them. The mind becomes the judge of evidence presented to the mind in support of the giving to man from God of a supernatural revelation. If the mind, however, after weighing this evidence decides that such a revelation has been given to man, then it has no right to set itself up as a

> judge to decide what things embodied in this revelation are reasonable, for in the nature of things, if there has been a revelation from God, it will concern those things which cannot be discovered by the unaided human reason. Since the mind has no actual experience with things which do not come to it through the senses, it has no right to deny truth which comes through revelation from a realm where sense perception is impossible. In regard to revelation, the legitimate sphere of the human reason is to investigate the evidence in support of such revelation and then to decide as to the meaning of that revelation (p. 28).

In the second chapter Hamilton invites us to advance with him "over the bridge of cause which we have erected" from ourselves to the external world. In the third he leads us even beyond the world by the same bridge to God. We know "that we must have been caused by someone other than ourselves who must have had sufficient power to produce our souls, which are the observed effect" (p. 44). This gives us "our first link in the chain of proof for the existence of God" (p. 46). One by one the other links are forged and soldered to the first. There is order in the universe (p. 47). There is design (p. 48). In man himself there is will. Will there not be a *Will* back of the universe? (p. 50). Man has a conscience. It is a "certain characteristic innate in the mind which enables a person who has reached the age of reasoning ability, to make a judgment as to the rightness or wrongness of any course of action which may be presented to the mind" (p. 53). "Shall we not then conclude with Bordon P. Bowne that man has a moral creator?" (p. 54.)

> The preceding arguments are so plain that the conclusion is inescapable. There is no alternative for thinking man in the face of such evidence but to fall upon his face before the wonderful Being who has created him, and to worship him. Let it be borne in mind that the arguments cited above are cumulative. Each adds proof to the others, and their force is only felt when they are taken together (p. 54).

Thus theism is supposed to have been established by a neutral process of reasoning. As has earlier been indicated, such a theism is not the theism of Scripture. Calvin's procedure is quite the reverse of Hamilton's. Following Descartes and others, Hamilton thinks that man can identify himself in terms of himself. Calvin says the knowledge of self immediately presupposes the relation of the self to God as its creator. No identification of the human self is possible in the realm of open chance. And no bridge of cause can be made from that which cannot be identified (the self) to something else that cannot be identified (the external world). The idea of causation cannot be taken as intelligible by itself in order by means of it to show that God has created the world. If God has created the world the idea of cause in the world must be determined from this its derivative nature. If it is first assumed to be working without God it cannot after that be shown to be working only in dependence upon God.

The same point is to be made about the ideas of order, purpose and morality. If any of them can function independently of God at the beginning why do they need God at all?

Moreover, how shall these several autonomous entities be forged into a chain? How shall there be cumulative force in the series of arguments if each argument is itself without force?

The whole procedure followed is out of line with the basic principle of the Reformed Faith. Only in God's light is there any light. The Psalmist (Psalm 94) teaches us to begin from above with God instead of from the bottom with man. If even a creature, *who is derivative,* knows, how much more shall the original know? That is the method of the Psalmist. Descartes assumes that man as the original knows, and that then God *also* knows. If man's knowledge is not from the outset defined as dependent on God's knowledge it never can be.

It was in line with Arminian and with Romanist thinking to use such a method as Mr. Hamilton uses. Wherever autonomy is hailed in theology why should it not also be welcomed in apologetics? But when autonomy is over and over regarded as the root of all evil in theology why then should it be welcomed in apologetics?

In chapter five of his book Hamilton deals with the Reasonableness of Supernaturalism.

God is shown to exist; therefore it is possible for him to

intervene in the universe (p. 87). He goes on to show the probability of such intervention.

> 1. In the first place, it seems strongly probable that God would not create man and leave him alone. A personal God, if he is at all like men in his fundamental characteristics, as the Bible says he is, having created a personal being, would most naturally want to have communion and fellowship with the being he had created.
>
> 2. It also seems unlikely that man should be left in ignorance of the ultimate destiny of the human soul. If it is true that there is a Heaven and a Hell, to one of which places every soul will go, then it seems unlikely that God would leave man in ignorance of these momentous facts. Especially is this true, if the corollary is true that man's ultimate destiny is decided by his actions upon the earth during a short lifetime, and that he will have no further chance after death to redeem his mistakes made during life on the earth. Most of all, if God intended as the Bible teaches, to have this redemption applied to a man's life through faith in a risen Lord, then he would most certainly tell men about this fact in some way or other. We thus see that there is a very great probability, if the God represented in the Bible exists, that he would reveal certain vital facts to man (pp. 93, 94).

From the question of probability we go on to that of actuality:

> Now a little reflection on the subject will be sufficient to convince one that the only way we can decide whether or not such a revelation has been given to us by God is by an examination of the evidence tending to show that such a revelation has been given. Since the matter is one purely of fact, and of fact alone, it can be decided only by the evidence. We may have a theory that it is impossible for the earth to revolve upon its axis, but no matter how plausible our theory may sound, our having the theory will not prevent the earth from turning on its axis once every twenty-four hours! In the same way, if God *has* given a revelation, no amount of theorizing to the contrary can change the fact. The only way those who do not believe God has given a

revelation to man can prove their case, is for them to show that the evidence for such a revelation is worthless (pp. 98, 99).

When we deal with the witnesses to supernatural revelation we ask: "Is the witness competent?" "Is the witness reliable?" "Was the witness in a position to know the facts?" (p. 99.) So we are ready as neutral observers to take up "the evidence for the Bible as the Word of God and decide for ourselves whether or not it contains such a revelation" (p. 100). In particular we are prepared to deal with the Bible and its claim to be the Word of God.

To be sure we must not make unreasonable claims for ourselves.

> If *God* teaches that a certain doctrine is *true*, then it is not man's place to decide whether or not it is *reasonable*! It is man's duty to *accept* it, even though he may not be able to *understand* all about it or to *prove* its *truth* by the *human reason*! If God has taught it, then all man has a right to do is to *accept* it. The whole question resolves itself into a question as to whether God *has* or *has not* taught it. In deciding *this* question man has a perfect right to use his reason to the fullest extent in judging the evidence on this point. It is purely a matter of fact, and as such must be judged according to the laws of evidence. But if the intellect is convinced that God actually did teach these doctrines in the Bible through inspired prophets and inspired writers of the various books of the Bible, then the intellect has no right to set itself up as a judge of the reasonableness of the doctrines which God teaches. The intellect can reason about the meaning of the doctrines taught, but it has no right to reason about the truth or falsity of the doctrines themselves after their meaning has been decided upon. To do so would be to put oneself above God himself and to question his own wisdom. Some men apparently do not hesitate even to do this, but to the man who has at least average intelligence, such a course is nothing less than blasphemy (p. 133).

It is our rightful business as men then to seek to identify

this body of literature as being the Word of God. We do not take it to be self-attesting from the outset. We do not accept it as the Word of God on its own assertion. On the contrary, by means of criteria not taken from the Scripture as self-attesting we test the Bible as to its claim to be the Word of God.

We must "approach the Bible as we would approach any other book" (p. 134). Then we find, step by step, link by link, that it meets all the demands which we legitimately make of any book claiming to be the Word of God. So on the question of Biblical ethics Mr. Hamilton says:

> We now wish to show that Christianity fulfils all the demands which must be made of any system which will work, and that the ethical system taught in the Bible is superior to any other system of ethics (p. 147).

In Chapter 10 Mr. Hamilton deals particularly with "the historic trustworthiness of the Bible." He tests the Bible by well established philosophical knowledge obtained independently of the Bible.

The Bible is not a textbook of philosophy, but the Bible in no wise contradicts the theories which are most accepted by philosophers of the present day (p. 167).

He finds that the historicity of the Bible is not contradicted by "the clearly discovered and well proved facts of modern science . . . " (p. 168).

In chapter 16 there is a discussion of the resurrection of Christ and in chapter 17 of the fulfilment of prophecy.

> We have reserved until last the two strongest proofs that the Bible is the Word of God and that Christianity is true. We believe that in fulfilled prophecy and in the resurrection of Jesus Christ we have positive proof that our claims are true. We believe that these two lines of proof are so strong that they will convince anyone whose mind is open to evidence, that we have as much positive proof of just as strong a character that the Bible and its contents are true and in very truth the Word of God, as we have that the Declaration of Independence was a genuine document produced in 1776 in Philadelphia, by the representatives of the thirteen colonies (pp. 283, 284).

In the resurrection of Christ we have a miracle that differs from all other miracles.

> Had there been no resurrection *there would have been no Christian Church.* The Christian Church as we know it was founded absolutely on the resurrection of Jesus Christ and all that it implied (p. 284). So we turn to the New Testament as containing the only historical documents attempting to explain the origin of Christianity or the belief in the resurrection (p. 286).

And when we are through we conclude:

> We have examined all possibilities and find that the only conclusion possible is that Christ actually rose from the dead. If he did rise, that fact carries with it, as was said at the beginning of the chapter, all the implications of supernatural Christianity. It is a fact that carries clouds of glory trailing through our Christianity. Nothing but a supernatural Savior is possible after he has risen from the dead. The fact of Christ's resurrection establishes beyond a doubt the truth of Christianity. But not only does it prove that Christianity is the one true religion. It also proves that all that Christ said and did was true, and this in turn proves that the Bible is the Word of God (p. 295).

The argument from fulfilment of prophecy again points to the truth of Christianity.

> God alone knows the future, and the future can be revealed only by God. When, therefore, we find a book unquestionably written hundreds of years before the prophecies recorded in it were fulfilled, can there be any question but that those prophecies were revealed by God himself? The prophecies which we shall cite will be those so detailed that there will be no question but that they were actual prophecies, and we shall show that no man unless he were speaking as the mouthpiece of God, could possibly have known or even guessed that the events prophesied would take place, both because of the unlikelihood of such events taking place at all, and because of the impossibility of a human being foretelling the events in such detail (pp. 297, 298).

So then after we have identified ourselves, then built a bridge of cause, order, purpose and morality to God, we approach the Biblical writings as we do any other book. The foundation fact to which they testify is the resurrection of Christ. Thus we have reached the risen Christ by neutral approach. *After that* we stand on his authority. He witnessed to the Old Testament as the Word of God. He promised the Spirit to his apostles so they might write the New Testament as the completion of the Word of God.

After that we bow before the Word of the sovereign God and require men to subject their reason to its verdict.

It was the *after this* that Kuyper so vigorously opposed in the sort of apologetics we have before us. If reason is not challenged at the outset it cannot fairly be challenged at all. Why should not "reason" be as anxious to suppress the evidence for the *fact* that the Bible is God's Word as to deny the system of truth of that Word? No one can recognize the *fact* of Christ's resurrection and the fact of the divinity of Scripture except in terms of the *meaning* of the resurrection and the *content* of the system Scripture presents. In all the stress on the fact that true faith is not blind but is faith in response to the presentation of evidence, this indissoluble unity of the *that* and the *what* of Christianity is overlooked.

It is impossible to discuss the works of Charles Hodge, Casper Wistar Hodge, Francis Patton and others. Suffice it to have dealt briefly with Warfield, with the sainted William Brenton Greene, Jr., and with his pupil, Floyd E. Hamilton.

Even in what has been adduced it is evidenced that the basic loyalty of these men is the full-orbed Reformed Faith. None the less it remains true that in their avowed apologetical procedure they embraced a method that resembled that of Bishop Butler, rather than that of Calvin.

To have a balanced view of the relation of the "old Princeton" and the "Amsterdam" apologetics, it is imperative that we turn to the question of "inconsistency" in the views of Kuyper and Bavinck. We have stressed the fact that in his main contention Kuyper strongly opposed the idea of a neutral area of interpretation between believers and unbelievers. And we have shown that Warfield was strongly insistent on the necessity of proceeding with unbelievers on a neutral basis with respect to the problem of theism and even with respect to the claims of Scripture to be the Word of God. But we have also indicated that Kuyper too sometimes reasons as though he were on neutral grounds with unbelievers. Even in his *Encyclopedia*, in which he so valiantly defends the idea of a twofold science, even in this work which Warfield so vigorously criticized, Kuyper sometimes does the same thing that Warfield does. Indeed Warfield has pointed out this very inconsistency in Kuyper.

We shall deal briefly with the evidence that indicates the presence of this inconsistency in Kuyper. We shall also deal briefly with Bavinck. As this inconsistency has to some extent been pointed out in *Common Grace* and in the syllabus *Introduction to Systematic Theology* we shall here deal with the matter chiefly in relation to the question of Scripture.

Both Kuyper and Bavinck have greatly stressed the fact that Scripture is *the* objective principle of knowledge for the Christian. The Christian must regard all the knowledge that he obtains from a study of nature and history in the light of the doctrines of creation and providence and of the work of redemption through Christ. Only thus is the Romanist doctrine of natural theology to be avoided. Apologetically this means that the Scriptures must be taken as self-attesting and the system of truth they contain as the light in which all the facts of experience are seen for what they are.

Therefore no corroboration is to be sought for the truth of the idea of Scripture, or for the truth of the system of doctrine it contains, by an appeal to the natural man as he interprets life in terms of his own principles. In fact it cannot be allowed that the natural man can in terms of his principles interpret any aspect of experience correctly. He does, to be sure, contribute to the edifice of true interpretation, but he does this because his principle is false and the Christian principle is true.

Yet while showing that the natural man is bound to seek to destroy the truth of God that speaks to him, Kuyper and Bavinck at times seek comfort in the fact that the natural man will approve their sayings even when he is not asked to change his assumption of autonomy.

IV

Kuyper

That such is the case with Kuyper is apparent from his treatment of the idea of formal faith. In the first section of his *Encyclopedia* he discusses the idea of wisdom as a check on skepticism. So he also speaks of general faith as restraining the natural tendency toward skepticism that has come into the world because of sin. He deals with faith, he says, in the purely formal sense of the term (Vol. II, p. 72). As such it is inherent in the human subject. All certainty about our own existence is based on this faith. It is independent of proof, it is prior to all proof (*idem*, p. 78). It is also the presupposition of our acceptance of the truth of our sensations of the external world. We must *believe* in the trustworthiness of our own sensations (*idem*, p. 80). Without this faith it is impossible to reach an object beyond ourselves. It is this faith that forms the bridge from the phenomena to the noumena (*idem*, p. 80). And this is of basic importance for science since science depends upon observation. Without this faith we should land in the subjectivism of Kant and Fichte (*ibid.*).

In addition to furnishing the foundation of certainty with respect to ourselves and with respect to our observations of the facts of our environment, faith is also the foundation of all logical proof. We cannot prove the truth of the ultimate axioms of logic; we must believe in them. It is unquestioned faith in them that forms the foundation of all proof (*idem*, p. 83). In particular the principle of identity springs from this faith (*idem*, p. 84). Still further, faith is the motivating power that helps in the building of the structure of science (*idem*, p. 84). One must believe in the uniformity of nature and in the idea of the universal knowledge of facts. Previous to investigation one must believe that the facts will fit into one universal pattern.

It will be observed that the procedure here followed is very similar to that of the old Princeton Apologetics. Kuyper insists that the concept of faith that he here speaks of is without content. It is inherent in the subject, therefore, not because the subject is unavoidably confronted with God, but simply as such.

By means of this purely formal faith the human subject is first to become conscious of its own existence. Then by means of this formal faith a bridge is to be laid to the external world. The laws of thought by which the environment of man is to be manipulated also rest on this formal faith.

All this is at variance with what Kuyper, following Calvin, has taught with respect to the sense of deity. Again and again Kuyper has insisted that man always confronts God in every fact that he meets. There is no such thing as formal faith. To be sure, all men have faith. Unbelievers have faith as well as believers. But that is due to the fact that they too are creatures of God. Faith therefore always has content. It is against the content of faith as belief in God that man has become an unbeliever. As such he tries to suppress the content of his original faith. He tries to reduce it to something formal. Then its content can take any form he wants it to have. Then its content is actually indeterminate. And thus there is no foundation for man's knowledge of himself or of the world at all. Identification of himself as the subject of knowledge is possible to man only in terms of the fact that in his very act of self-identification he identifies himself as the creature of God. If one allows that identification of the human self as the subject of knowledge is possible without God's identifying himself to man as his Creator and judge in the same act, there is no basis for knowledge.

It then also becomes impossible to maintain consistently what Kuyper has so stoutly championed, that the non-regenerate subject will seek, because of its ethical hostility to God, to suppress the truth that comes to it. Kuyper speaks as though the merely formal idea of faith is a dam against skepticism since it meets that skepticism in the subject itself (*idem*, p. 73). But how can this be? For this very formal idea of faith says nothing about the content or object of faith. Or rather, by its formality it allows for and even demands the correlative notion of pure non-rational factuality and of logic as an abstract system that includes both God and man. Thus the formal idea of faith is the very source of skepticism itself. Skepticism in the subject cannot be met otherwise than by the way Kuyper himself meets it elsewhere, namely, by insisting that faith always has content. And this constent is inherently belief in God as man's Creator and as the one who controls whatsoever comes to pass. Then when this faith turns into unbelief this unbelief cannot succeed in suppressing fully the original faith in God. Man as man is inherently and inescapably a believer in God. Thus he can contribute to true knowledge of the universe. Add to this the fact of common grace and he can in a measure cooperate with the believer in building the edifice of science.

Kuyper is in any case unable to carry through the idea that faith is merely formal. He says that faith is formal only in the field of the exact or external sciences. In what he calls the spiritual sciences he asserts that the fact of sin makes its presence felt. He speaks of a "unifying power of the object" which operates in the external or exact sciences but which does not operate in the case of the spiritual sciences (*idem,* p. 98). And in the spiritual sciences faith always has content. And the moment faith has content diversity appears (*idem,* p. 94).

But how are we to draw the line between physical or objective and spiritual sciences? In both cases the human subject is involved. There is no "unifying power of the object" that can do away with this fact. Kuyper himself has insisted that even in observation of facts the subjective element enters into the picture. There is not the least harm in this. It is a purely metaphysical and psychological fact. It is not the fact that a subject is involved in the knowledge situation that makes for skepticism. It is only when this subject does not want itself interpreted in terms of God that skepticism comes about.

By starting off with the idea of faith as a purely formal something, and then turning off into the idea of faith as having content in the spiritual sciences, Kuyper caused himself great trouble. It made it impossible for him to present his main contention without ambiguity. His main contention is that, as created, every man has faith in God. Therefore faith always has this content. The only alternative to acceptance of God is the denial of God by means of an effort at suppression. It is this suppression by the sinful subject, it is this ethical subjectivism that must be removed and is removed in principle through Christ in his people. Through Christ's work science is saved, its unity preserved and its object attained. And common grace suppresses the sinful man's attempted suppression of his faith in God and thus enables even sinful men to contribute to the progress of knowledge.

Kuyper's idea of formal faith is out of line with this his main line of reasoning. For by this idea of formal faith he speaks as though the metaphysical subject as such has a tendency to misinterpret the objects of its environment. He speaks as though this tendency can be stopped by means of a "unifying force of the object," which object has in the first place to get its very objectivity from the subject that somehow identifies itself even though it has no content.

The result is that Kuyper cannot carry through the idea that the believer must challenge the unbeliever in his interpretation of the universe at every point. He is vague in his discussion of the natural sciences. His main principle requires him to say that every science is possible only on the presupposition of the truth of Christianity. His main principle therefore requires him to insist that the principle of Scripture be self-attesting. And this involves that man's self-identification and the uniformity of nature be based upon this identification of God's identification of himself to man. If Kuyper is to have an internally consistent picture of the Christian view of things that he has so valiantly set forth, he must dispose of the idea of faith as purely formal. Wherever he maintains this formal idea of faith, he virtually grants that the man who works on the assumption of human autonomy has the right principle with which to interpret not only the external phenomena but even the causes of things (cf., p. 95).

Ridderbos and Masselink both appeal to Kuyper in support of their idea that there is a territory of interpretation that is virtually common to the believer and the unbeliever. They appeal especially to Kuyper's assertions with respect to weighing and measuring and formal logic. Any man, says Kuyper, can deal with external matters effectively. And man's reasoning powers have not been influenced by the fact of sin. The non-Christian can reason as logically as can the Christian.

So far, then, as scientific knowledge deals only with externals or so far as it is controlled by those subjective factors that did not undergo any change because of the fall of man, it is common to believer and unbeliever (*idem,* p. 116).

It will be observed that Ridderbos and Masselink quite

rightfully appeal to Kuyper. They might well have added Kuyper's idea of formal faith. For the idea of formal faith and the idea of a virtually common territory of interpretation between believer and unbeliever are involved in one another. It is only if one takes the idea of faith as formal that one can also consistently hold that the creation idea with respect to fact and logic need not be taken into consideration. Then those who believe that the universe is run by chance and at the same time think that logic is the means by which men should seek the exhaustive penetration of the relation of God to man can cooperate with Christians who believe none of these things. But it should be added that in that case the non-Christian has the logical right to claim that he may interpret the whole of reality in terms of his principles.

It is to this inconsistency in Kuyper that Ridderbos and Masselink appeal in support of their position. But progress in Reformed apologetics will come only if this inconsistency is dropped and Kuyper's main position be maintained. Then there is a sense in which all men have faith and all men know God. All can contribute to science. And there is then another sense in which the same subject becomes "subjective" in the ethical sense through sin. This ethical subjectivism includes weighing and measuring and reasoning. It includes all the activities of the process of interpretation. For then the philosophy of fact and the philosophy of logic maintained is such as would destroy all possibility of identification and of ordering of experience (cf. Kuyper: *op. cit.*, p. 562).

Kuyper himself has told us that the natural man lacks true self-knowledge (*idem*, p. 564). Only in the light of the Word of God does he know himself for what he really is (*ibid*). "Natural theology therefore must not stand next to Scripture but must be taken up into Scripture. Only through the Scripture does it bring us into true contact with nature" (*ibid*).

V

Bavinck

It is from Bavinck as much as from Kuyper that we have learned to stress the Scriptures as the *principium unicum* of the Christian.

"The true concept of revelation can only be taken from revelation itself; if no revelation has ever taken place, then all reflection on its concept is labor expended in vain; if revelation is a fact then it alone must provide us with its concept and indicate the criterion to be employed in our research with respect to religions and revelations" (*Gereformeerde Dogmatiek*, Vol. I, p. 309). The ground of faith, says Bavinck, is identical with its content and cannot be separated from it (*idem*, p. 644).

When the believer is asked why he thinks of the Bible as the Word of God, he may point to the *notae* and *criteria* of Scripture. He may speak of the majesty of its style, the elevated nature of its content, the depth of its thought, the blessedness of its fruits, etc.; but

> . . . these are not the grounds of his faith, they are but characteristics and evidences which are later discovered in Scripture by believing thought, even as the proofs for the existence of God do not precede and support faith, but spring from it and have been devised by it (*idem*, p. 634).
>
> The *Deux dixit* is the *primum principium*, to which all *dogmata*, including that pertaining to Scripture, can be traced (*idem*, p. 634).

In spite of this stress on the Scripture as self-attesting and as such the primary principle for the interpretation of man and the world, Bavinck too sometimes reverts to the idea that man can without this principle interpret much of experience truly.

In his *Philosophy of Revelation* as well as in his work on dogmatics Bavinck stresses the fact that the idea of revelation must spring from revelation itself (*Wysbegeerte der Openbaring*, Kampen, 1908, p. 21). Yet when defending this Christian idea of revelation against various forms of philosophy Bavinck sometimes leaves this high ground and argues neutrally with them. He wants to reason philosophically with modern philosophers and therefore starts with them from the fact of self-consciousness as such, without at once setting this fact, as he does elsewhere, in the context of its relation to God and Christ.

How shall we show that various modern philosophies, and in particular pragmatism, are mistaken in their views of reality? By pointing out that there are "more elements, more fact" than those with which they construct their universe. "The only path by which we are able to attain reality is that of self-consciousness" (*op. cit.*, p. 46). On this point idealism is right. But idealism is mistaken if it deduces from this fact the conclusion that perception is a purely immanent act (*idem*, p. 47).

> In self-consciousness, therefore, we have to deal not with a mere phenomenon, but with a noumenon, with a reality that is immediately given to us, antecedently to all reasoning and inference. Self-consciousness is the unity of real and ideal being; the *self* is here *consciousness*, not scientific knowledge, but experience, conviction, consciousness of self as a reality. In self-consciousness our own being is *revealed* to us, directly, immediately before all thinking and independently of all willing (*op. cit.*, p. 61).

In the chapters from which these passages are taken Bavinck seeks for incontrovertible reality in the idea of human self-consciousness as such. He does not bring into the picture the fact so greatly stressed in his theology, that the reason why men find reality in self-consciousness is because it is at the same time consciousness of God as Creator and controller of all things. Bavinck leaves out this fact in order to meet non-Christian philosophers on their own ground.

Of special interest is the fact that Bavinck thinks he finds in self-consciousness as such the "unity of real and ideal being." On the basis of his theology Bavinck elsewhere asserts that unity of real and ideal being can be found only in God. Of course it is true that the human self has a legitimate consciousness of itself as really existing. It cannot but know *that* it exists. And it cannot know *that* it exists unless it knows *what* this existence means. But the latter man does not know by some immediate, direct identification with "thought" or "ideal being." Man knows *what* he is and therefore *that* he is only if he takes himself to be analogical of God. Thus man's self-identification is analogical self-identification. The terms "real and ideal being" are abstractions unless given content in terms of the Christian system. And if we say that in self-consciousness noumenal reality is *revealed* to us, this revelation must be taken to mean that the self is a self to itself because it speaks of the Self of its Creator.

Moreover, to abstract the self-consciousness of man from its world as though in this self-consciousness, more immediately or more certainly than elsewhere, *reality* is found, is again to go contrary to Bavinck's own theology. Has he not shown how innate knowledge and acquired knowledge involve one another? Has he not pointed out that even in the *status integritatis* God's revelation to man through the facts about him and through his consciousness within him was conjoined with supernatural thought-communication by God to man? (*Gereformeerde Dogmatiek,* Vol. I, p. 321.) The revelation of God to man through his environment and the revelation to man through his own self-consciousness is equally, and equally clearly, indicative of reality as God has made it and as he controls it. It is this ever and everywhere present face of God that Descartes virtually denied when he made the human self the ultimate starting point in predication. This was forgotten by the old Princeton Apologetics; it is also, for the moment, forgotten by Bavinck when he would start with the *cogito* as such as the foundation of human knowledge.

After Bavinck has discussed the relation of revelation to philosophy, to science, to history and to religion, he introduces his chapter on Revelation and Christianity with the following words:

> The arguments for the reality of revelation, derived from the nature of thought, the essence of nature, the character of history, and the conception of religion, are finally strengthened by the course of development through which mankind has passed, and which has led it from paradise to the cross and will guide it from the cross to glory (*idem,* p. 144).

This summation indicates, as the text itself in each instance establishes, that Bavinck has to some extent sought the proof of the identity and significance of the system of truth found in Scripture in an interpretation of the universe in terms other than those of Scripture.

The "course of development through which man has passed" points to the idea of revelation. Tradition points to revelation as back of it (*idem,* p. 144). To be sure one cannot speak with certainty on the past. "Nevertheless there are phenomena which point back with great probability to a common origin" (*idem*, p. 157). Here again Bavinck seeks to understand the universe first in order to introduce the necessity of revelation for the understanding of it. And in doing so he naturally lowers the claims of God's general revelation on man. His approach on this point is the same as that which he makes again and again in his *Gereformeerde Dogmatiek*. In it he sometimes grants that Thomas Aquinas was right in maintaining that supernatural revelation is necessary for man because natural revelation is uncertain.

> For that reason Thomas was quite right when he said that even with respect to those truths, which general revelation makes known to us, there is a necessity for revelation and authority because natural knowledge is fit only for the few, would take too long a time to search out, and moreover is imperfect and uncertain (*op. cit.*, Vol. I, p. 325).

Bavinck here fails to distinguish between the revelation which is clear and the interpretation of that revelation which is worse than uncertain, but is a perversion of the revelation.

It is in accord with this admission that the theistic position can be said to be probably, but only probably, true when Bavinck asserts that the Christian's belief in Scripture is no less defensible than belief in other religions. The believer has no compelling proofs for his position. He must accept the Scriptures on their own authority. But he has at least as much to say for his defense as others have for their attack.

> Unbelief, too, in the last analysis does not rest on proofs but has its roots in the heart. In this respect believers and unbelievers are in the same position, the convictions of both are bound up with their personalities, and these convictions are supported *a posteriori* by proof and ratiocination. When they debate with one another in this *a posteriori* fashion, the believers are in no worse case than they who do not believe. God is sufficiently knowable to those who seek him and sufficiently hidden for those who flee from him (*idem*, p. 635).

Again Bavinck says:

> Historical and rational proofs will not convert anyone,

but are for all that as powerful for the defense of the faith as are the arguments of the opposite party in justification of its unbelief (*ibid.*).

It is evident that in thus lowering the claims of both general and special revelation, Bavinck is again inconsistent with the main thrust of his own as well as of Calvin's theology. Again and again Bavinck has pointed out that God's revelation to man, whether general or special, is inherently clear. Again and again he has emphasized the fact that whenever God speaks—and he speaks everywhere—men must in spite of themselves admit the truth of what he says. It is their creation in God's image, their sense of deity that compels them to do so.

> It is God himself who witnesses to all men. And it is man himself, created as he is in God's image who must, in spite of himself, listen to this testimony and consent to it. In this light the so-called proofs for the existence of God must be taken. That will safeguard both against their over- and against their under-estimation (*op cit.*, II, p. 55).

It is when Bavinck reasons thus that he does full justice to the objective claims of God in both general and special revelation. Every man must recognize God's voice. No man can escape it. The Word of God "finds support in the rational and moral nature of man" because man is what he is as the creature of God.

Therefore it is not true that the arguments of those who seek to flee the voice of God are rationally as good as the arguments of those who admit and insist that God's voice is everywhere present.

The former start with the "cogito" as though it were a rock in a bottomless ocean. They cannot individuate. They cannot show how one fact, if it could be found, can be related to another fact. They cannot account for the uniformity of nature. They cannot use the law of contradiction except they abuse it, making it destroy individuality as it succeeds in its reduction to abstract unity. They cannot find intelligible meaning in the words *cause*, *substance*, or *purpose*; there is no coherence in all their thought.

It is thus to hold high the claim of God and to point out the utter irrationality of unbelief that is in accord with the main thrust of Bavinck's theology. It is out of accord with this his main view when Bavinck starts from the "cogito" as such, then builds up the theistic position piecemeal, link by link, the causal argument proving one point (*idem*, p. 61), the teleological argument proving another point (*idem*, p. 62, 63), and the ontological argument proving still another point (*idem*, p. 65); but together having failed to bring us to God, the God who alone exists. Of the ontological argument he says that it does not take us across the gulf between thought and being (Over de klove van denken tot zyn brengt het ons niet heen, *idem*, p. 62). Surely we must follow Bavinck when he presupposes the unity of thought and being in God. The presence of such a God cannot but be clearly apparent to man. And surely we must not follow Bavinck when, starting from man as ultimate, he leads on to an ultimate Cause that is not clearly God, to an ultimate Purpose that is not clearly God's, and to an ultimate Being who does not help us out of the vicious circle of our thought. In this latter case we would also find response in the "rational and moral nature of man" but this time it would be this as interpreted by those who seek, in vain, to flee from God. For it is quite to their liking to be told that the voice of God is not clearly heard and the face of God is not clearly seen in the phenomena of human experience. And they find it quite to their liking too to be told that by faith in God and in his Christ, nothing dissimilar to faith in that which is not yet known or in that which is wholly unknowable is meant.

It is impossible to deal more fully with either Kuyper or Bavinck at this time. And we cannot touch on the works of their colleagues and followers, nor is this necessary for the main purpose in hand.

Our main purpose was to indicate:

1. That the theology of old Princeton Seminary and that of Amsterdam is essentially the same. The Hodges, Warfield, DeWitt, Greene, and others are insistent as are Kuyper, Bavinck and their followers that the Scriptures are the Word of God and that its system of truth is an analogical system. All of human experience must therefore be interpreted in terms of it. Supernatural revelation was, even before the Fall, supplemental to natural revelation. Hence the Scripture is supernatural revelation providing for men as sinners.

Sinners cannot presume of themselves to know their needs. They are bound to misinterpret these needs. They must be diagnosed by the great Physician. Therefore only when the Holy Spirit convicts the sinner of his sin does he in the same act convince him of the Bible as the Word of God. To him whom the Spirit regenerates does the Bible appear for what it really is.

The *indicia* of divinity in Scripture are therefore part of the same process and act of the self-attestation of God. All the facts of the universe attest God. They are all inter-related in their testimony. If there is a cumulative effect produced by the evidence for the existence of God and for the truth of Christianity it is cumulative because each fact says the same thing, proves the same point in a different manner.

2. Inherent in this common theology there is a common opposition to every form of Romanist or evangelical reasoning in theology. All such reasoning assumes that the Scriptures cannot teach anything that is out of accord with the idea of man's ability to turn aside the plan of God. Romanism and Evangelicalism therefore cannot effectively challenge the wisdom of man that is built on the idea of autonomy.

Both the men of Princeton and the men of Amsterdam constantly make this point plain. When they speak of the "common consciousness" of man, they mean the sort of thing that Calvin means by the sense of deity. When they speak of the self-consciousness of man, they mean what Calvin means on the first page of his *Institutes* when he says that man knows himself in the same act whereby he knows God. When they speak of the proofs of the existence of God they mean that the heavens declare the glory of God and the firmament shows forth his handiwork. They hold to the objective validity of the Christian religion. When either of them reasons with the unbeliever, he tells this unbeliever that unbelief destroys the uniformity of nature and intelligent predication in any field. Over and over again all of these men do all these things by direct assertion or by implication.

It is therefore upon this common basis held by old Princeton and Amsterdam alike, that we build when we contend:

a. That in apologetics we must use the same principle that we use in theology, namely the principle of the self-attesting Scripture and of the analogical system of truth which it contains.

b. That therefore we must not make our appeal to the "common notions" of unbelievers and believers but to the "common notions" that, by virtue of creation in God's image, men as men all have in common.

c. That when appeal is thus to be made to man as man, this can be done only as we set the principle of Christianity squarely in opposition to the principle of the unbeliever. Only when the principle of autonomy with its irrationalist-rationalist principles of identity and contradiction, is rejected in the name of the principle of analogy, is appeal really made to those common notions which men have as men.

d. That therefore the claim must be made that Christianity alone is reasonable for men to hold. And it is utterly reasonable. It is wholly irrational to hold to any other position than that of Christianity. Christianity alone does not crucify reason itself. Without it reason would operate in a total vacuum.

e. That the argument for Christianity must therefore be that of presupposition. With Augustine it must be maintained that God's revelation is the sun from which all other light derives. The best, the only, the absolutely certain proof of the truth of Christianity is that unless its truth be presupposed there is no proof of anything. Christianity is proved as being the very foundation of the idea of proof itself.

f. That acceptance of the Christian position on the part of sinners who are *in principle* alienated from God, who seek to flee his face, comes when, challenged by the inescapably clear evidence, the Holy Spirit opens their eyes so that they truly see things for what they are.

Intellectually sinners can readily follow the presentation of the evidence that is placed before them. If the difference between the Christian and the non-Christian position is only made plain to them, as alone it can be on a Reformed basis, the natural man can, for argument's sake, place himself upon the position of the Christian. But though in this sense he then knows God more clearly than otherwise, though he already knew him by virtue of his sense of deity, yet it is only when by the grace of God the Holy Spirit removes the scales from men's eyes that they know the truth existentially. Then they know him, whom to know is life eternal.

g. That therefore the remnants of the traditional method of apologetics that have been taken over from Romanism and Evangelicalism, in greater measure by old Princeton, in lesser measure by Amsterdam, must no longer be retained.

Standing on the shoulders of Warfield and Kuyper we honor them best if we build on the main thrust of their thought rather than if we insist on carrying on what is inconsistent with their basic position. Then are we most faithful to Calvin and to St. Paul.